CANADIANS ON THE NILE, 1882–1898

CANADIANS ON THE NILE, 1882–1898

*Being the Adventures of the Voyageurs
on the Khartoum Relief Expedition
and Other Exploits*

Roy MacLaren

UNIVERSITY OF BRITISH COLUMBIA PRESS
VANCOUVER

CANADIANS ON THE NILE, 1882–1898

BEING THE ADVENTURES OF THE VOYAGEURS ON THE KHARTOUM RELIEF EXPEDITION AND OTHER EXPLOITS

Canadian Cataloguing in Publication Data

MacLaren, Roy, 1934–
Canadians on the Nile, 1882–1898

Bibliography: p.
Includes index.
ISBN 0–7748–0094–1

1. Sudan—History—1862–1899
2. Canadians in the Sudan—History.
I. Title.
DT156.6.M22   962.4'03   C78–002014–6

International Standard Book Number: 0–7748–0094–1

Printed in Canada

For Anne Graham MacLaren

Contents

Illustrations

Photographic Credits

Plate 1 is from the National Army Museum, London. Plates 2, 5, 16, 24, 27, 28, and 31 are from illustrations in the *Graphic*. Plates 15, 17, 18, 20, and 21 originally appeared in the *Illustrated London News*, and Plates 29 and 30 are from *Scribner's Magazine*. Plates 3, 4, 6, 7, 8, 9, 11, 12, 13, 14, 25, and 26 are from the collections of the Public Archives of Canada, and Plates 10, 19, 22, 23, and 32 appear courtesy of the Toronto Public Library.

Acknowledgements

I am grateful to Celia Metrakos and to Pat Tuck for their accurate and reliable typing—and re-typing—of the manuscript of this book. Peter Robertson of the Public Archives of Canada was, as always, kindly and perceptive in providing assistance, attitudes happily characteristic of that admirable institution. Finally, my wife, Lee, was as patient, imaginative and in every way as helpful during the gestation of this book as she has been during similar writing fits of the past.

Roy MacLaren
Toronto
May 1978

Introduction

To have been born into the upper strata of Victoria's England was a guarantee of at least some comfort and respect but not, however, of adventure. To the young noblemen of Tudor England, adventure had been readily at hand. And it had never been far from those who had served the House of Hanover. But a young Englishman of the latter half of Victoria's long reign had generally to go far in search of adventure, to seek it out in distant lands.

At home there was excitement enough for those who saw challenge in parliamentary, church, or social reform or in burgeoning industrial or scientific advance. But for those who equated adventure with the sword and the bugle, the camp and the quarterdeck, adventure was only to be found across the seas. Even Edward, the Prince of Wales, felt bored and smothered in England—his mother did not, of course, help matters—and he too longed to share in the overseas exploits open to less regal gentlemen, exploits that were rapidly colouring a quarter of the world a bright British pink. To such gentlemen as these, life in England since the Crimean War had seemed seized with the dull monotony of peaceful prosperity. On the continent, a Prussian here, a fervent nationalist there might cause armies to be mobilized or even battles to be fought, but it was really only in the out-of-the-way places of his own Empire that an Englishman could hope to find military adventure.

Whether their intent was pacific or bellicose, many Englishmen sought escape from their placid homeland. In satisfying their desires to escape dull prosperity, Thomas Cook was making a fortune, while the books of Rider Haggard or Rudyard Kipling told those who had to stay at home of strange lands south or east of Suez where fuzzy-wuzzies fought like heroes or Burmese girls smoked black cheroots. Even people who could not leave Britain on one of Mr. Cook's increasingly imaginative tours, or who were tied to the dull, colourless routine of a desk in London or of a factory bench in Birmingham, could at least share vicariously in the adventures of others in distant and romantic lands. Everywhere the army went, so went that new phenomenon, the war correspondent. A by-product of the recently invented telegraph and universal postal system, the war correspondent, in providing some of the sensationalism which was increasingly an antidote for the heavy dullness of much of Victorian England, generally failed to report the more sordid face of imperialism. The war correspondent—and the war artist—helped both to create and to whet the appetite. And each year a spate of illustrated travel

books and memoirs—much of it worthy stuff for the *Boys' Own Paper*—
appeared on the market, all designed to pander to growing imperial romanti-
cism and jingoism. Here was escape of a sort; all Englishmen could—in their
mind's eye—visit distant spice islands or follow the explorer into the hinterland of black Africa. Gradually the Little England of Gladstone was ignored
or rejected in the growing sense of Empire. Of this imperialism, G. M. Young
has said,

> perhaps the greatest part, was no more than adventurous. We must
> consider the influence of the telegraph and the war-correspondent, in
> vivifying messages which had once trailed through, months after the
> event, in official dispatches borne by sail; of the newer, livelier press,
> rapidly surrendering the make-believe that newspapers were the instruc-
> tors of the people or that the Board-school population desired to be
> instructed; of the ever-growing literature of travel and adventure,
> always pushing farther into the unknown and always leaving something
> for the next pioneer. Still armies might march into the mountains and
> be lost for weeks, as Roberts marched on Kandahar; into the desert
> and be lost for ever, as Hicks was lost at El Obeid. Still false prophets
> might arise in the wastes beyond Wady Halfa, still Lhassa was un-
> visited, and a man might make himself as famous by riding to Khiva
> in fact, as by discovering King Solomon's Mines in fiction. The ways
> of adventure stood wide open.[1]

The motives of the imperialists were many and varied, but whatever they
were, imperialism, like all power, corrupts. The love of adventure which had
originally inspired some gave way in time to more sordid motives. Greed
had always been present, but by the last years of the nineteenth century,
imperialists of a baser type had typically replaced the earlier adventurers in
Africa and Asia. In her imperial expansion of the latter half of the nineteenth
century, Britain had started down the road that led eventually to the debacle
of the Boer War.

But to many in 1880, to bring order and justice to distant lands was simply
the "white man's burden." Sometimes—and occasionally to the surprise
of the British—the native people did not welcome traders or administrators.
Skirmishes large and small frequently preceded, or followed, the opening
of trade. Exploitation presupposed no opposition. Order accordingly became
the first prerequisite of prosperity. And this is where the British army and
navy came in. To be a young officer promised adventure, since such a career
entailed a share in shouldering the white man's burden. One subaltern well
put the feelings of his fellows when he wrote that they regarded the world

as having been "specially created for their own wild pleasures, of which war, with all its sudden changes, and at times its maddening excitement, was the greatest."[2] For such men, war posed no moral dilemmas. It was not so much that they disregarded the moral problems inherent in warfare or colonialism; they simply remained unaware of them. They had nothing but scorn for those who questioned Britain's imperial course. To any who might have enquired, they would have replied that it was for the glory of Britain that they killed other men. That their answer was insufficient, that it simply put the question one step back, never occurred to most of them. It was clear to them, as they passed through Asia and Africa on their imperial progress, that the British were a most superior race. The world had been created for them.

Even the outward trappings of the military life looked promising. Splendid scarlet, blue, and gold uniforms marked the members of the officer corps, an élite branch of the Victorian establishment that combined for its members some of the best features of a private club and a mutual aid society. One of the most satisfying features was that the same fine fellows kept turning up again and again—occasionally in the most unlikely places. Britain's small army was, in a way, a closed shop. A soldier might find that the captain who led his company in the muddy trenches of the Crimea was later the colonel leading his regiment along the Great Lakes of Canada or his general defying the jungles of West Africa. And within the regiment, or in brother regiments, other officers were always eager to share in a bit of work or adventure in any remote and romantic place. Even during the long periods of leave which the army so generously provided, it was easy to find a brother officer delighted at a proposal to penetrate the Moslem preserves of Imperial Russia, the upper reaches of the Nile, or the mountains of Afghanistan.

The world had become the Englishman's playground—or his field of adventure—thanks to the steamers that now carried him with speed to his distant destination and the telegraph that kept him informed of what was happening at the centre and the centre informed of what he was doing in his particular corner of the Empire. The great stretches of the world over which his Lady Sovereign reigned were becoming a complicated network of trade routes and coaling stations that science held together and industry sustained. That is not to say, of course, that each colony was developed and self-sufficient. The older colonies, like Canada, had achieved internal self-government. But others—the non-white ones—were both politically and economically held firmly between the thumb of the governor and the forefinger of the Royal Navy. The centre of the Empire was still greater than the sum total of its subordinate parts. Yet no colony was entire unto itself. The component parts had begun to interact on each other. When this story begins, a major event in any part of the Empire had repercussions in other parts, even in the most distant colonies.

The role of the military in fostering a sense of Canada's place in the Empire or of Canadian national consciousness has not received much attention from historians, yet the expeditions of the latter half of the nineteenth century —the Fenian Raids, the two Riel expeditions, the Nile contingent and the volunteer units sent to South Africa—all contributed to a greater awareness by Canadians of themselves as a distinct and identifiable society. So it is with the participation of individual Canadians in imperial enterprises. Two examples may suffice for several: the Indian Mutiny saw the recruitment of Canadian volunteers to help put down the insurgents and a young man from Upper Canada College won the Victoria Cross in the charge of the Light Brigade in the Crimean War. They too contributed to a heightened sense of Canada as an entity, whether as a component of an Empire or eventually as a nation unto itself. All such military service was a little like holding up a mirror to oneself to be certain how one looked—and how one was changing.

This book is an account of how men from one of the larger colonies, Canada, helped to secure one of the lesser dependencies, the Sudan, within the realm of the Island Queen, how rough, turbulent Canadian woodsmen joined with the officers and gentlemen and the sometimes equally rough but always brave and long-suffering Tommy Atkins of Victoria's army in the most remarkable adventures of the latter half of her long reign. More unlikely companions for imperial excursions into the then largely unknown Sudan can scarcely be imagined. Certainly few episodes in Canadian history are more incongruous. Why should Canadians sail to war in the Sudan? Why should they leave their new world, their homes in the young land of Canada, to journey half way around the world to join in distant campaigns? What was the Sudan to Canadians? What called them across the ocean? Later observers might explain that the desire for trade, extension of national prestige, or imperial security were the underlying motives for the British expeditions in Egypt and the Sudan. However, for many Victorians—whether British or Canadian—there was simply something both natural and splendid in the way in which all the good fellows gathered together to make the daring attempt to save a beleaguered brother officer, something gratifying in the scene of Canadian boatmen guiding milord the English captain up the great River Nile, in the way in which the skills of the railroad engineer, developed to a unique pitch in North America, were later employed by the Crown to consolidate its tenuous hold over the Sudan. The fact that such diverse elements could be readily brought together for imperial adventures was, among other things, a mark of the power of science to shrink the world. The fact that Canadians were involved in such undertakings half-way around the world was an indication that Canada was coming of age in the imperial era of Victoria, a roadmark on the meandering way to a new status. Somewhat paradoxically, participation in an imperial expedition contributed to the impetus to full Canadian nationhood.

The primary purpose of the Nile expedition of 1884-85 was to rescue a famous British general besieged in Khartoum. To many Victorians, that officer, Charles George Gordon, was the personification of the ideals that they valued most highly. There had always been a strange combination of high drama and Christian humility in Gordon's military career. There was something marvellous in the plight of the evangelical Gordon closed up in that hot and dusty city, surrounded by fanatical Muslims who stubbornly refused to acknowledge the superiority of British arms and aspirations. Here was a situation to appeal strongly to those who had followed with pride Gordon's earlier exploits in China and Africa. Here was high adventure to relieve for a moment the drabness of daily existence. Here was material with which Kipling could later please the British public:

> We took our chanst among the Kyber 'ills,
> The Boers knocked us silly at a mile,
> An' a Zulu *impi* dished us up in style:
> But all we ever got from such as they
> Was pop to what the Fuzzy made us swaller;
> We 'eld our bloomin' own, the papers say,
> But man for man the Fuzzy knocked us 'oller.
> Then 'ere's *to* you, Fuzzy-Wuzzy, an' the missis
>   and the kid;
> Our orders was to break you, an' of course we
>   went an' did.
> We sloshed you with Martinis, an' it wasn't
>   'ardly fair;
> But for all the odds agin' you, Fuzzy-Wuz,
>   you bruk the square.

Here was imperialism at its most romantic. And Canadians were no more immune to its appeal than the British. Certainly Canadian imperialism was neither expansionist nor aggressive. It was basically an expression of affection for Britain, a basically romantic sense of belonging to an admirable Empire, which in turn arose from a variety of sources. For some Canadians, imperialism was simply an unquestioned part of their United Empire Loyalist heritage. For more recent arrivals from Britain, it was a manifestation of a lingering love for the "Old Country." At home, some saw the Empire as the bulwark against expansionist pressures from the United States. In return,

Canada owed the Empire its support elsewhere. For yet others, the Anglo-Saxon was naturally superior to other races and, accordingly, qualified to lead the world. A racial unity transcending mere geography bound together Anglo-Saxons everywhere. This view came close to mixing up gold, God, and glory in one splendid, confused mélange. God was an Englishman in the late nineteenth century—if He ever was one. More moderate Canadians shunned the emotionalism of racial superiority, but they did reason that Britain deserved their support since it represented the most liberal political system yet devised. Still others, like Stephen Leacock, proclaimed "I . . . am an imperialist because I will not be a Colonial." For them, Canada would gain a leading role in the Empire as its weight and influence grew. "Just as warfare was seen as a rather strenuous sport and an expression of national self-assertiveness and fitness, so too the martial spirit appeared to be synonymous with a masterful and upright manhood, order and stability, a necessary aspect of vital national feeling, and an antidote to the follies of the age."[3] The last decades of the nineteenth century were, in a sense, a period of adolescence for Canada. And adolescence is normally a period of uncertainty and misgivings, a time of testing. One of the few things that did seem certain in a Canada where the tempo of change was accelerating was the Queen at the centre of a great and still growing Empire. To serve them appeared to be both a splendid ideal and a great adventure to some young Canadians, an excellent place to test what one had become.

Some said that imperialism was basically "Gold, God and Glory." Certainly many of the Canadian volunteers wanted to go to the Sudan for no more complicated reason than that the pay was good. Their special skills were in scarce supply, and the money offered was more than they could earn in Canada. For several generations, British officers stationed in Quebec City, Montreal, or Kingston or Canadians serving in the British army had recorded the skills of the Canadian boatmen. As a result, somewhere in the totality of British military knowledge, the fact had been stored away that the *voyageurs* were superb boatmen. Accordingly, when experts were needed for a desperate dash up the Nile River to relieve Khartoum, Canadians were eagerly sought by Garnet Wolseley, the general appointed to lead the expedition, who had spent many years in Canada. But this is by no means the whole reason why Canadians were involved in what became the greatest adventure story of the nineteenth-century Empire.

By 1882, when the story begins, Canada was no longer an unknown land, the Rockies had been penetrated, the buffaloes and Indians of the prairies were being displaced by railroads and settlers. Even Vancouver and Victoria were growing towns. In short, the last frontier was disappearing. The settlement and economic development of Canada during the sixty-four years of Victoria's long reign help to explain why, for the first time, an imperial interest began to manifest itself among young men who, generations before, would have responded to the challenge of the frontier rather than the call of overseas adventure. Sir John A. Macdonald and the other Fathers of the Canadian Confederation had created a dominion that governed itself internally and that was slowly beginning to take a place in the comity of nations. Some young Canadians, still lacking any clear sense of national direction or of their own nationhood, envisaged exciting roles for themselves in the great Empire of which they were a part. Some shared the yearnings of their British cousins for valorous adventures and military glory beyond the seas. The boredom of industrialized England was beginning to seep across the Atlantic. When these young Canadians set about translating their dreams into reality, they were able to bring to imperial forces special skills that life in Canada had taught them. And these skills were not only the sylvan skills of the boatman; in addition to *voyageurs* who helped in the attempt to relieve Khartoum, this book is about how a young Canadian engineer later won fame through building the railroads which opened the way to the final pacification of the Sudan and its subjection to Anglo-Egyptian rule for fifty years. This book is also, in an incidental way, about young Canadians (several from the Royal Military College in Kingston) who achieved high rank in Victoria's army. There were a surprising number.

From these experiences came impetus to nationhood. Young Canadians began to judge themselves against others. By learning to know other men and other lands, they learned to know their own. As a result of their service in imperial wars from the Indian Mutiny to the Boer War, they came to see Canada either as a significant and increasingly important part of a growing Empire—not merely as a colony but rather as a part of what would become an imperial federation—or as an incipient nation, capable of standing on its own feet internationally as well as domestically. Canada's experience in World War I would confirm this latter perception, but in the last decades of the nineteenth century the choice had not yet been made. The route to nationhood still lay through imperial experience.

1

Egyptian Prologue

In his first interview with the Governor of St. Helena, Napoleon said
emphatically, "Egypt is the most important country in the world."

ROSE
LIFE OF NAPOLEON

By 1875 it was obvious that the thirty-nine-year-old Khedive Ismail of Egypt
was fast becoming bankrupt. A profusion of palaces in Cairo and Alexandria
and such Western innovations in the rural areas as railroads and elaborate
canal systems attested to his extravagance. What extensive and sometimes
ill-conceived public works did not absorb of the country's resources, corrupt
officials did. The Khedive's nominal suzerain, the Sultan in Constantinople,
was in no position to provide any financial help or even to stand as an example
to his sleek, plump, and bankrupt vassal. The Turk himself was in debt to
half the bankers of Europe, and Ismail had emulated him. When Ismail
became Khedive in 1863, the Egyptian national debt was approximately
£3,000,000. Twelve years later, he had run it up to £90,000,000. What was
especially distressing was that there was so little of a productive nature to
show for this massive spending. There was, however, no lack of creditors.
Investors in most of the countries of Europe—especially in Britain and
France—held vast quantities of Egyptian bonds. So many, in fact, and so
powerful were these bondholders that, when it became obvious that Egypt
was in serious financial difficulties, they were able to induce their own
governments, on the grounds of what was called financial probity and
international morality, to take an increasingly active interest in Egyptian
affairs.

The British and French governments had, in any case, another reason
for keeping an eye on what was happening in Cairo in 1875. Whichever
European power controlled Egypt could play a leading role in the Mediterranean—and beyond. With the construction of the Suez Canal, Egypt had
assumed the importance that the Cape of Good Hope had formerly possessed.
In 1869, the great French engineer, de Lesseps, had completed the Suez
Canal. In November of that year, amid dazzling celebrations and in the
presence of members of several royal families of Europe, the Khedive had
declared the canal open. It was an immediate success. The length of the

passage to India was reduced by one-half. Proceeds from tolls mounted rapidly. But the profligate Khedive Ismail, who held a large number of shares in the great enterprise, spent his sizeable dividends even faster than he received them. By 1875 he brought himself to make a painful decision. Both to meet his more pressing debts and to maintain his lavish lifestyle, he had to have more cash. There was only one sure way of getting it. He sold his shares in the Suez Canal company to the British government for £4,000,000. As a result of this deal with Disraeli, Ismail gained sufficient money to hold off his creditors and to continue his extravagances for a few years more. And Britain gained a major voice in the operations of the Suez Canal, hitherto the preserve of certain French investors and the Khedive. Liberals in Britain attacked Disraeli for involving their country in another imperialist entanglement. Yet if anything is inevitable in the history of nations, it was predictable that, sooner or later, London would want to participate in the management of the Suez Canal. It was the strategic route to Britain's great Indian Empire and to her other extensive holdings in the Far East. Once it was actually built, Britain could no longer afford to stand aloof from Egyptian affairs as she had done when de Lesseps had first begun to advocate the construction of the canal. Following the purchase of the Khedive's shares, Britain was, for better or for worse, intimately involved in Egypt.

The Khedive used part of his £4,000,000 from Disraeli to further his efforts to create a new Cairo, a transformed city worthy of the new Egypt that he fondly hoped had been inaugurated with his reign. As a result of his spending, Cairo began to change yet more rapidly from a dusty, crowded oriental town to the Western city an English traveller had described in the early 1870's:

> The city is lighted by gas; it has public gardens in which a native military band performs every afternoon; an excellent theatre for which Verdi composed Aida; new houses in the Parisian style are springing up by streets, and are let out at high rents as soon as they are finished. No gentleman wears a turban.... Already there is telegraphic communication between Cairo and Khartoum, and a railway is about to be commenced. As for the Sudan, it was formerly divided among a number of barbarous chiefs almost incessantly at war. It is now conquered and at peace, and trade is seldom disturbed.... The traffic in slaves is abolished.[1]

The traveller's account of the transformed Cairo was reasonably accurate. His description of the Sudan was, however, wide of the mark. The large-scale traffic in Africans from the hinterland to the slave markets of the Turkish lands was far from abolished. What little legitimate trade there was in the million square miles of desert and jungle that made up the Sudan remained subject to constant harassment by predatory chieftains. A sort of tribal anarchy was the only form of government in a primitive land where, not many years before, a white man had penetrated for the first time. Despite his continuing debts, the Khedive decided that, with a little money in his treasury from his share in the Suez Canal profits, he must firmly establish his rule over the Upper Nile as well as the Lower. He had a shadowy legal claim to the Sudan, and now was the time to enforce it. Once he had made up his mind, the remarkable Ismail was not to be deterred by any obstacle, financial or otherwise. He first engaged the great African explorer, Sir Samuel Baker, to establish Egyptian rule where the Blue and White Niles join and, from there, into the lands bordering Uganda and the Congo. Baker was partly successful in his own humanitarian efforts to suppress the Arab slave trade and, on behalf of Ismail, to organize a rudimentary Egyptian administration in the northern part of Sudan. He was, however, unwilling to extend his contract beyond two years. Hence, the Khedive began to cast about for another brave and honest European explorer or soldier who would be prepared to undergo hardships and deprivations to plant firmly the Egyptian flag in what was called the Equatoria Province of the Sudan, a largely unknown area in the south where the source of the great River Nile was concealed. No reliable Egyptian would undertake such a daunting task.

The name of an Englishman who might be the very person he wanted reached the ears of Ismail. He authorized his prime minister to interview a colonel in the Royal Engineers when both happened to be visiting Constantinople in 1872. The name of the short, stocky Englishman was Charles George Gordon. A member of the Victorian establishment by birth (his father was an artillery officer), but by choice isolated from it, Gordon embodied several of the virtues that his contemporaries cherished most. These virtues were, of course, the very ones that Victorians knew themselves to be least capable of achieving. In a society increasingly rich with the things of this world, many prosperous Victorians longed for the treasures of another, for the peace of Christian simplicity and devotion. Charles George Gordon appeared to have achieved such peace. His high ideals and simple piety were the envy of many. Gordon was, in fact, a complex man, moody and impulsive, determined and incredibly brave, and frequently rebellious against human (although not Divine) authority. His bright blue eyes, it was noted, had a disconcerting way of seeming to look into the heart's secrets. Others read different things into Gordon's complex character. Lytton Strachey and one or two others among his many biographers were later to hint at an addiction to liquor. But all who knew Gordon personally or who have investigated his extraordinary career have agreed that he remains one of the great figures of the Victorian age, a saint—and occasionally a sinner—of the sort that only nineteenth-century Britain produced.[2]

As a sapper subaltern in the Crimean War, Gordon seemed to live a charmed life. Even in the exposed front lines at the siege of Sebastapol, Russian bullets and shells left him untouched. His courage and devotion to duty won the admiration of all who knew him. None admired him more than another young subaltern who became his fast friend during the long siege. Much later, this officer was to play the leading part in the great undertaking organized to save his life, a life of which Charlie Gordon was himself notoriously careless.

Gordon's close friend in the Crimean War and his exact contemporary, Garnet Wolseley, was already marked as an outstanding officer, destined to rise to the very top.[3] Many years later, Wolseley was to write about his comrade-in-arms, "In these material days of money grubbing, when the teaching of Christianity is little practiced and the spirit of chivalry is wellnigh forgotten, I cling tenaciously to every remembrance of our intimacy, because he was one of the very few friends I ever had who came up to my estimate of the Christian hero. He absolutely ignored self in all he did, and only took in hand what he conceived to be God's work. Life was to him but a Pilgrim's Progress between the years of early manhood and the Heaven he now dwells in, the Home he always longed for."[4] Like most other Victorians, Wolseley revered in Gordon those qualities that he himself most conspicuously lacked.

It was only by the greatest good luck that Russian shells did not carry Gordon off to the home he had always longed for before he was twenty-five. His cool conduct under Russian bombardment both invited destruction and attracted the favourable notice of his superiors. Because of his record of skill and courage in the Crimea, Gordon's offer to serve in China from 1860 to 1864 was immediately accepted. In the Anglo-French force sent against the Celestial Emperor as part of the general and persistent Western efforts to pry open the closed door of China, Gordon's energy, efficiency, and courage brought him again to the attention of his superiors. They were so impressed by the young engineer that they gave him command of a small independent force of Chinese levies which before very long was dubbed the "Ever-Victorious Army." Soon London newspapers were describing for their eager readers the feats of the romantic "Chinese" Gordon. The publicity given to Gordon's exploits in China during the Taiping Rebellion firmly secured his fame among his countrymen. His sobriquet became known to every household. The reputation of Chinese Gordon did not diminish even when he accepted the obscure appointment of superintendent of fortifications at the mouth of the River Thames upon his return to England. This post was no promotion. Gordon was too eccentric an officer to be fully trusted and accepted by the military establishment. His six years at Gravesend were uneventful, but they did provide Gordon with an opportunity for intense biblical study that confirmed him in the simple but profound Christian mysticism and charity which he had already begun to exhibit. The not very exalted appointment as British member of the International Danube Commission followed his technical duties on the Thames, a further expression of the lingering question in the official mind about Gordon's judgment. It was from Romania in 1872 that he travelled to Constantinople where he had his fateful appointment with the Egyptian prime minister.

The Khedive's offer of employment in the Sudan was just the sort of challenge that Colonel Gordon sought as an escape from the uneventful and personally unrewarding course his army career had taken. Both as a staunch opponent of slavery and as a devout Christian mystic, he eagerly accepted the governorship of Equatoria, that ill-defined and turbulent southern province where maladministration and slavery were even more prevalent than elsewhere in the Sudan. Here, Gordon believed, was an opportunity to do something tangible for some of the most neglected of all God's children.

After having obtained indefinite leave from the British army, Gordon assumed his gubernatorial duties in Equatoria in February 1874. In the deserts and in the jungles, he drove himself tirelessly for the next two years to open the largely unexplored country to the benefits of Western civilization, to abolish the slave trade, and to establish a just administration. The effects of his boundless energy and personal conviction gradually became evident. Peace, a hitherto unknown blessing, descended on the southern Sudan. Alan Moorehead has described the success of Gordon's mission in Equatoria well:

> If he had failed in his grand design—the annexation of the Nile from Gondokoro to its source and the launching of his steamers on Lake Victoria—he had only just failed. The river was accurately mapped and explored for the first time to within sixty miles of its source, the "Nyanza" was afloat on Lake Albert and the "Khedive" was soon to join her there; the Arab slavers had been driven out of Equatoria, and his military forts held a secure control from one end of his province to the other. Even more important, perhaps, than all this, he had prevented his own soldiers from pillaging the inhabitants, and had converted the tribes along the river from enemies into friends. It was now possible for a single traveller to move about armed with nothing more than a walking stick. That was something of a marvel for Central Africa.[5]

But this remarkable achievement had exacted a heavy price on Gordon's spiritual and physical equilibrium. By the end of 1876, after almost three years of incessant labour, he was travelling down the Nile on his way back to England, exhausted by his almost superhuman efforts to establish justice and good administration in the southern Sudanese wilderness and discouraged by the absence of Egyptian support for his efforts to abolish the slave trade.

Yet the Sudan was now in Gordon's blood. He could not stay away for long. Prosperous and pedestrian Britain was no place for Chinese Gordon. The Khedive Ismail probably sensed his feelings. Certainly he was the first man the Khedive thought of when, in the year following Gordon's resignation, he required an incorruptible, conscientious officer to assume the post of governor general of the whole of the Sudan. Ismail had already spent a fortune—even by his own extravagant standards—in attempting to impose his rule over that vast and chaotic land. Nevertheless, he had failed. His costly failure was partly the result of the colossal dishonesty and indifference of the Turkish and Egyptian officials whom he had sent to Khartoum. Only Gordon's province of Equatoria had stood out from the murky background of corruption as a bright example of good government. Obviously Gordon was the very man to attempt to organize and impose order on the whole of the unstable dependency that was larger than Egypt itself. Ismail was an astute man despite an unprepossessing appearance caused by one drooping eyelid and a rather absurd reddish-brown beard. He cleverly appealed to Gordon's high sense of duty, and soon the eccentric Gordon was on his way back to the Sudan. From 1877 until 1880, Gordon, careless both of his health and personal happiness, strove to give the nine million Sudanese their first honest administration, to abolish slavery, and to instil in his Arab and black subjects the same high ideals of duty and responsibility that he so manifestly embodied. In his efforts to achieve his goals, he rode his camel prodigious distances across the desert sands of the Sudan—he is estimated to have covered by camel alone between eight and nine thousand miles in less than three years—and, at forty-five, drove himself in a fashion that fatigued men half his age. From his capital of Khartoum, he dispensed severe but generally just orders to his young European and Egyptian provincial officials. He made the city into the funnel through which the trade of black Africa flowed to the Mediterranean. In doing so, however, he alienated many officials in both Egypt and the Sudan who did not welcome either his strict standards or his autocratic methods. Nor was Gordon in favour of foreign intervention in the Sudan. A year after resigning his appointment, he wrote of Egypt, "I do not think that it has altered at all except in improving its finances for the benefit of the [foreign] bondholders. . . . the lot of the fellahin and the inhabitants of the Sudan is the same oppressed lot as before."[6]

What the final synthesis of all Gordon's efforts in the Sudan would have been is a matter for speculation. In February 1880, after almost three years in office, events in Egypt and his own exhaustion combined to bring to an abrupt end Gordon's remarkable and erratic career as governor general.

2

England in Egypt

The Grand Old Man went out to fight
Spite of Midlothian's lingo,
L with an I, N with a G, -LIN-go,
Lingo!

The Grand Old Man fought Arabi
And gave him regular Stingo,
S with a T, I with an N, -STIN-go,
Stingo!

ANON

Again the trouble was money. By resorting to one dodge after another, the Khedive Ismail had managed to stave off financial disaster for a number of years. The patience of his European creditors was, however, fast running out. More important, they began to feel that their vice-regal debtor, having exhausted all possibility of further manipulations, might now attempt to reduce the high interest rates arbitrarily. Worse still, he might even repudiate the payment of the interest altogether. Such an idea was so shocking to Victorian businessmen that the Khedive's many creditors told each other that any indication of gross irresponsibility would immediately become a matter for their governments. The French government readily listened to the financiers' fears. In Britain, however, Gladstone and his Liberals were, by and large, opposed to anything which smacked of imperialism, financial or otherwise. Both France and Britain had hitherto exercised an indirect control over Egypt through their influence at Constantinople, influence used largely to help prevent the entry of Russia into the Mediterranean. But with Egyptian financial chaos as well as a general Ottoman collapse in sight, Britain and France began to grope about for new policies which would support their common interests in the Mediterranean.

France was all for direct intervention in Egypt. Paris was convinced that a few European troops in Cairo would soon ensure that there were no sudden and unpleasant financial or political surprises. But "since Egypt remained of lesser importance than Asia Minor, the British had no higher ambition in the crisis of the Khedivate than to restore its finances and to keep the old parity of influence with France.... 'The question for us,' Derby, the Foreign

Secretary, explained, 'is not one of establishing an exclusive interest, but of preventing an exclusive interest from being established as against us.'"[1] The foreign secretary described what was essentially a passive position. By taking this attitude, the British were, in fact, handing to the French the initiative in Egyptian affairs. Paris was not long in taking it. As early as 1876, the Khedive had been impelled, largely at French insistence, to turn much of his revenue over to an international *Caisse de la Dette Publique*. Additionally, British and French debt commissioners had been appointed to the Egyptian ministry of finance to attempt to reduce the financial chaos and to protect the interests of the European bondholders. At first the British government dissociated itself from what it chose to call "these private arrangements." But private or official, Britain had taken an irrevocable step into Egypt by permitting a British controller to be placed in the ministry of finance in Cairo. This step looked innocuous enough to most contemporary observers, but in fact it marked the beginning of a British presence in Egypt that was to last for seventy years.

The next step soon followed. When it became obvious that this first intervention in the economic life of Egypt was insufficient to protect the interests of the European bondholders, the aggressive French government insisted on further interference. In London, the Liberals were reluctant to become drawn deeper into the morass of Egyptian problems. Yet even their misgivings had to give way in face of the overriding importance of preventing France from gaining sole ascendancy in Cairo and independent control over the Suez Canal. Turkey, the sick man of Europe, was powerless to intervene in the affairs of its Egyptian province or to deflect further French intervention. London acquiesced in most of the plans made in Paris. British and French ministers were eventually introduced into the Egyptian cabinet and further reforms into the Egyptian financial system. One of these reforms resulted in a reduction in the size of the Khedive's overgrown army. Considerable savings were soon made, but the sudden discharge of a large number of army officers added a third and very articulate group to two classes in Egypt already discontented by French and British intervention: the peasants, who suffered greatly from oppressive new taxes, and the privileged classes, who opposed foreign financial reform and control. In one last desperate gamble to retain some influence over his people, the Khedive Ismail attempted to place himself at the head of the growing number of nationalist malcontents. Not surprisingly, Ismail failed in his ill-considered and tardy effort to pose as a great Egyptian nationalist. How could he hope to succeed against the combined opposition of a determined France and a reluctant but acquiescent Britain?

Ismail soon found himself being packed off to spend the remainder of his life in luxurious exile in Turkey. After his son, the more pliable Khedive Tewfik (or Taufiq), had ascended the vice-regal throne in 1879, the British and French cabinet members were withdrawn, but the financial controllers with a large European staff were re-established, an arrangement approved by the four other interested European nations who acted in concert with the two intervening powers. Egypt was in effect "tied hand and foot, unable to move, almost unable to breath, without the consent of Europe."[2] There were, however, a large number of Egyptian nationalists who felt that a popular revolution might yet succeed. But the new Khedive would provide no leadership against the British and French. Soon Tewfik, who proved to be little more than a puppet in the hands of the European powers, lost even the limited popular support his unrepentant and obstinate father had formerly commanded.

Once it had become clear that they could expect no leadership from Tewfik, a group of Egyptian army officers decided to put themselves at the head of all those Egyptians who wanted to purge the country of foreign control. After an abortive attempt at revolt in 1879, the officers, under the leadership of Colonel Ahmed Arabi, began a series of more subtle moves in early 1881.

Arabi had been born in lower Egypt about 1840, the son of a prosperous peasant. Largely by his own efforts, he had risen rapidly in the army, eventually being promoted colonel, and, as a special mark of favour, Ismail gave him one of his many concubines as a wife. Nevertheless, Arabi had not been satisfied with either his own lot or that of his homeland. Gradually the peasant's son had become the hero of both the exploited masses and the frustrated nationalists. His popular support eventually became such that Tewfik felt compelled to appoint him his minister of war in 1882. However, the creation of a nationalist cabinet did little to placate the restless or counter the rumblings of discontent in Egypt. They became so loud that France began to urge armed intervention by a joint Anglo-French expeditionary force to protect European interests, a policy opposed in London by the pacific Gladstone yet supported most notably by Lord Hartington, his secretary of state for India, who became secretary of state for war in December 1882.[3]

Hartington, the heir to the Duke of Devonshire, was one of the most prominent members of the "Marlborough House Set," the circle of which the Prince of Wales was the centre. Their tastes in horses and women were similar. The immensely wealthy "Harty-Tarty" was a rather heavy and ponderous man, yet he had enough dexterity to keep several mistresses in London at the same time without the fact becoming common knowledge. And from his experience as secretary of state for India, he was as conscious as anyone in the Liberal cabinet of the overriding importance to British imperial interests of the Suez Canal. No foreign army could be allowed to threaten it. Hartington began to bring all the pressure that he could muster on his cabinet colleagues to persuade them to pursue a more forward policy in Egypt. In the London press and among the general public that fateful phrase, "national honour demands it," was increasingly heard. Finally, in the face of possible resignation by Hartington—the first of many occasions when Hartington seemed on the point of resigning and thereby of destroying the fragile balance between Whig and Radical, the two wings of the Liberal Party—the prime minister gave his reluctant agreement to an Anglo-French naval demonstration off Egypt's principal port, Alexandria.

It seemed to Gladstone the lesser of two evils; he saw the naval demonstration as the only way of giving a warning to Arabi and his nationalist followers that neither ran the risks involved in outright occupation of Egypt nor raised the possibility of a rupture with France. However, the Anglo-French show of naval force failed completely of its purpose. It only succeeded in making the Egyptional nationalists, safe in Cairo, more than ever determined to free their country from foreign domination and humiliation. That the cry of "Egypt for the Egyptians" became more persistent was only one result of the demonstration. It also provoked a savage nationalist riot in Alexandria on 11 June 1882. With wild cries of "O Moslems! Kill him! Kill the Christian!" a mob bludgeoned or stabbed fifty Europeans to death and injured as many more, including the British consul, almost under the guns of the Anglo-French fleet.

Officials in London and Paris were deeply shocked by the way in which the recalcitrant Egyptians had flouted the solemn warnings and had disregarded the naval show of force. However, at this crucial point the French, increasingly preoccupied with other problems at home and abroad and suddenly uncertain about Bismarck's intentions in Europe, ended their participation in the Egyptian venture. From having been the protagonists of armed intervention, they suddenly became little more than interested spectators. One morning in late June 1882, the French warships, without much warning, weighed anchor and steamed away from Alexandria, leaving the British ironclads to face the growing batteries of Egyptian artillery that Arabi was hastily assembling along the shore. To the British admiral the guns appeared increasingly threatening to his anchored ships. On 10 July he wired to London for permission to bombard the Egyptian fortifications.[4] Preoccupied with plans for parliamentary reform and Home Rule for Ireland, Gladstone was nevertheless mindful of the popular desire for revenge for the British lives lost in the Alexandria riots. He was, moreover, dismayed by Arabi's political immorality in attempting to establish a military government and by his financial immorality in seeking to repudiate Egypt's foreign debts. In finally agreeing to the bombardment of the Alexandrine defences, Gladstone took yet another step into Egypt. He took it reluctantly, and, France having suddenly withdrawn, he took it alone. As a result of this further intervention, Britain was in Egypt to stay until 1955.

Royal Naval gunnery was not very accurate in the late nineteenth century. However, no great skill was required to destroy Arabi's hastily prepared shore batteries. British marksmanship was also assisted by information that a most ambitious lieutenant of the Royal Engineers, Horatio Herbert Kitchener, had collected surreptitiously ashore in Alexandria.[5] Eventually, like the equally ambitious Wolseley, Kitchener was to reach the highest posts in the British army. In 1882, however, he was simply one of many young officers in search of adventure and opportunity to distinguish himself in his chosen career. Speaking fluent Arabic as the result of determined study during an earlier period of service in the Middle East, the slim, six-foot two-inch Kitchener was convinced, when he first learned of the Anglo-French display of force off Alexandria, that he could perform some remarkable feat in Egypt if he could but get there from his uneventful survey post in Cyprus. He thereupon took unauthorized leave in the hope of seeing active service. Such service was all too rare for ambitious officers, who could hope for early and rapid promotion only from outstanding conduct in the field, and Kitchener's espionage was later recalled to his advantage.

After a ten-hour naval bombardment, all the Egyptian guns had been silenced. But then the question naturally arose, what were the British to do now? Arson and pillage had immediately followed the bombardment. Part of the city was in flames. What little Egyptian civil authority remained was obviously powerless to prevent the wholesale crime that had broken out. The youngest captain in the Mediterranean fleet, "Jackie" Fisher (later Admiral of the Fleet Lord Fisher), and an ebullient and daring commander, Lord Charles Beresford, who, like "Harty-Tarty" Hartington, was a crony of the Prince of Wales,[6] were sent ashore with Royal Marines and bluejackets to help restore order in the narrow and half-destroyed streets of Alexandria. They were aided in their efforts by a heterogeneous collection of Italian, German, Greek and United States marines landed from the various men-of-war in the harbour. Fisher and his naval brigade and Beresford and his motley contingent of marines soon pacified Alexandria. But Arabi remained unintimidated and unrepentant. Not surprisingly, he regarded the bombardment of the city as tantamount to a British declaration of war. It was clear to Arabi that Britain relied heavily on her seapower for her international prestige and influence. The one place where he might be able to damage that maritime power was the Suez Canal. Hence he immediately dispatched part of his army in the direction of the canal. This action was just what Hartington had feared. With the canal threatened, the imperial life-life to India was in danger of being cut. A clash between British and Egyptian armies, likely before, now rapidly became unavoidable. Hartington and the more aggressive members of the British cabinet pressed with renewed vigour for a final show-down with Arabi. The reluctant Gladstone once again yielded. "The insecurity of the Canal, it is plain, does not exhibit to us the seat of the disease," he explained in a somewhat uneasy way to the House of Commons on 24 July 1882. "The insecurity of the Canal is a symptom only, and the seat of the

disease is in the interior of Egypt, in its disturbed and anarchial condition."
If the canal were to be rendered safe from attack by dissident Egyptians,
the authority of the Khedive would have to be restored by British arms and
the rebels put down once and for all.

Charlie Gordon's old friend from the Crimea, Garnet Wolseley, was
selected as the physician to cure the disease that Gladstone had described.

3

Enter Wolseley

For my military knowledge, though I'm plucky and adventury,
Has only been brought down to the beginning of the century,
But still in matters vegetable, animal, and mineral,
I am the very model of a modern Major-General.

GILBERT AND SULLIVAN,
THE PIRATES OF PENZANCE

Twenty-five years after he had served with Gordon in the wretched trenches of the Crimea, Wolseley was a seasoned veteran of campaigns in Burma, India, China, Canada, and West and South Africa. During those twenty-five years, he had won rapid promotion and a reputation as a brave, capable officer. He was also vain, pompous, and scheming, eager to participate in the *beau monde* of London, both to advance his career and to satisfy his *amour propre* (his father had been a bankrupt Irish major). In addition, the future field marshal was an author and president of the Society for the Prevention of Bad Language, and he achieved sufficient notice with a truncated life of Marlborough for Thomas Hardy to recommend him as one of thirty English writers to sign a letter congratulating George Meredith on his seventieth birthday. Wolseley was also a friend of Henry James, Edmund Gosse, and Alfred Austin, the poet laureate, but these friendships do not appear to have increased his own literary talents. Wolseley's published letters to his wife,[1] his "dearest little Rumteefoozle," have occasional passages of charm and felicity but these qualities are entirely wanting in his autobiography.[2] Even Wolseley's official biographer, Sir George Arthur, admitted that the autobiography "as a whole is defective in construction and diffuse without being satisfying; it suggests the holding up of a blurred mirror instead of what should have been a strong and arresting portrait."[3] Something of the flavour of the autobiography and, more important, of the man can be gauged from this passage in which Wolseley describes his feelings in the Crimea on overhearing a fellow officer berating the incompetent Lord Raglan.

On the first stretcher that Lord Raglan encountered lay a young officer
—I withhold his name and regiment for the sake of the old and historic

corps to whose ranks he was a disgrace. As to himself, I hope his hateful and undistinguished name has been forgotten as he himself should be. Lord Raglan, going up to him in the kindest way, said in the most feeling and sympathetic tone and manner, "My poor young gentleman, I hope you are not badly hurt?"...This brutal cur—I subsequently knew the creature well—turned upon him, and in the rudest terms and most savage manner, denounced him as "responsible for every drop of blood that had been shed that day." Wounded though this ungenerous fellow was, I could with pleasure have run my sword through his unmanly carcass at that moment.[4]

Whatever his literary and personal shortcomings, Wolseley helped to make a number of major improvements in the British army, although not, perhaps, so many as he liked to claim. He alienated conservative elements in the War Office—especially the venerable commander-in-chief, the Duke of Cambridge—by his advocacy of certain radical measures to increase the efficiency and well-being of the army. But at the same time he earned popularity among many other professional soldiers and the public generally, who were convinced that he had at heart the best interests of the army. When Wolseley was appointed quartermaster-general in 1881, he was able to exploit his popularity—he was, for example, the model for "the modern Major-General" in *The Pirates of Penzance*—to institute some of the measures which he was certain were necessary if the army was to meet the dual challenge of a global empire and the implications of modern science. For Wolseley, the campaign in Egypt against Arabi was an opportunity to put into effect some of his innovations and to demonstrate how he believed an army in the field should be organized, fed, and led. Naturally he selected for his staff in Egypt two of his staunchest supporters and intimates: Gerald Graham, an old friend from the Crimean War, and Redvers Buller, a large, florid, and aggressive officer whose skill and fortitude Wolseley had greatly admired both in Canada in 1870 and in West Africa in 1873.[5]

There had early formed around Wolseley a devoted band of followers—known as the "Wolseley" or even, inevitably, the "Garnet Ring"—who served with him in distant parts of the Empire. In addition to finding appointments for friends upon whom he believed he could rely absolutely, Wolseley was faced with a flood of applications from officers who had found that the dull prosperity of Victoria's England was little to their liking and who wanted to serve in Egypt under "England's only general." Such men were constantly volunteering for any minor engagement or border war; for them there was seldom enough fighting to go around. Wolseley's campaign against Arabi promised excitement and, if an officer were lucky, quick promotion. For these professional soldiers, men like Kitchener, considerations of career

were paramount. In addition, young members of the nobility often maintained tenuous connections with the army and, upon occasion, employed
such connections as a means of serving in a particular campaign. The
Egyptian War of the summer of 1882 was a particularly fashionable event;
the season in London was over and a brief campaign in the desert promised
more excitement than racing or hunting in the English countryside. Everyone
wanted to participate in such a splendid outing, even the Prince of Wales.
For a few weeks, shops in Mayfair did a brisk trade in the air mattresses
and champagne that would make campaigning in the desert bearable.

The Queen herself prevented her heir from going with Wolseley, but
another son—one of two future governors general of Canada—was among
the officers who were successful in their efforts to be appointed. Elaborate
arrangements had to be made for the future tenth governor general of Canada,
the Duke of Connaught. Trained as an army engineer, the third son of Queen
Victoria had nevertheless served as an infantry officer in South Africa and
had spent a winter in Montreal in 1862, the same winter that had brought
Wolseley to Canada for a much longer period of service. Wolseley took
special precautions to ensure that the duke's service as commander of the
Guards Brigade in Egypt was as safe and as comfortable as possible. He wrote
to his wife that the royal duke "is really one of the most active Brigadiers
I have, and is very keen. I am distressed in my mind as to what I shall do,
for I want to shove the Foot Guards into a hot corner, and they want this
themselves, and they are the best troops I have, but I am so nervous that no
injury shall befall the favourite son of the Queen that I am loath to endanger
his life."[6] Wolseley had not, in any case, a very high opinion of the duke's
stamina. From Ismailia, he had written archly to his wife, "The Duke of
Connaught was *hors de combat* yesterday when I left him: a heavy march
in the sun, no dinner, and a bad bivouac had done him up."[7]

The other future governor general, Lord Melgund, later the fourth Earl
of Minto, was a former officer in the Scots Guards who had early decided
that his avocation as a jockey or "gentleman rider" meant more to him than
a military career.[8] Even breaking his neck in the Grand National did not, on
the one hand, prevent "Rollo" from continuing to race nor, on the other,
from participating in an unofficial way in the Russo-Turkish War of 1877
and the Afghan War of 1879. No longer in the army, Lord Melgund's arrival
in Egypt in 1882 was entirely on his own initiative. However, Wolseley soon
found a job for his old friend.

By the second week of September 1882, when most of his forty thousand
troops had arrived, Wolseley decided upon a daring night march over the
desert from the Suez Canal towards Arabi's troops, who were known to be
strung out across the route to Cairo. Night marches and particularly night
actions were rare and considered risky. Wolseley knew that he was gambling.
He wrote to his wife, "I fully realized the danger of the operations I had

determined upon, and I knew that if I failed every wiseacre in England would have said what a fool I was to have attempted a night attack."[9] But Wolseley also held a low opinion of the military skill of his opponent and a firm belief in the ability of his own trusted staff to carry out his plans without error. The one and only battle of the campaign to quell the revolt of Arabi, the Battle of Tel-el-Kebir, was fought at dawn on 13 September.

One of the main factors in the success of the attack on Arabi's lines at daybreak was the navigating skill of a young Canadian lieutenant in the Royal Navy who was one of Wolseley's aides-de-camp. Wyatt Rawson was born in 1850 in Quebec City, where his father and, later, his brother were Anglican clergymen. Educated at Bishop's College in Lennoxville, he had entered the Royal Navy as a cadet in 1867. Rawson won promotion to lieutenant in 1874 when he was serving under Wolseley in the Ashanti War in what is now northern Ghana. His bravery there at the battle of Amoaful, where he was severely wounded, brought him to the notice of Wolseley, who did not forget him when he needed a naval aide-de-camp in Egypt eight years later. Between his adventures on the Gold Coast and in Egypt, Rawson had returned to Canada in H.M.S. *Discovery* as a member of the Arctic expedition of 1875-76.[10] For his services in the Arctic, Rawson was elected a fellow of the Royal Geographical Society and was appointed to the comfortable and coveted, if not very active, post of lieutenant aboard the Royal Yacht *Victoria and Albert*.

It was from H.M.Y. *Victoria and Albert* that Rawson was named naval aide-de-camp to Wolseley. Wolseley always attempted to encourage Canadians serving in imperial forces, a habit that he had formed during his service in Canada from 1862 until 1870. For his purposes in Egypt, Wolseley could hardly have made a happier choice. Rawson had gained expert knowledge of celestial navigation during his service afloat, especially during the long night watches under the clear, cold skies of the Arctic. It was, therefore, with confidence that Rawson volunteered to guide the leading brigade of Wolseley's column across the desert on the silent night march (one wonders whether Rawson recalled, as he did so, that it was exactly 123 years since other British troops had gambled on a major night attack and had won victory—and a whole colony—near his hometown of Quebec).

An anonymous sergeant in the Highland Brigade later vividly described the unique service that Rawson performed in the desert near the small village of Tel-el-Kebir:

About 1:30 a.m., the march was resumed. The 79th was appointed the directing regiment, and Lieutenant Rawson, R.N., had the duty of guiding it by the stars. Clouds obscured the sky occasionally, but the North Star and part of the Little Bear remained visible. Another non-commissioned officer and myself had the honour of being told off to march on the flank, and we were, consequently, close to the directing guide, Lieutenant Rawson. We were ordered to take off our helmets and keep our eyes fixed on a certain star, and if it should disappear to inform him in a whisper. In less than an hour several disappeared, and, as they did so, Lieutenant Rawson indicated others for us to watch. The strictest discipline was now maintained, and silence rigorously enforced; save that occasionally a horse would neigh and another answer, not a sound was to be heard but the slow trampling of many feet on the sand, resembling the fluttering of a flock of birds. Once a man on whom the rum had taken effect or whom the weird silence had made ungovernably nervous, suddenly broke out into wild yells. Sir Garnet immediately rode up and ordered the offender to be bayoneted, but the regimental surgeon interposed and begged leave to chloroform him instead. This was granted—the man was drugged into insensibility and left lying on the sand.

After marching at a funeral's pace for about two hours, a twenty minutes' halt was commanded. As the orders were slowly passed from company to company, in a low tone of voice, they did not reach the flanks of the brigade, which continued in motion, retaining the touch till the extremities all but met in front of the centre, so that the brigade in effect formed a great hollow circle. This line had to be labouriously straightened out and reformed in the pitchy darkness, and in all but silence, and it was a fine proof of discipline that this was accomplished in twenty-five minutes. The advance was resumed at 4:30. The slowness of the pace was very tiring, and, but for the necessity of the steady watching of the stars, I certainly should have been nodding in sleep as I moved, as many men were doing. Sir Archibald Alison, commanding the brigade, was close to Lieutenant Rawson, and, as the night waned and nothing was discerned, he was clearly beginning to fear that something was wrong. "Are you sure, Rawson," he asked in a low tone, "that we are on the right track?" "Yes, sir!" said Rawson, "we have the North Star on our right, and"—another whose name I did not catch—"in our front, and soon we ought to be there or thereabouts." Dawn was just breaking. I could dimly see some objects in the front of us, looking like a lot of Kangaroos, hopping backwards and forwards— they were Egyptian cavalry we afterwards learned. I nudged my companion, and Rawson whispered "we are not far off now." Suddenly a shout was heard, then two shots were fired from opposite our left front and a man of F company fell dead. No notice was taken of this, and the brigade marched on silently; every man was on the alert. All at once a whole sheet of musketry flashed out, lighting up the scene far to right and left. Above the crackle of the rifle-fire sounded loud the roar of artillery. Regardless of these portents, our regiments marched silently and steadily on. The order to fix bayonets was given; when it had been obeyed and the men sloped arms, the rattle of the bullets on the bayonets was like the sound of hailstones striking against glass.

. . . the 79th had marched quite one hundred yards with their rifles at the slope when the command, "prepare to charge!" was given. Down came the rifles of the front rank of the unbroken line. The "charge" sounded, and as the last note of the bugle died away, a tremendous cheer was raised, the pipes struck up the slogan, and with our gallant colonel in front, shouting "Come on, the Camerons," the ranks broke into double time, and still cheering, with all their power swept forward on the enemy's position. One of the pipers, just as he began to play, had his bag-pipes pierced by a bullet, and most discordant sounds escaped from the wounded instrument. "Guid faith", cried the piper philosophically, "but the bullet's a deevilitch sicht better through her wame than though mine."[11]

Another of the Egyptian bullets, however, found its mark, and Rawson fell mortally wounded as he clambered up the Egyptian earthworks and sprang over the trenches. He was carried to a hospital ship at Port Said where, two days before his death on 20 September, he learned of his promotion to commander in recognition of his bravery. Wolseley missed his Canadian aide-de-camp and noted sadly in a letter to his wife on 15 September, "I fear poor Rawson cannot live. He was shot through the body leading the Brigade to the point of attack. Such a fine, plucky fellow!"[12] A nineteen-year-old Scot in the Black Watch, who had admired greatly Rawson's good humour and spirit on the troopship taking them to Egypt in August 1881, recalled how, "ignoring the fact that when by his extraordinary genius he had so skilfully led us across the desert that although our charge was in the darkness of night we faced Egyptian muzzles in the morning light, his duty was ended, he joined with us, in the fight for possession of the trenches and was one of the first to reach them. . . . Serene were his last days and bright. I have been told that when General Wolseley visited him, from his bed of pain he looked up, smiling, and . . . exclaimed, 'Didn't I lead them straight, General!' "[13]

Charles Francis Winter, another Canadian, lived to describe with pride and admiration the great contribution his compatriot had made to the success of the campaign. Having become bored by his work in Canada as a bank clerk and a purser aboard a Lake Ontario steamer, Winter sought adventure by sailing to England and joining the 7th Royal Fusiliers. As a nineteen-year-old corporal, Winter saw service throughout the campaign of 1882 and remained with the British army of occupation until the following summer. Thirty years later, writing in the *Canadian Magazine*, Winter could still recall the profound silence and suppressed excitement in which the British army had marched across the desert, guided by the navigating skill of Rawson.[14]

One other young Canadian had hoped to participate in the campaign against Arabi, to join in the excitement of an imperial campaign, but before he could do so, he had succumbed to typhoid fever, a disease which killed more of Wolseley's soldiers than Egyptian bullets. Lieutenant P. O. J. Hébert of "B" Battery of the Canadian Regiment of Artillery had, like so many British officers, applied for permission to serve in the campaign against Arabi. The Canadian government, eager to see its new permanent force officers as well trained and experienced as possible, successfully recommended Hébert's application to the imperial authorities.[15] After a hurried farewell to his relatives near St. Jean, Quebec, the ambitious and adventurous Joseph Hébert arrived in England in August 1882 and sailed at the end of that month for Egypt. Upon his arrival at Suez, he was attached to "N" Battery of Wolseley's Second Brigade, the same brigade in which Corporal Winter served. However, before Hébert could join his new unit, he contracted the enteric disease, which soon proved fatal. He was buried with full military honours in Cairo in late September 1882.

While Hébert languished in a Suez military hospital a week before his death, Wolseley won the Battle of Tel-el-Kebir. Arabi's army had been quickly and decisively beaten. No further resistance to the advance of the British was offered by the Egyptian nationalists. They entered Cairo unopposed. Soon the Khedive Tewfik was placed back on his throne, and Arabi was sent off to exile in Ceylon.[16] It had all taken only a few weeks. It was, Wolseley believed, "the tidiest war in British history." The problem of Egypt, however, continued to plague Gladstone's government. And the problem of Egypt became more than ever a British problem. The destruction of the rebellious Egyptian army had in fact compounded the difficulties already caused by continuing Egyptian bankruptcy.

From their very first and reluctant intervention in Egyptian affairs, factors partly outside their control had resulted in Gladstone's Liberals becoming increasingly involved in Egypt. Now with garrisons in Cairo and Alexandria, the British government began to think about consolidating its influence before carrying out the withdrawal from Egypt which it had repeatedly promised. Queen Victoria urged upon the home secretary "the absolute necessity... of... securing to ourselves such a position in Egypt as to secure our Indian Dominions and to maintain our superiority in the East."[17] To do this, the British cabinet set itself the goal of creating a stable, self-governing Egypt with a well-trained army and an efficient civil service. The resultant benefits, Gladstone hopefully recorded, could only make the Egyptian people permanently grateful to Britain, and through such gratitude and friendship, the supremacy of British influence in the eastern Mediterranean would be so firmly established that never again would the Suez Canal be threatened by a rebel such as Arabi. On these broad lines of principle the cabinet more or less agreed. The details of how best to implement this wildly optimistic policy were, however, to be considered only after Lord Dufferin had visited Egypt and reported on the situation there.

Frederick Temple Hamilton Temple Blackwood, the first Marquess of Dufferin and Ava, was one of the most capable of British diplomats of the nineteenth century.[18] An accomplished linguist, famous for his tact and discretion, an explorer in the sub-Arctic, and an experienced administrator, Dufferin had been better qualified for his appointment in 1872 as the third governor general of Canada than most of his successors, who were more often selected for their social position than for their personal qualifications. An indefatigable traveller, he had done much to foster whatever sense of unity there was in the young Canadian nation. Following his departure from Canada in 1878, Dufferin, a staunch Liberal, had been appointed British ambassador to Russia and subsequently to Turkey, whence he travelled to Egypt.

While compiling his long report about the state of Egypt following the climacteric of the Battle of Tel-el-Kebir during the winter of 1882, Dufferin had to bear in mind that his recommendations for the administration of the country, especially the financial arrangements, should, if possible, be acceptable to the French, who were both jealous of growing British influence in Egypt and the most vociferous spokesman for the ubiquitous European bondholders. Any attempt to reconcile a continued British presence in Egypt with French ambitions, however, soon proved impossible. Equally difficult were the efforts that Gladstone was making to reconcile conflicting views in his cabinet about British involvement in Egypt, with the Radicals calling for prompt withdrawal and the "annexationists" (some of whom believed that only in that way would better government for the masses result and others of whom were simply imperialists) calling for the inclusion of Egypt in the growing British Empire. The prime minister finally settled doubts about British policy in Egypt by adopting the idealistic recommendations Dufferin submitted in early 1883. A sound administration was to be established in Egypt and the foundations thereby laid for liberal constitutional advance. A new Egyptian army was to be trained and partly officered by Englishmen. These policies were what Gladstone wanted to hear. He could not bring himself to recognize that he had placed Britain in a position where it could not depart from Egypt without creating an unacceptable vacuum. He convinced himself that the Egyptians could be trained to govern themselves in the best liberal traditions. British troops would then be withdrawn, Egyptian friendship and, consequently, the security of the Suez Canal having been secured. However, events in the distant Sudan soon led Gladstone's government to recognize the futility of considering as a practicable policy the early evacuation of the British garrison in Egypt.

Egypt had, in fact, become a part of the Victorian imperial tapestry. In theory it was still part of the ailing Turkish domains, but to such as Wolseley and his "Ring," Egypt had passed under British suzerainty. For them and for many in Canada as well as Britain, the Empire had a unity which led them to see the dominions and colonies as parts of a whole. Talent could be recruited anywhere in the Empire and employed anywhere in imperial enterprises. Wolseley and his two lieutenants in Egypt, Graham and Buller, had all served in Canada. Two future governors general of Canada and a commanding officer of the Canadian militia served under Wolseley in Egypt in 1882, and a former governor general was assigned the conundrum of what to do with Egypt. And Egypt in 1882 did not merely involve British officers who had served in Canada. Canadians serving in British forces were also present: Rawson, Hébert, and Winter. Within the Empire, a growing sense of unity was embodied in the persons, careers, and attitudes of such men as these, all embarked upon imperial ventures, all part of the imperial fabric.

4

Gordon and the Sudan

Let all show penitence before God, and abandon all bad and forbidden habits, such as the degrading acts of the flesh, the use of wine and tobacco, lying, bearing false witness, disobedience to parents, brigandage, the non-restitution of goods to others, the clapping of hands, dancing, improper signs with the eyes, tears and lamentations at the bed of the dead, slanderous language, calumny, and the company of strange women. Clothe your women in a decent way, and let them be careful not to speak to unknown persons. All those who do not pay attention to these principles disobey God and His Prophet, and they shall be punished in accordance with the law.

FROM AN EARLY PROCLAMATION OF THE MAHDI

About 1840 a son was born to a Sudanese boat-builder on the banks of the Upper Nile. As the boy, Mohammed Ahmed, grew older, his devotion to Islam became increasingly pronounced. The renown of his zeal, piety, and asceticism spread. Eventually, from a retreat in the desert, Mohammed Ahmed announced that he was none other than the long-awaited "Mahdi," the guide of the faithful whom God had "placed upon His Throne above princes and nobles. And He has also told me that whosoever doubts my mission, does not believe in God or His prophets." This bold claim from the self-styled messiah was received with disdain by the Egyptian governors of the Sudanese provinces. The desert had produced false prophets before. No doubt the local Egyptian officials reassured themselves that this was just another such fraud. But to many Sudanese, Mohammed Ahmed's proclamation of early 1881 seemed to be a call to devotion by the true Mahdi. Had not this ascetic teacher shown the profound piety with which the Mahdi would be endowed? Did not the prophecies and certain traditions of Islam teach that the messiah would appear in the Muslim year 1300 (approximately the Christian year 1883) and that he would be a man of great asceticism and learning? Even the folklore of the people of the desert taught that the Mahdi would bear such marks as a mole on his cheek and a gap between his front teeth—characteristics that Mohammed Ahmed clearly possessed.

In the eyes of increasing numbers of Sudanese tribesmen at least, it was evident that the eloquent Mohammed Ahmed embodied all these characteristics. The Sudanese became convinced that the true Mahdi had at last arrived to call them to his earthly kingdom. Life under brutal Egyptian rule was one of deprivation and hardship. Around the sacred green banner that the Mahdi unfurled gathered the forces of religious fervour and popular unrest. Religious and national fanaticism joined together in the immense, silent land of the upper Nile at the moment when the confusion in Cairo caused by Arabi's revolt loosened the already tenuous Egyptian hold on it. The Egyptian governor general in Khartoum was himself a devout Muslim, but he began to realize that this gifted religious teacher in the desert, of whom he heard more and more, this so-called Mahdi, presented a double threat to his civil administration. The message that Mohammed Ahmed preached was not only religious; it was also, at least by implication, political. The followers of the Mahdi pledged themselves to make a *Jihad*, a Holy War, on the oppressive Egyptians, on the Turks, and on infidels everywhere—all, in short, who denied the true faith and who were exploiting the Sudanese poor. An alien government that employed rhinocerous whips to enforce its will became as much a target as those who refused to believe in the divine message of the Mahdi. At first the governor general attempted through conciliatory messages to persuade his brother Muslim, the Mahdi, of his error in inciting his fellow Sudanese to revolt. But when the Mahdi replied with an invitation to the governor general himself to embrace the true faith or ensure the eternal torment of his soul, the insulted Egyptian decided to use force where his attempts at persuasion had failed.

But force too failed. Victory followed victory for the Mahdi. At first mainly with spears, but later with the firearms largely captured from his enemies, the Mahdi, his three lieutenants (the "Khalifas"), and his small irregular forces defeated two punitive expeditions sent against them by the governor general. Thereafter even more Sudanese flocked to join the Mahdi and to don the distinctive garment of his followers, the *jibbah* or loose night-shirt of Egypt with patches added as a mark of humility—or, in some cases, decoration. The Mahdi's first major opponent soon suffered the humiliation of being recalled by the Khedive for his incompetence. The·new governor general, Abdel-Kader (or Abdul Qadir), having served with the French army in Mexico and with Sir Samuel Baker in the Sudan, felt confident that he could defeat the obstreperous rebel. But Abdel-Kader, like his vanquished predecessor, failed to recognize the real strength of the religious and political fanaticism the Mahdi had aroused by his teachings. In June 1882, a large but ill-equipped force sent against the Mahdi was decisively defeated.

The Mahdi was not always victorious. His attempt to capture the provincial capital of El Obeid the week before Wolseley's victory at distant Tel-el-Kebir failed at the colossal cost of about ten thousand of his followers killed and wounded. The firearms of the Egyptian garrison had proven—as they were often to prove later—their superiority over spears and sticks. But the setback to the Mahdi's forces was brief. The Mahdi explained to his followers that the defeat at El Obeid had been fore-ordained by God to test the zeal of true believers. It was part of the necessary suffering which must precede great victories. And in a short time, the Mahdi had again proved himself right. Governor General Abdel-Kader was unable to obtain anything like the necessary reinforcements from Egypt, now in near chaos following Arabi's revolt and his defeat at Tel-el-Kebir. As a result, the Mahdi was able to starve the garrison town of El Obeid into submission in January 1883.

As soon as the Khedive Tewfik reascended the Egyptian throne with the support of British arms, he turned some of his attention to his rapidly disintegrating dependency of the Sudan. He decided to send to the Sudan a large—but badly equipped—army (some of the soldiers were no more than convicts still in chains) under a former Indian army officer, Colonel William Hicks, to put down the Mahdist rebellion once and for all. Gladstone and his foreign secretary, anxious not to become yet further involved in Egyptian affairs and committed to peace, retrenchment, and reform, refused to support such a forward Egyptian policy in the Sudan, despite a specific recommendation to the contrary that Lord Dufferin had included in his report:

> It is probable that, if only some person like Colonel Gordon could be found to undertake its administration, fairly good government could be maintained in the Sudan. Colonel Gordon, I believe, has already broken up and disorganized in a great measure the former centres of the slave traffic, and the same energy and ability which has gone so near to effecting this difficult task ought to be sufficient to keep the country in order.[1]

After reviewing the many intractable problems of the Sudan and acutely conscious of demands at home for reform, Gladstone advised abandonment. The Mahdi was causing more trouble than the Sudan was worth.

The Khedive, however, had already decided on one more effort to subdue his rebellious province, which had been nominally a part of Egypt since 1819. "Hicks Pasha" was appointed a general in the Egyptian army and commander-in-chief in the Sudan and given orders to destroy the Mahdists. The colonel, however, although a competent officer, was not the "person like Colonel Gordon" whom Dufferin had in mind. After a few initial victories, his campaign against the Mahdi rapidly deteriorated and ended in disaster. The whole of his army, his ten thousand miserable Egyptian soldiers, his dozen European officers, and the governor general all died with him on 5 November 1883, while attempting to penetrate deeper into the Mahdi's stronghold in the southern Sudan. After being led astray by treacherous guides, the Egyptian troops suffered three days of terrible thirst in the desert south of Khartoum before their annihilation. Their defeat was rendered all the more certain by their panicking when the Mahdists suddenly attacked (a *Times* correspondent had described Hicks's army as "9,000 infants, that 50 good men would rout in 10 minutes"). As a result of Hick's defeat, the Mahdi's hold on the Sudan was further strengthened. The faith of his followers now became so complete that, among other acts of simple piety, they drank his wash water in the hope of curing themselves of sickness.

The catastrophe to Hicks's force changed the whole Egyptian problem. The Khedive now had no more troops to send into the Sudan and few enough for service at home. He had gambled with his last army and had lost. The Sudan, it now appeared, would have to be abandoned, at least for the time being. Paradoxically, however, as Egyptian influence in the Sudan diminished, British interest and involvement grew. Following Hicks's dramatic end, Gladstone found it increasingly difficult to ignore the Sudan. Egyptian problems became and remained prominent in every London newspaper. Willy-nilly Britain was being dragged into the affairs of the Sudan in much the same way that it had earlier become entangled in the problems of Egypt. Hicks's costly campaign had been preceded by the defeat of a small force of Egyptians, officered by Englishmen, on the Red Sea coast of the Sudan. Since the Red Sea was part of the Suez route to India, Britain could not let the coast fall into unfriendly hands, even those of such ill-equipped rebels as those led by Osman Digna, a somewhat independent-minded follower of the Mahdi.[2] There could be no doubt about the necessity of holding the Red Sea coast. Even the hinterland of the Sudan intruded itself on British thoughts. If the Mahdi established his control over the whole of the Sudan (and now that Hicks's forces had been vanquished that hitherto remote possibility seemed increasingly likely), the borders of Egypt itself would be threatened. For the Suez Canal to be safe, Egypt had to be safe; for Egypt to be safe, the border with the Sudan had to be safe. Turkish troops might be available but few British statemen wished to see them in Egypt. Britain certainly did not want to see Turkey dead, but it was content to see the sickness of the Turk continue indefinitely. A resurgence of Turkish influence in the eastern Mediterranean could be detrimental to British interests. The strategic needs of the British Empire again began to erode Gladstone's resolution not to become further involved in Egyptian affairs. The prime minister was beginning to understand Napoleon's cryptic hyperbolic statement that Egypt is the most important country in the world.

Finding it difficult to decide, the British government asked its representative in Egypt what he thought should be done about the Sudan. The newly appointed British agent and consul-general in Cairo was the type of man who was seldom in doubt about what policy should be followed in any given situation. Despite his modest title, Sir Evelyn Baring was to be the virtual ruler of Egypt for the next twenty-four years.[3] Strong and self-reliant, "Over-Baring," as some in Cairo called him, was the epitome of the British overseas administrator who had learned his trade in India. He firmly believed that the "scientific" administration which Britain had applied with considerable success in India would be equally felicitous in Egypt. Good administration and unparalleled efficiency were always the goals of those such as Baring and Wolseley (both of whom had served under Cardwell during that war minister's reforms of 1870-71). Prosperity and justice in Egypt, Baring was certain, would lead to the same apparent contentment, tranquillity, and consolidation of British influence that had occurred in India. Good administration was one more safeguard of imperial interests. The personification of the calm, conscientious, and efficient administrator, Baring was in many ways the opposite of the volatile Gordon, who not surprisingly wrote of him after their first meeting, "he has a pretentious, grand patronising way about him. . . . When oil mixes with water we will mix together."4 Gordon's description was candid but incomplete. It neglected those outstanding abilities which made Baring one of the greatest administrators that the British Empire ever knew and which helped to establish the British position in Egypt for more than half a century.

In reply to Gladstone's cabinet's request for advice on the bothersome problem of the distant and little known Sudan, the consul-general wired that if Khartoum fell, there would be danger to Egypt. The sublimely confident Mahdi had long before announced that after he had placed himself at the head of the liberated people of the Sudan, he would next attack Egypt, then Turkey, and subsequently that little country called Europe that lay beyond its borders. Already the British generals in Cairo and even some Egyptian officials were beginning to question whether the hot, dusty capital of Khartoum could be held. The Egyptians had some time previously decided to abandon the southern and western provinces of the Sudan. The Egyptian government was, however, still determined to make further efforts to hold at least the Red Sea littoral and the two routes to Khartoum which ran from the coastal town of Suakin and from the inland town of Berber on the Nile north of Khartoum. To a pessimistic report from Baring about the security of Egypt, Lord Granville, the foreign secretary, replied that, in view of the uncertain conditions, the planned reduction in the British garrison in Cairo would be delayed. "Egypt proper" and the Red Sea coast must be held—if necessary by British arms. But, the reply from London added, "Her Majesty's Government can do nothing which would throw upon them the responsibility of operations in the Sudan."5 Nevertheless, in January 1884, Baring reported that, "the Egyptian Government would feel obliged if Her Majesty's Government would sent at once a qualified British officer to go to Khartoum with full powers, military and civil, to conduct the retreat [from Khartoum]."6

All this Gladstone attempted to pass off as an Egyptian problem, but wriggle as he would, he was caught. Try to deny responsibility as he might, try to concentrate upon domestic affairs as he would, each successive event made it yet more difficult for Gladstone to extricate Britain from involvement. Once upper Egypt and the Red Sea coast appeared to be threatened by the Mahdi's hordes and once the British press and public opinion were aroused by the Hicks disaster, Gladstone found it increasingly difficult to maintain his indifference to the fate of the Sudan. Moreover, as Sir Philip Magnus has noted, "The exotic glare of the upper Nile fascinated late-Victorian England. The rich and little-known Sudanese hinterland of Egypt offered a tempting field of adventure; and the dramatic appearance of a false Messiah exercising despotic authority over a gigantic territory, and claiming supernatural powers at a time when the controversy between science and religion was at its height, posed a romantic challenge."[7] Victorian Britain could not neglect such a challenge. In London, the name of an officer who had boldly confronted and quelled fanatical hordes in China twenty years before and who had more recently given the Sudan its only honest administration was heard ever more frequently as the saviour of a rapidly deteriorating situation. He was clearly a brilliant leader in irregular warfare. He might again be able to perform miracles. "Chinese Gordon for the Sudan!" became a popular panacea for all the ills of the land of the Upper Nile. With increasing urgency, newspapers repeated the demand. Even Sir Samuel Baker, the great African explorer, named Gordon as the one man who could fill successfully the office of British high commissioner in the Sudan.

Gordon, in 1882 promoted a major-general, had, since his departure from the Sudan three years earlier, added to his already large public following by helping to settle a dispute with native tribes in South Africa. In Mauritius, where he had commanded the Royal Engineers, the intensity of his Christian faith had become yet more pronounced through lonely meditation; in the Holy Land, where he spent almost the whole of 1883, his mysticism had increased as a result of his studies, including a search for the burial place of Christ. He was finished, he announced upon his return to London in late 1883, with the falsity and hypocrisy of life in England. At the moment when his return to the Sudan began to be urged, Gordon intended to resign his army commission so that he might enter the service of the King of the Belgians to help suppress slavery in the Congo.

By December 1883, the deterioration in the Sudan had proceeded so far that Gladstone and his cabinet finally came to a decision of a sort. They decided to avoid any further commitments by the simple expediency of calling upon Egypt to abandon the Sudan and to establish a strong line of defence along her southern border near Wadi Halfa. If the Egyptian government would agree to abandon the Sudan, Britain would undertake the defence of both the Red Sea coast and of Egypt itself. (Britain had really no other choice but to defend Egypt since it had destroyed one Egyptian army and had not yet completed the organization of another.) "We are satisfied," Baring's cousin, Lord Northbrook, the First Lord of the Admiralty, noted in explaining the British insistence on abandonment of the Sudan,

> that Egypt should no longer be hampered by the attempt to govern a piece of the world as long as Europe when she cannot find a Corporal's guard fit to fight...or...a hundred thousand pounds to pay troops without plunging deeper into bankruptcy....We are not going to spend the lives of Englishmen or of natives of India in either supporting Egyptian rule in the Soudan or of taking half Africa for ourselves and trying to govern it.[8]

The "hundred thousand pounds" was a principal factor in the British decision. Britain was not going to pay for any Egyptian adventures in the Sudan, and clearly Egypt could not afford to take the offensive again in the foreseeable future. After the chaos caused by the Arabi revolt, Egypt was once again on the verge of bankruptcy. In the eyes of British statesmen, the Sudan was one major charge on the Egyptian budget that was clearly expendable.

But there was more than just money involved in the Sudan problem. There were men's lives at stake. It was all very well to say that the Sudan should be abandoned and the line of defence established at the Egyptian border, but there remained the problem of how to remove the twenty-one thousand Egyptian soldiers who formed the fourteen scattered garrisons in the Sudan. If the British were going to force the Egyptians to surrender the Sudan to the Mahdi, they assumed a moral responsibility for the evacuation of the Egyptian garrisons at the same time. This was a dilemma that could not be avoided. For this reason Gladstone and his Liberals began to listen to the now incessant call of "Chinese Gordon for the Sudan!"

After a number of false starts and misgivings, the British government finally muddled into sending Gordon to Khartoum in a manner which was entirely in keeping with its previous ill-considered fashion of wading ever more deeply into Egyptian affairs. Once again the members of Gladstone's cabinet could not agree. This time their disagreement centred on what exactly it was that Gordon was to do in the Sudan. The cabinet moved to obtain his agreement to forego his appointment to the Belgian Congo, but it went on debating what he should be instructed to do in Khartoum.

It was at this point that the paths of Wolseley and Gordon again crossed. The careers of the two old friends had differed greatly since the days when they had stood together before the walls of Sebastapol. Gordon had taken unusual jobs in out-of-the-way places; Wolseley had sought quick promotion through service in the many little wars that Britain fought during the latter half of the nineteenth century. Nevertheless, Gordon and Wolseley had met from time to time, they had corresponded intermittently, and now they were brought together once again in London. By 1884, Wolseley was adjutant general, a methodical and efficient officer still eager to rise to the very top of the service. Since the commander-in-chief, whom he despised, the old Duke of Cambridge, was interested mainly in military tradition and ceremonies, Wolseley had been able to become the secretary of state for war's chief adviser. Gordon, on the other hand, was careless of the opinions of this world, indifferent to the attentions of the great, and happiest when helping neglected and oppressed peoples. At their meeting at the War Office on 15 January 1884, Wolseley took the initiative of asking his old friend whether he would be willing to go to Suakin to enquire into the general state of Sudanese affairs and to recommend what steps should be taken in the light of the prevailing circumstances. This was the role of a reporter, an essentially passive role that required no initiatives, and a role which Hartington, the secretary of state for war, was prepared to envisage for Gordon. However, there was another idea abroad both in the cabinet and, more especially, in London newspapers; Gordon must be sent to the Sudan to withdraw—somehow—the Egyptian garrisons and civilians. It is, therefore, not surprising that, in the general confusion surrounding the formulation of his sudden mission, vague instructions which implied both reporting and supervisory functions were finally issued at a meeting between Gordon and four cabinet ministers on the afternoon of 18 January.[9] Gladstone, preoccupied with problems of parliamentary reform and Ireland, was given the impression by the four cabinet ministers that Gordon would be asked to go to the Sudan merely to report on local conditions. At the meeting with the ministers (including Hartington and Northbrook), Gordon was asked, according to his own laconic version, "'Had I seen Wolseley and did I understand their ideas?' I said 'Yes,' and reported what Wolseley had said to me as to their ideas, which was: 'they would evacuate the Sudan.' They were pleased and said, 'That was their idea, would I go?' I said, 'Yes.' They said, 'When?' I said, 'Tonight,' and it was over."[10]

Gladstone gave his general approval to these curious proceedings, but no precise agreement about Gordon's mission had ever been reached by the prime minister and his cabinet colleagues. Later, misunderstandings and costly delays were caused by differences about whether they had asked Gordon to go to Suakin simply to report and recommend or whether he had been commissioned to attempt the infinitely more difficult task of evacuating the Khartoum garrison (as Gordon understood). In either case, Gladstone should have known better than to agree to send such a brilliant and perverse officer to carry out what amounted to a vaguely defined policy of retreat. Gordon was the most unsuitable person imaginable for a task which demanded great patience and consistency. Baring summed up well—if some-

what uncharitably—Gordon's eccentric character when he later recalled
how the decision to send Gordon to the Sudan had been reached:

> a more unfortunate choice could scarcely have been made than that
> of General Gordon to carry out the policy of evacuating the Soudan.
> The execution of that policy should have been in the hands of a man
> who could fight if necessary, but who would devote all his efforts to
> turning his mission into one of peace rather than of war; he should
> have been cool, self-controlled, clear-headed, and consistent, deliberate
> in the formation of his plans after a careful study of the facts with
> which he had to deal, and steadfast in their execution when once his
> mind was made up. He should have had sufficient knowledge of English
> public life to have been able to form some fairly accurate conjecture
> of the motives which were likely to guide the British Government,
> even if no definite expression of opinion had been conveyed to him.
> General Gordon possessed none of these qualities. He was extremely
> pugnacious. He was hot-headed, impulsive, and swayed by his emotions.
> It is a true saying that "he that would govern others, first should be
> the master of himself." One of the leading features of General Gordon's
> strange character was his total absence of self-control. He was liable
> to fits of ungovernable and often of most unreasonable passion. He
> formed rapid opinions without deliberation, and rarely held to one
> opinion for long. His Journal, in which his thoughts from day to day
> are recorded, is...a mass of inconsistencies. He knew nothing of
> English public life.... He appears to have been devoid of the talent,
> so valuable to a public servant in a distant country, of transporting
> himself in spirit elsewhere. His imagination, indeed, ran riot, but when-
> ever he endeavoured to picture to himself what was passing in Cairo or
> London, he arrived at conclusions which were not only unworthy of
> himself, but grotesque, as, for instance, when he likened himself to
> Uriah the Hittite, and insinuated that the British Government hoped
> that he and his companions would be killed or taken prisoner by the
> Mahdi. In fact, except personal courage, great fertility in military
> resource, a lively though sometimes ill-directed repugnance to injustice,
> oppression, and meanness of every description, and a considerable
> power of acquiring influence over those, necessarily limited in numbers,
> with whom he was brought in personal contact, General Gordon does
> not appear to have possessed any of the qualities which would have
> fitted him to undertake the difficult task he had in hand.[11]

Gordon, quixotic and elusive though he was, might himself have agreed with Baring's description, if he had lived long enough to read this unflattering analysis of his character. He himself once wrote in his journal, "I own to having been very insubordinate to Her Majesty's Government and its officials, but it is my nature, and I cannot help it. . . . I know that if *I* was chief, I would never employ *myself*, for I am incorrigible."[12]

The fateful decision had, however, been made. No matter how unsuitable or incorrigible, Gordon had been asked by the British government to go to the Sudan on an ill-defined and ill-considered mission. For months past nothing had been done by London as much of the Sudan gradually passed under the control of the Mahdi. Then, suddenly, a decision had been made that something had to be done, that Chinese Gordon was the man to do it, and that it had to be done at once—a decision that was warmly welcomed in the London press as soon as it became known.

True to his word, on the same evening that he had seen the four cabinet ministers, Gordon left Charing Cross Station on the "Brindisi Mail," bound for Italy. It was a curious scene. The foreign secretary, Lord Granville, carried Gordon's ticket to the carriage for him, the commander-in-chief, the Duke of Cambridge, held its door open for him, and Wolseley, having learned that his old friend had only a few shillings with him, pressed on him his own watch and the cash he had been able to collect during hurried visits to several London clubs. That strange little farewell on the station platform was, somehow, a fitting departure for the rather lonely, stocky major-general who had, for many years, so consciously shunned this world's rewards.

Less than one month later, an onlooker in Khartoum would have seen Gordon, in his red fez and white uniform and accompanied by his aide, Lieutenant-Colonel J. D. H. Stewart,[13] watching the records of debtors being burned, the chains of convicts being struck off, and prisoners being set free. The gates of the city were opened and any who wished to join the Mahdi were told that they were now free to do so. This was Gordon's dramatic way of marking the beginning of a new era in Sudanese history, an era in which, he was determined, the Egyptian garrisons would be withdrawn in accordance with what he understood to be the British government's wishes. At the same time, however, he was also determined that a local and a just administration, able to withstand the Mahdi, should be established in the place of the departing Egyptians. By interpreting his orders in this wide fashion, Gordon had gone far beyond what Gladstone and his colleagues had envisaged as his assignment. He was acting as plenipotentiary governor general with full powers to impose and depose. On his way to Khartoum, Gordon had stopped only briefly in Cairo (he had been persuaded by Baring to forego Suakin and travel by the Nile to Khartoum), but it was long enough for him to convince both the Khedive and a somewhat sceptical Baring that he should be reappointed governor general. None in the Sudan would then be in any doubt about his supreme authority.

Gordon was optimistic that he could achieve his basically impracticable dual goal of evacuation of the Egyptian garrisons from Khartoum and the establishment of a stable native government. Yet there was, in fact, little reason for his optimism. It was true that Gordon was back again as governor general among the people for whose welfare he had worked so diligently in the past. He was back again in the country which had never been far from his thoughts in the years that he had been away. His personal reputation in the Sudan was still high, and the welcome of the people of Khartoum, enthusiastic. Yet these factors, potent though they might be, were no longer enough to restore order throughout the Sudan. The Sudan in 1884 was not the country that Gordon had known so well ten years before. In the understatement of one of Gordon's ablest biographers,

> In retrospect, the idea of sending two men, foreigners and Christians, with a very rudimentary knowledge of the local language and only a limited knowledge of the country, alone, with a credit of £100,000 and an Egyptian secretary, to conduct the peaceful evacuation of a demoralized garrison of some 6,000 men, plus 10,000–15,000 unarmed civilians, including a large proportion of women and children, through some 500 miles of desert, in face of a victorious enemy and through the midst of an armed, hostile and predatory population, does not seem to have been a very promising one.[14]

Gordon might have been warned of the enormous power of religious fervour, particularly when joined with incipient nationalism, by an event which had occurred only a fortnight before his arrival in Khartoum. On the Red Sea coast, an Egyptian force of four thousand under the command of a former British cavalry officer, Valentine Baker (who had left the army after having been convicted of assaulting a girl in a railway carriage),[15] was decisively beaten as it broke in terror in the face of a wild charge by the Mahdists. Colonel Fred Burnaby of the "Blues" (the Royal Horse Guards), who accompanied Baker on the debacle, later recorded his impressions of the massacre resulting from the blind fear that overcame the badly trained Egyptian soldiers.

> The sight was one never to be forgotten some four thousand men running pell-mell for their lives with a few hundred Arabs behind them spearing everyone within reach; General Baker and Colonel Hay, with the Arabs between themselves and the Egyptians forcing a passage through their foes; Egyptians on their knees praying for mercy; English

and foreign officers at the guns surrounded by numerous assailants selling their lives dearly. Here an Egyptian, who had thrown away his rifle and had run two or three hundred yards, could be observed undressing himself in order to run the faster; there a Bashi-Bazouk galloping as quick as his horse could go and firing his carbine, regardless of whether he hit friend or foe; around us nothing but butchery; English officers doing their best to rally the Egyptians, who had been the first to leave the field of battle. Several of these cowards were shot, but nothing would induce the others to oppose the Arabs.[16]

The six-foot-two-inch Burnaby was well known as a colourful officer even in the colourful army of Victoria's later years. Like many of his contemporaries, he sought adventure in out-of-the-way campaigns. A daring balloonist, a visitor to Gordon in the Sudan in 1875, an observer of wars in Bulgaria and Spain, Burnaby used on the Red Sea coast a massive double-barrelled shotgun to slaughter Mahdists, some of whom were armed only with spears or even sticks.[17]

Burnaby alone counted for many "fuzzy-wuzzies," yet the victory was clearly the Mahdi's. Two small towns near the port of Suakin subsequently fell to his able lieutenant, the ex-slaver Osman Digna. As a result a small British force was shut up in Suakin itself. Khartoum became yet more isolated. Now the route to the Red Sea coast was cut off; only the Nile and the telegraph line to Cairo remained open. Somewhat belatedly, London acknowledged that no further deterioration on the Red Sea coast could be permitted; the British government formally declared that its retention in friendly hands was essential to imperial interests. After the defeat near Suakin, it was obvious that Egyptian soldiers could not be relied upon to hold it. Accordingly, in late February 1884, partly at the urging of Wolseley, four thousand British soldiers were despatched from Cairo to Suakin under the command of two prominent members of his "Ring," Sir Gerald Graham, a friend of Gordon and Wolseley from Crimean War days and a veteran of service in China and Canada (where he had been posted as senior engineering officer in the Montreal Military District from 1866 to 1869) and Redvers Buller, who had served under Wolseley in the Red River Expedition of 1870. By March, after Graham had fought two battles with Osman Digna, Suakin and the Red Sea littoral could once more be considered secure. That was, however, anything but true of the rest of the Sudan.

In Khartoum, as the dervishes gradually closed in around the city after having invested or defeated the Egyptian garrisons further south, Gordon set about carrying out his vague instructions as he interpreted them. With his Bible never far from him, the Victorian "chevalier sans peur et sans reproche" made arrangements for six hundred Turkish and Egyptian sick and aged, children and widows, to travel down the Nile to safety. At the same time, he urged upon Baring in Cairo and, through him, on the government in London, a variety of ways in which he believed that a native administration might be successfully established in the Sudan. However, despite his apparent optimism, Gordon soon realized the extreme difficulty of what he was attempting to do. He also clearly foresaw the danger to Egypt if the Mahdi were allowed to capture Khartoum. He telegraphed to Baring on 26 February:

> My duty is evacuation and the best I can for establishing a quiet government. The first I hope to accomplish. The second is a difficult task and concerns Egypt more than me. If Egypt is to be quiet, Mahdi must be smashed up.... Remember that once Khartoum belongs to Mahdi, the task will be far more difficult; yet you will, for the safety of Egypt, execute it.... I repeat that evacuation is possible, but you will feel the effect in Egypt, and will be forced into a far more serious affair in order to guard Egypt.[18]

Gordon understood far more than the vacillating cabinet in London that the safety of Egypt could not be secured by the simple expedient of evacuating the Sudan. That would only embolden the Mahdi to attack Egypt proper. Gordon was increasingly convinced that there could be no real peace for Egypt or security for the British position astride the Suez Canal until the Mahdi had been in his words finally "smashed up."

Gordon did, however, take every precaution not to become involved in any fighting with the Mahdists who were gradually closing in on Khartoum. The Mahdi was fully aware of the importance of Khartoum; if it fell, the few other Egyptian garrisons would soon succumb. Yet Gordon, a man who had always attempted to avoid bloodshed whenever possible, managed to prevent any clashes between his Egyptian and Sudanese troops and the Mahdists during the first month he was in Khartoum. With incredible energy, he did everything possible to put his seven thousand Egyptian and Sudanese soldiers and approximately fifty thousand civilians in the best possible position to defend themselves against the dervishes. Earthworks were built, mines were laid, the arsenal expanded, and his small steamers armed. In these steamers and on foot, Gordon sent out reconnaissance parties, but he refrained for as long as he could from undertaking any offensive. However, on 10 March 1884, tribes now declaring for the Mahdi cut the telegraph to Cairo. Although a few messages were later successfully sent by other means, it was on that day in March 1884 that the siege of Khartoum began in earnest.[19]

With the telegraph line out, it became clear to Baring in Cairo, to Wolseley and the government in London, and to the British public generally that Gordon was now in danger in his hot, white, flat-roofed city of Khartoum. News of the siege and the dangers confronting Gordon filtered through to London. Britain thrilled at the thought of a man whom they regarded as a sort of knight-errant defying the Muslim fanatic and inspiring the people of Khartoum with his own infectious courage. Baring, who despite his deep reservations about Gordon's eccentricities, had supported him vis-à-vis London, now telegraphed the foreign secretary, "Having sent Gordon to Khartoum, it appears to me that it is our bounden duty, both as a matter of humanity and policy, not to abandon him."[20] Queen Victoria was in no doubt what must be done. She wrote to Hartington, "Gordon is in danger; you are bound to try and save him.... You have incurred fearful responsibility." After his offer of going himself to the Red Sea coast was rejected, Wolseley wrote to Hartington on 13 April 1884 (in a letter perhaps intended for Gladstone's eyes), "I presume the Government is not prepared to allow General Gordon and his garrison to fall into the hands of the cruel and barbarous enemy now besieging Khartoum ... if you contemplate sending an expedition in the autumn to Gordon's relief, the sooner he is informed the better it will be for our interests ... the British people will force you to do this whether you like it or not."[21] Gladstone and several of his ministers were not so certain. The prime minister was not even certain that he had incurred *any* responsibility for Gordon. What exactly that fearless, obstinate soldier was attempting to do in Khartoum or why he insisted on staying there if he was, in fact, in danger remained throughout an enigma to Gladstone. As stubborn and strong-willed as Gordon himself, he could not understand the soldier's rigid sense of honour and his concept of Christian duty which kept him at his post even after it had become obvious that he would be unable to withdraw the Egyptian garrison.[22]

Such conduct only fed the flames of jingoism in Britain which Gladstone felt were already burning far too high. In any case, he was extremely reluctant to be sucked yet further into the seemingly bottomless bog of Egyptian affairs by Gordon's unpredictable conduct in the Sudan. He did agree with Gordon —but could not convince a majority of his colleagues—that the administration of the Sudan should be turned over to a brave and efficient Egyptian officer and ex-slaver named Zubair and then Gordon himself should withdraw. But he remained adamantly opposed to Britain sending any troops. The divisions in the prime minister's mind reflected the differences in approach by members of his cabinet. The foreign and home secretaries were strongly opposed to any rescue expedition, apparently believing that Gordon could escape if he so chose, while the secretaries of state for war and for the colonies favoured the despatch of a relief force on the grounds that the government had incurred a responsibility for Gordon and that British honour demanded no less. While the cabinet was divided, the London press were united in their demand that any expedition to save Gordon should be organized without delay. *The Times* spoke for them all when on 1 April it stated flatly, "We absolutely refuse to believe that the Government means to abandon Gordon." The newspapers only differed about the best means to rescue Gordon. Some urged that Sir Gerald Graham should be instructed to despatch at once part of his small force over the desert from the Red Sea coast, a plan given tentative support by Baring but already rejected by the government, while other newspapers began to suggest sending an expedition up the Nile during the cooler months of the autumn (assuming that Gordon could hold out until then). Prayers for Gordon began to be offered in churches, mass meetings were held, and the irrepressible Colonel Fred Burnaby, campaigning as a Tory parliamentary candidate in Birmingham, declared, "Gordon may die in order to let Mr. Gladstone's Government live. Allow me, my friends here, Radicals as well as Conservatives, to make an appeal to you ... unite together and force this cowardly Government of time-servers to rescue General Gordon. ... The distinguished General who so ably conducted the expedition on the Red River would, I feel convinced, if it were offered him, at once accept the command of such an expedition."[23] It can be assumed that Burnaby made such a pointed suggestion only after consulting the now anxious Wolseley.

Increasingly, Wolseley began to be spoken of as the one man who might be able to save Gordon. The widespread clamour for an expedition had now advanced to the point of including a specific demand for "England's only general" to lead it. Clearly the government could not procrastinate much longer. "By 23 April, 1884, there were six [cabinet] ministers for an autumn expedition and five against it. Northbrook's diary breathes the tension in the Cabinet: 'Cabinet 3 till 7. Great difference of opinion. Question of immediate steps for consideration of expenditure to support Gordon deferred. ... I think Government will probably break up.' Saving Gordon was put off, and his fate became entangled in the Liberals' disagreement about Egypt's future."[24] Northbrook noted a majority of one in the cabinet in favour of an expedition in the autumn to rescue Gordon. But it was only Gladstone who could decide the question.

Throughout the late spring and early summer of 1884—and particularly during a major parliamentary debate in May—he remained opposed. However, in view of the public clamour, the urgings of the War Office, the pleas of Baring, and the insistent messages of the Queen, Gladstone finally agreed during the last days of July that the government would have to do something for Gordon, if for no other reason than to save its electoral position. On 1 August, parliament was finally asked for money to organize an expedition—and even then only "in case it might be needed." The sole purpose of the expedition would be to rescue Gordon and *not*, it was stated explicitly, to vanquish the Mahdi. Hartington, the secretary of state for war, had led those in the cabinet who had pressed most strongly for an expedition. His threat of resignation—a threat which he often made—was the straw which had broken the back of Gladstone's opposition. Since Hartington's support was essential in keeping the Whigs and Radicals together, Gordon's fate had become bound up not only with the Liberal's continuing disagreement about the future of Egypt, but also with the future of Gladstone's government.

5

Red River Interlude

Happy, happy days were those . . . the scenes through which our course was laid were such as speak in whispers, only when we have left—the whispers of the pine-tree, the music of the running water, the stillness of the great pine lakes.

SIR WILLIAM BUTLER
THE GREAT LONE LAND

Long before the approval of the House of Commons had been obtained on 5 August for "certain expenses" of an expedition, Adjutant General Wolseley had been involved in the War Office's consideration of various plans for the relief of Khartoum. Throughout the early summer of 1884, he was never in any doubt that an expedition would, sooner or later, be required. The one doubt in his mind concerned the time that would be available to organize it. Driven partly by ambition, by a sense of his own responsibility for having helped to place Gordon in his predicament, and by his affection for him, Wolseley had, with Hartington's knowledge, been for some time considering how the beleaguered Sudanese capital might be relieved. But it was all very difficult. The dearth of information about the true position of Gordon or even about the Sudan itself made planning little better than considered guesswork.

The few messages that were smuggled out of Khartoum told a confusing story. In some, Gordon described the situation of the city in hopeful terms; in others, he seemed to anticipate serious difficulties in holding the city for very long. The problems of knowing the real state of affairs in Khartoum compounded the complexities which confronted Wolseley when he considered plans for the expedition. Not only did the desert between Suakin on the Red Sea coast and Khartoum—the shortest route—present great natural obstacles, but also the dervishes now controlled it. It was only too easy to picture a British force being attacked in the desert and losing some or all of its water wagons and then dying in much the same miserable fashion as Hicks's army had in the southern Sudan two years earlier. There was, of course, all the water that any army could possibly want in the Nile. But that much longer route also presented great problems. During the early summer of 1884, as Wolseley pondered, prepared, and reviewed memoranda about the two alternative routes, his thoughts went back fifteen years and across five thousand miles of ocean.

Under the high ceilings and the gaslights of the War Office on Pall Mall, Wolseley remembered his long period of service in Canada. He recalled in particular its culmination during the summer of 1870 when he had led an Anglo-Canadian expedition through five hundred miles of wilderness to re-assert federal authority at Fort Garry where, it seemed to some, Louis Riel was attempting to create an independent republic. The expedition was the high point of Wolseley's service in Canada where he had spent nine years. He had come to know its people, its pioneers, its trappers, its militiamen, its farmers, and its businessmen in a way that few other British officers before him had done. Unlike many of his fellow officers, Wolseley had arrived in Canada with an open mind, eager to learn whatever the new world had to teach him and, being a keen soldier, to consider ways in which the special skills and aptitudes of Canadians might be adapted to the military needs of the Empire.

After serving in Burma, the Crimea, India, and China, Garnet Wolseley had arrived in Montreal in late December 1861 to assume, as a lieutenant-colonel of only twenty-eight, his appointment as assistant quartermaster-general on the staff in British North America. He had arrived at a crucial time. The dream of many Canadian statesmen to see the several British colonies in North America united in one self-governing nation was then beginning to assume tangible form. One potent catalyst in the involved formula of Canadian confederation was the threat of invasion from the United States. As Wolseley soon discovered, no single element was more powerful in making for Canadian unity than the recurring fear of absorption by the United States. When Wolseley arrived in Canada, however, the threat was particularly worrisome because the states south of the unfortified border were far from united. Their attitude toward Canada was, in these circumstances, less predictable than usual.

In late 1861 and early 1862, eleven thousand British reinforcements, of whom Wolseley was one, had suddenly been sent to Canada to strengthen the garrisons and small forces along the border and to demonstrate Britain's commitment to defend its colonies in North America. One month before Wolseley's arrival, the *Trent* affair—involving the seizure by a Union warship of Confederate representatives travelling on a British ship on the high seas—had clearly indicated where the sympathies of many British lay. The *Trent* incident only aggravated the hostile feelings which already existed between Britain and the Union states. Fanned by militant Irish nationalists in the United States, this hostility made an invasion of British North America a recurrent possibility throughout the American Civil War. Against this disturbing background, it was clear that in greater unity there lay whatever strength the British colonies in North America could muster to defend themselves. Britain itself, eager to see its colonies become as self-supporting as possible, was on hand to encourage the movement toward Canadian confederation.

Wolseley had been ordered to join in the urgent task of improving the meagre defences of the great and sparsely populated area of British North America. His first appointment in Canada was to head a militia officers' training school at La Prairie, across the St. Lawrence River from Montreal. Wolseley probably learned as much as his students. Theirs were formal lessons in the profession of war; his were more informal and included careful observation of the breed of men the new world produced.

Near La Prairie was the Iroquois village of Caughnawaga. There Wolseley first met that unique Canadian type, the *voyageur*. The Iroquois departed each spring for distant western wilds to employ their special skills. But before the St. Lawrence froze in the winter and occasionally between their long trips to the West, Wolseley was able to watch demonstrations of their highly developed skills. A little further south, across the nearby border, Wolseley was determined to see at first hand the great struggle that wass raging between the Northern and Southern states. Accordingly, during the autumn of 1862, his first long period of leave, and at some personal risk, he managed to cross through the Northern lines to visit—and subsequently to praise highly— Robert E. Lee and his Confederate forces.

Wolseley did not, however, have much time to observe at first hand how the tragic struggle was being fought out across the border. With the threat of invasion constantly hanging over Canada—the only place where the Union states, if they so decided, could attack the British with any hope of success— the Canadian militia had to be improved rapidly. Canada's amateur soldiers had been neglected during the fifty years of peace since the last war with the Americans. By 1862 competent Canadian officers were particularly scarce. Wolseley, however, was delighted with the raw material on hand. He soon found his flexible, imaginative pupils at his militia officers' school were deserving of high praise.

> I found they made excellent officers; they were thinking and yet practical men, without any of the pedantry which too often clings to the young officers of all Regular Armies. ... A considerable number of those trained at La Prairie subsequently accompanied me in the expedition I led in 1870 from Lake Superior to the Red River, and no commander could wish to have better soldiers than those of the two Canadian militia battalions who constituted the bulk of the brigade I then had with me. Our young officers of the regular army are too prone to depend upon regulations which are apt to dwarf their natural military instincts

in positions where the Canadian officer would act according to the common sense that is within him.[1]

Before long, Wolseley had an opportunity to see whether his students at La Prairie had learned their lessons. During the Fenian Raids of 1865, twelve thousand ill-organized and ill-equipped Irishmen and adventurers, many of them Civil War veterans, made a half-hearted attempt to invade Canada from the United States. Britain had favoured the Confederate side in the Civil War, and, more important to Irish veterans, the road to Dublin might, paradoxically, be found through an invasion of Canada. Here was a test to show exactly where the strengths and weaknesses of the Canadian militia lay.

The "invasion" itself came to nothing. In fact, it had the beneficial effect of helping to ensure that, subsequently, there was a body of officers and men in Canada who could respond rapidly to a further call to arms. And that call came only five years after the abortive Fenian Raids and three years after the new Dominion of Canada had been created by the union of four provinces of British North America. The challenge to the newly established federal authority occurred in the Northwest, presenting Ottawa with both difficult and complex political questions and its first military problem.

The banks of the Red River, in what was later to become southern Manitoba, had been settled largely by French Canadians, many of whom had married Indian women. Their descendents, métis, became fearful of what the transfer of the great prairie lands of the Northwest from the control of the Hudson's Bay Company to the distant authority of the new government in Ottawa would mean for their traditional, if ill-defined, property rights and privileges. Many supported a protest movement led by a persuasive and popular leader, Louis Riel. He placed himself at the head of a "provisional government" of the Northwest pledged to protect the traditional property claims of the Red River settlers and, by implication, to oppose the establishment of Canadian federal authority. Here was a bold challenge to its status and claims which the government could not afford to ignore. In addition to Riel's assertion of independence, Ottawa was worried by growing evidence of United States interest in the vast empty lands that stretched from the Great Lakes to the Rocky Mountains. Unless the Canadian government clearly established its control, that huge area might pass into the hands of the United States. Accordingly, it was clear to Ottawa that something had to be done and done quickly when in 1870 the insurgents on the Red River began to take the law into their own hands.

Since the very first days of unrest at Fort Garry, Prime Minister Sir John A. Macdonald had considered the unwelcome possibility that troops would have to be sent there to establish Ottawa's authority and to maintain order.

The British government, eager to withdraw its remaining garrison from Canada (now that the threat from the United States had receded) and to have them available for service elsewhere in an ever-growing Empire, was reluctant to become involved. However, under pressure from Macdonald, London finally agreed to a mixed force of British regulars and Canadian militiamen, if the despatch of such a force were to become necessary. Macdonald was anxious to have British troops, partly because the insurgents would be likely to regard them as more impartial than Canadians, whom the métis suspected, sometimes with reason, of prejudice or even animosity.

The difficulties in forming the expeditionary force, when Ottawa reluctantly decided that one would have to be sent, proved less troublesome than selecting the best route for it to follow. A descent from Hudson Bay was impracticable because of late ice, which hindered travel until the beginning of the short summer. The easiest route would be by rail to Minneapolis and down the Red River to Fort Garry. But such a route was out of the question because of American hostility to the idea of a foreign force crossing United States territory, especially a force intended to suppress a self-proclaimed republic. There remained only one possible route and it was a difficult one: overland through the wilderness from the head of Lake Superior to the Winnipeg and Red rivers.

It was, at best, a dangerous way to reach the Red River settlement. Canoes and boats could easily be used on the many lakes, but morasses, rapids, bogs, waterfalls, and dense virgin forest separated them. The natural obstacles were not only a great hindrance to a military force; they also provided advantages to its enemies. The thick woods could provide safe shelter for guerrillas if Riel decided to resist the passage of the Anglo-Canadian force. The expedition was clearly going to be a major challenge to whoever was appointed to lead it. It was evident to the authorities in Ottawa that Lieutenant-Colonel Garnet Wolseley was the only British army officer available in Canada who combined youthful energy with understanding of Canada and Canadians and the skill, experience, and resource necessary to lead twelve hundred soldiers to Fort Garry along the wilderness route of the old Northwest fur traders.

Once this route had been selected and final approval received from London for the participation of British troops and for Wolseley's appointment as commanding officer, there was little time left before the ice would melt on the rivers, marking the beginning of the few months available to the expedition to complete its unique task. Wolseley immediately set about organizing his force with his characteristic energy. The Canadian soldiers were drawn from the Quebec and Ontario militia, the British from the 1st Battalion of the 60th Rifles, the Royal Engineers, and the Royal Field Artillery. The natural obstacles along the route from Thunder Bay at the head of Lake Superior to the Winnipeg River formed the major problem confronting Wolseley: no prolonged fighting was anticipated, given the weakness and hesitation known to be widespread among Riel's followers. The transport problems in the wilderness were, however, so formidable as to give any but the most determined officer considerable doubts about the possible success of the expeditionary forces. The force had to carry all its supplies; the virgin forest could not be depended upon to yield food readily, and none of the time remaining before the arrival of winter could be lost in hunting for food. Wooden boats twenty-five feet in length were readied for the expedition, each to carry about twelve soldiers, two expert Canadian boatmen, and up to four tons of food and other supplies. The route was a challenge even to men already skilled in the use of boats in swift rivers and wide lakes; to novices encumbered by a large amount of military equipment, impediments that never burdened the old fur traders, it was a route that seemed almost impassable. Wolseley had to make the most careful calculations and preparations, a duty for which, fortunately, he was well suited by both training and inclination.

One of his first tasks was to arrange for the recruitment of almost four hundred *voyageurs*, mainly Indian, French-Canadian, and métis, to help his soldiers over the rivers, the rapids, and the forty-seven major portages which would confront them along their 500-mile route to Fort Garry. Wolseley himself went out of his way to ensure the recruitment of Iroquois boatmen from Caughnawaga. From his own observations of their skill, Wolseley knew that the Iroquois were unsurpassed among that famous and special breed of short, stocky, wiry boatmen who, in 1870, were still to be found in Canada. The *voyageurs* were the last professional descendants of the canoemen of the seventeenth and eighteenth centuries who had been employed by Montreal traders and fur merchants. *Les vrais hommes du nord* had known intimately for more than two centuries the lakes, large and small, the rivers, placid and dangerous, the portages, easy and difficult, of the old Northwest trade routes. Wolseley got his skilled *voyageurs* largely from among the Iroquois from Caughnawaga and French Canadians from Trois Rivières. But he also found later that, given the haste in which the boatmen had to be recruited, a number of land-hungry adventurers had managed to pass themselves off as experienced *voyageurs*. The imposters were, however, soon culled out.

> As rations had to be carried in the boats for every man . . . so it became an object of importance that none but skilled *voyageurs* should be taken. The most stringent orders on this head had been issued by Colonel Wolseley, and officers commanding brigades were directed to leave at the first portage they came to, all *soi-distant voyageurs* whom they found to be incapable of managing boats. The object of having *voyageurs* was not to pull an oar, a duty which the soldiers were quite

competent to perform, but to take the management of the boats in rapid water and to instruct the soldiers. Many men had engaged themselves under the high-sounding title of *voyageur*, with the object of working their passage to the Red River by their manual labour at the oar; consequently when they had to take hold of a paddle or a pole, they were found to be quite ignorant of its use.[2]

It was annoying to have imposters among his boatmen, but Wolseley was delighted with the skill of the true *voyageur*. On 16 July 1870, after arrival by steamer at Thunder Bay, the leading units of his small force launched their canoes and boats onto the waters of the first major lake on their route. Navigation on the largely uncharted lakes in northwestern Ontario was sometimes a problem, but crossing them was at least a respite from the labour of portages and from the danger—and thrill—of the swift rivers that formed a large part of the route. Almost every day the boats had to be carried, dragged, or rolled over portages that sometimes were more than a mile long or they had to be guided through foaming, rock-strewn rapids where a wrong turn meant disaster. "No one who has ever descended the Winnipeg River in a boat or canoe is ever likely to forget that experience," Wolseley later wrote:

As for myself, the falls, the rapids, the whirlpools, the great rushing angry waters, and the many hair-breadth escapes its navigation involved, are indelibly stamped upon my memory. We had one or two boats wrecked, but no life was lost. The pleasurable excitement of danger is always an agreeable experience, but the enthralling delight of feeling your frail canoe or boat bound under you, as it were down a steep incline of wilding rushing waters into what looks like a boiling, steaming cauldron of bubbling and confused waters, exceeds most of the other maddening delights that man can dream of. Each man strains for his life at oar or paddle, for no steerage-way can be kept upon your boat unless it be made to run quicker than the waters. All depends upon the nerve and skill of the bowsman and steersman, who take you skilfully through the outcropping rocks around you. But the acme of excitement is of short duration, and the pace is too quick to admit of self-examination. No words can describe the rapid change of sensation when the boat jumps through the last narrow and perhaps twisted passage between rocks, into an eddy of the slack water below! You had—perhaps unknowingly—held your breath, whilst every nerve was nigh to breaking point, during the moment of supreme danger; but in

Plate 1. The aftermath of the 10-hour British bombardment of Alexandria in July 1882. The Egyptian fortifications—strengthened following the U.S. Civil War by ex-Confederate officers—are in ruins in the foreground. British warships and merchantmen are at anchor in the harbour.

Plate 2. "Victory: the scene immediately after the capture of Tel-el-Kebir," 13 September 1882 —the jubilation of British infantry in which Corporal C. F. Winter of Montreal joined.

Plate 3. The "pugnacious ... hot-headed, impulsive," and very brave Major-General "Chinese" Gordon of the Royal Engineers, in the tarbush and court dress of the Governor General of the Sudan. Gordon served in the Sudan from 1874 to 1876, 1877 to 1880, and 1884 to 1885.

Plate 4. Garnet Wolseley, in the campaign uniform of a general, at the time of the Gordon Relief Expedition of 1884–1885 which he commanded.

Plate 5. "A last good-bye": the departure for Khartoum of General Charles Gordon and Lieutenant-Colonel J. D. H. Stewart from Charing Cross Station, London, on 18 January 1884. The Duke of Cambridge (left) and Gordon shake hands, with Wolseley between them. Colonel Stewart is at the right.

Plate 6. The Manitoba wheelsmen photographed in Ottawa before their departure for Egypt in October 1884. The four wheelsmen are Captains William Robinson, J. Weber, R. A. Russell, and John S. Seeger (the latter three were United States citizens).

Plate 7. The Ottawa wheelsmen photographed at the same time as those from Manitoba: Captains William M. Jones, John A. Williamson, James McKeever, and Thomas Anson Cummings.

Plate 8. The composite picture produced in early 1885 by an enterprising Ottawa photographer, "a tout ensemble gotten up in first-class style, well worthy of being kept as a souvenir of the Contingent."

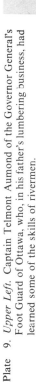

Plate 9. *Upper Left.* Captain Telmont Aumond of the Governor General's Foot Guard of Ottawa, who, in his father's lumbering business, had learned some of the skills of rivermen.

Plate 10. *Upper Right.* Lieutenant-Colonel Frederick Charles Denison sometime after his return from Egypt. He is wearing the C.M.G., a campaign medal, and an Egyptian decoration he won for his service on the Nile.

Plate 11. *Lower Left.* William Nassau Kennedy, the second mayor of Winnipeg, in the uniform of a lieutenant-colonel of the 90th Battalion of Rifles. He was paymaster of the Canadian contingent on the Sudan expedition and died in London at its conclusion.

Plate 12. *Below.* Captain Alexander MacRae of the Seventh Battalion, Fusiliers, of London, Ontario. The Governor General's Secretary noted of MacRae and Aumond, "we certainly have succeeded in sending two of the toughest customers [to the Sudan] but I believe they are both well suited to the work."

Plate 13. *Lower Right.* The monocled and bilingual Lieutenant-Colonel John Louis Hubert Neilson, a Laval medical graduate and future director general of the Canadian Militia Medical Service.

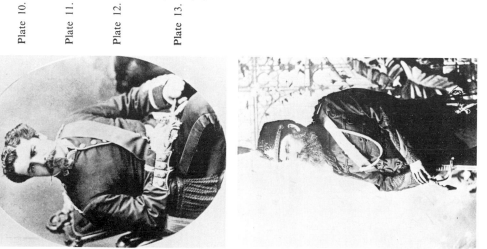

Plate 14. A group of Ottawa *voyageurs* (who are not yet wearing their issued work clothes) photographed before the Centre Block of the Parliament Buildings, Ottawa, before their departure for Montreal on 13 September 1884. Two foremen stand in the foreground.

Plate 15. "The Nile Expedition: Arrival of the First Division of the Camel Corps at Wadi Halfa." This easy way of travelling was only possible until the cataracts were reached.

Plate 16. "The Canadian Voyageurs' First Touch of the Nile." Immediately below the Second Cataract, a steamer (presumably the *Ferooz*) has cast off the whalers it has towed. The *voyageurs*, mainly in slouch hats, are for the first time taking charge of them (one *voyageur* is offered a melon by an Egyptian child).

Plate 17. "The Manitoba Boys (Canadian Boatmen) at breakfast."

a few seconds of time afterwards a long breath of relief comes that enables you to say, "Thank God!" with all heartfelt sincerity.[3]

Wolseley retained throughout his later life a profound admiration for the boatmen who could perform such feats. That admiration was to have practical effect when, fourteen years later, the Empire needed boatmen on the distant Nile.

Wolseley never forgot the endurance and quiet efficiency of several Canadian and British officers who served under him during this arduous expedition. They were destined to serve with him again and again in the future. Once Wolseley was convinced of a man's worth, he became a member of that select clique, "Wolseley's Ring," and his career was furthered by all means at his mentor's disposal. The names of such men recur frequently both in Victorian military history and in the accounts of service by Canadians in the imperial wars of the last decades of the nineteenth century. For example, John McNeill joined Wolseley's staff for the Red River expedition from his post as military secretary to the governor general. A veteran of service in India and New Zealand, McNeill had also seen action during the abortive Fenian Raids of 1867.[4] Redvers Buller, a lieutenant of the 60th Rifles, impressed his commanding officer with his intimate knowledge of the Canadian woods (where he had chosen to spend his leave while serving in eastern Canada) as much as by his hearty and brusque manner. Captain William Butler was, like Wolseley himself, of Irish descent but, unlike his colonel, Butler had not risen rapidly in the army. As soon as he learned of the projected Red River expedition, he had paid his own passage to Canada in search of adventure and promotion. Appointed by Wolseley to reconnoitre ahead of the expedition, Butler travelled overland through the United States and actually entered Fort Garry where he coolly interviewed the rebel. Butler's bold, resourceful, and yet reflective nature is evident in his own delightful account of his Canadian adventures, *The Great Lone Land*.[5] The young captain commanding the detachment of Royal Field Artillery on the Red River expedition, James Alleyne, later saw action under Wolseley in the Zulu War of 1879 and, like McNeill, Buller and Butler, in the Egyptian War of 1882.[6]

Several other future members of "Wolseley's Gang"—as its detractors called it—were among the British officers appointed to the Red River expedition (the "Ring" always thereafter to have veterans of Canadian service at its centre), but one young Canadian stood out even in such a galaxy of capable and brave officers. Wolseley had first met Lieutenant Frederick Charles Denison of the Governor General's Body Guard—one of the foremost Canadian militia units—during the Fenian Raids. Denison came from one of the few families in Canada that could claim a long military background in Canada itself. Denison's ancestors, United Empire Loyalists, had fought on the British side in the American Revolution, in the War of 1812, and in the Rebellion of 1837. Both he and his older brother, George, had come to Wolseley's notice as a result of their outstanding conduct during the Fenian raids. Buller was sometimes full of bluster and Butler of impetuosity, but Frederick Denison always combined his military skills with such a degree of quiet confidence and efficiency that Wolseley soon appointed him one of his aides-de-camp for the Red River expedition. Wolseley was in no way to regret his choice. Denison proved able and imaginative, free from the stultifying traditions which sometimes inhibited British officers. Wolseley probably had just such men as Denison in mind when he spoke of Canadian officers as being "without any of the pedantry which too often clings to the young officers of all Regular Armies." He was to utilize this rare quality in an imperial cause in attempting to solve the Sudanese puzzle fourteen years later.

For thirteen weeks, Wolseley and his men toiled with their supplies and boats over portages drenched in rain—it rained the equivalent of seven of the thirteen weeks—and through the clouds of mosquitoes and black flies that can make life in the Canadian woods almost unbearable. The trip across Lake Superior had been uneventful and even comfortable in small lake steamers, but from the Lakehead westward, the route proved to be a trying ordeal for the soldiers, whether from Britain or eastern Canada. For most of them, this was their first encounter with primeval forests, lakes, rivers, and rapids. But with Wolseley in confident and competent command, they persevered and arrived at their goal almost as tough and as knowledgeable from their odyssey as skilled and experienced woodsmen.

On a rainy day in late August 1870, when Colonel Wolseley and his expectant force at last stood before the wooden gates of Fort Garry, they found that Louis Riel and his two principal lieutenants had given up any thought of armed resistance and had that same morning bolted to the United States, making the first part of their journey on a raft of logs and fence posts lashed together in part by their neckties and trousers. Fifteen years later, when Wolseley was commanding another river expedition half-way around the world—this time on the Nile—Riel was to return and defy for a second and last time federal authority on the prairies. It was not, however, Wolseley's fault that Riel escaped on this first occasion. He had carried out his difficult task with boldness, economy, and despatch. Shortly before he returned to England, he wrote to his wife, "The Franco-German War, of course, deprives this expedition of all possible interest; who on earth will care two straws for us, or for news from the Red River, when great events are being enacted on the Rhine."[7] Wolseley was largely right in his prediction. The Red River expedition holds no prominent place in the long annals of the British army. The little expedition had, nevertheless, three far-reaching results which greatly affected Wolseley's own later life and that of many Canadians. One was that the War Office noted the admirable way in which Colonel Wolseley had led his forces. Not one shot had been fired and not one life lost. Perhaps best of all, it had not cost very much. It was obvious that the ability, imagination, and energy of its commander had been the principal element in ensuring the success of the expedition. Wolseley (who now became Sir Garnet) had added to his already growing reputation. He was again marked out for early promotion. The second ramification of the Red River expedition was that Wolseley never afterward forgot the skill, fortitude, and adaptability of the Canadian *voyageurs*. Their complete mastery of rivers and rapids was a consummate performance which greatly impressed him. The special skills and attitudes which life in the woods taught and which Canadian boatmen and many Canadian soldiers embodied were thereafter always highly valued by Wolseley and would be drawn upon by him in a later imperial venture. The third result of the expedition was Wolseley's conviction that what he had accomplished, often through improvisation, in the unique circumstance of the Canadian wilderness, he could reproduce in entirely different circumstances—a dubious assumption that was later to be tested in the Sudan.

It was the skills of the *voyageur* that Wolseley recalled as he sat in the War Office during the late spring of 1884, considering ways in which the attempt might best be made to save the life of his old friend, Charlie Gordon. Rivers, wherever they are in the world, Wolseley reasoned, cannot differ so very much. The white water of the rapids on the Upper Nile cannot be so very different from the white water of the Canadian rivers over which the *voyageurs* had clearly demonstrated their mastery. Although more than fourteen years of distinguished service in the War Office, in West and South Africa, Cyprus and Egypt had intervened since Wolseley (now General Lord Wolseley) had seen *voyageurs* at work, he had no doubt that they could perform the same feats on the Nile as they had on their own rivers. He recalled the skill that they had shown in conquering the Slave Falls in Manitoba; it was not difficult to imagine them vanquishing the Nile cataracts. Nothing on the Nile could exceed the Slave Falls, Wolseley was convinced. Even thirty years after the event, he was able to recall every detail of his first encounter with those terrifying rapids:

The portage by which travellers...take their canoes round these falls begins some few hundred yards above them, and is reached without danger. But to my horror the guide took my canoe into midstream where the current runs down a considerable decline at a most exciting pace. My first wild notion was that he had mistaken these falls for some others, and that nothing then could save us. I sat motionless, speechless and awe-stricken as we raced along the last and swiftest decline into the column of mist and spray, which rising from below seemed to mark the point where the water jumped from the edge of the falls into the steaming frothing jumble of bubbling foam and boisterous waters below. My bowsman was a portly Iroquois [*sic*] whom I did not like much, but he had a jowl that bespoke courageous determination to a remarkable degree. As he dipped his broad paddle far out into the stream upon one side to draw the canoe hard over after it, he had, like most Indians when excited, thrown off his hat, and as his long straight hair flew back behind his neck and shoulders, I saw his face clearly. It was enough. His lips closely pressed together, and there was an unmistakable expression of satisfied determination, of assured triumph, about him that said without words, "All is well." In less time than it has taken to write this, the bow turned sharp in towards the shore, and the canoe was in fairly slack water, where two of the crew jumping out held her secure. My bowsman, throwing his broad paddle into the air and catching it again, gave a shout of victory, and all the crew burst out into hilarious and triumphant laughter. Nothing could have saved us from destruction had that paddle broken when he held on to it in the current—as if it were a fixed iron pillar—to draw the canoe's head in towards shore. Nothing pleases or satisfied these Iroquois more than such trials of strength, such victories over dangerous water, which is truly their element.[8]

The excitement of such days in the wilds of Manitoba returned to the bemedalled general. The skill of the Canadian *voyageur* seemed to be the answer to the dilemma which now faced him. They might be able to get a river expedition up the Nile to save Gordon. The alternative route across the desert seemed to Wolseley, if not to others, to present even more difficulties.

Unlike Gordon and other British officers who had served for prolonged periods in India or Egypt, Wolseley had little experience of deserts. The brief impression that he had formed of seemingly endless miles of Egyptian sand when he had defeated Arabi in 1882 was most unfavourable. The crucial supply problems of water and food for both men and animals appeared to him insurmountable objections to an expedition being sent over the 245 miles of desert from the Red Sea coast to Berber and thence another 200 miles up the Nile to Khartoum. Yet the general commanding the British garrison in Egypt, Frederick Stephenson,[9] in response to enquiries from the War Office, had emphatically advocated the desert route, which would be supplied from the port of Suakin. His position on the spot and the prevailing ignorance of the Upper Nile lent weight to his arguments. Moreover, a Royal Navy officer had recently made a hurried survey of that part of the

Nile still in Egyptian hands. Supported by the commander-in-chief of the Mediterranean fleet, he too contended that the Nile was barred to major movements of troops because of the fierce rapids and the constantly changing depths of the river as it passed through its seasonable variations. The navy concluded that an expedition transported by boats was out of the question. Finally, both the War Office and Admiralty intelligence departments came down on the side of the Suakin-Berber desert route.

But as early as 8 April 1884, Wolseley had made up his mind. He supported the river route in a report prepared at the request of Hartington.[10] To reassure himself that he was not unreasonably opposed to the Suakin-Berber route, he wrote to General Sherman who, during the Civil War twenty years before, had conducted a long overland march across Georgia to the sea. He now wrote to him, without, apparently, any consciousness of the irrelevance of Sherman's experience to the problem he was considering, to enquire whether he had any useful suggestions about how the supply problems of a long over-land march might be overcome. Sherman, not surprisingly, could offer Wolseley no advice or suggestions of any value since he had not operated across a desert.[11] Nor could the railway experts whom Wolseley also consulted offer any hope of being able to lay a track quickly enough from Suakin to Berber to be of much use in rescuing Gordon. And the Royal Navy was opposed to any attempt to use boats on the Nile. Something of an impasse had been reached by the end of July.

But Wolseley, backed by his "Ring," especially its "Canadian" members, was convinced that the river was the only route. On 5 August, when the government finally called for a small financial allocation to undertake "if necessary" an expedition, Wolseley was in a position, as adjutant general, to help ensure the adoption of his plans for an assault on the Nile. Once the tenacious little general had made up his mind, he was to be deterred neither by further adverse comments from men on the spot, nor, later, when the plan to transport the expedition by boats up the Nile became public, by the ridicule of certain London newspapers. Leading the criticism about the river route which appeared in some London newspapers was the *Army and Navy Gazette*, an old critic of the British army in the Crimea and of Wolseley's "Ring." On 13 September it stated bluntly,

A more wicked waste of money was never perpetrated, a more silly quackery was never devised by any public department than that of which Lord Hartington and the Duke of Cambridge, representing the War Office and the Horse Guards, have really and truly been guilty in ordering that monstrous armada of boats, that unfloatable flotilla for the Nile. Burn them for firewood! Send them to Jericho, to ply on the Palestine canal of the future! Make matches of them—do anything with them! Put men in them, and try to send them up the Nile cataracts—never, we beg of you!

Wolseley was not perturbed by such criticisms—as an outspoken army reformer, he had been engaged in both public and private controversies many times before—nor was he deflected by more cogent arguments such as the simple facts that rocks which could be seen in the clear waters of Canada were invisible in the muddy waters of the Nile or that portages in Canada were facilitated by readily constructed corduroy roads whereas there was nothing but sand and rock along the banks of the upper Nile or that there were shifting sand bars and a constantly changing volume of water in the Nile and not on most Canadian rivers. Wolseley had conquered some of the most turbulent rivers of Canada and, he contended, given the help of Canadian boatmen again, he could also conquer every one of the 1,650 miles of the Nile between Alexandria and Khartoum. Even before Gladstone's divided cabinet finally reached its decision in principle to send a force to rescue Gordon, the War Office had quietly appointed a three-man committee to review the relative merits of desert and river routes. From his key position, Wolseley was able to ensure that all three members were officers who had served under him on the Red River expedition. Redvers Buller and John McNeill, now major-generals, and William Butler, now a colonel, reported on 29 July 1884:

> In 1870, a force consisting of about 1,400 men proceeded from Thunder Bay on Lake Superior to Fort Garry on the Red River, a distance of over 600 miles through a wilderness practically destitute of supplies, and where no native labour was obtainable.
>
> Remembering this, we believe that a brigade can easily be conveyed in small boats from Cairo to Dongola in the time stated by Lord Wolseley, and further, that should it be necessary to send a still larger force by water to Khartoum, that operation will present no insuperable difficulties.
>
> From all we can learn about the Nile, and the difficulties of desert journeys where water for all the men and animals employed has to be conveyed on camels, we are convinced that if it is necessary to take a fighting force to Khartoum before the end of the year, or the end of January, the Nile will be found the easiest, the safest, and immensely the cheapest line of advance to adopt.[12]

There was no doubt in the minds of the three committee members about which route the expedition should follow. For good measure, they went on to argue that the Royal Navy, when it had reported adversely on the project, had been erroneously thinking of large boats to carry the troops and supplies, whereas what was desirable were much smaller, shallow-draft boats, like those used on the Red River. The constantly changing level of the Nile would not endanger them. It seemed to the three members of the committee that the principal question was not whether small boats could be taken through to Khartoum but whether they could be constructed in time to rescue Gordon, whose position was rapidly becoming desperate.

Five days before the committee presented its report, Wolseley, strongly opposed to Gladstone's cautious policy, had written with candour to Hartington,

> Remember we cannot command things. All the gold in England will not affect the rise and fall of the Nile or the duration of the hot and cold seasons in Egypt. Time is a most important element in the question, and indeed it will be an indelible disgrace if we allow the most generous, patriotic and gallant of our public servants to die of want or to fall into the hands of a cruel enemy because we would not hold out our hands to save him. . . . At any rate, I don't wish to share the responsibility of leaving Charlie Gordon to his fate, and it is for this reason that I recommend immediate and active preparation for operations that may be forced upon us by and by.[13]

Colonel Butler submitted a separate memorandum entitled "Notes on the Advantages of the Use of Small Boats for the Ascent of the Nile" to supplement the report of the committee and to counter the discouraging comments of the Admiralty. He noted that there were four ways in which a small boat can be moved against the current of a river: sails, oars, poles, and track-line, the latter two being employed in especially swift water. Three or even all four methods could occasionally be used at the same time, but if the first two were of no avail, poles could be used in shallow water or track-lines in deeper water where the boats could be hauled from the shore. Butler echoed Wolseley's own conviction when he arrived at the deceptively simple conclusion, "Water is water, and rock is rock, whether they lie in America or in Africa, and the conditions which they can assume towards each other are much the same all the world over."[14]

Committees and reports take time. Precious days and weeks were rapidly passing. Finally, largely as a result of Wolseley's persistence and the convincing way in which he marshalled his arguments, the bold decision to follow the river route was made. Once parliament had voted the funds for an expedition, steps were taken to implement the decision with the greatest speed.

What was wanted now was action. On 8 August 1884 the general commanding in Egypt, Stephenson, was informed by the secretary of state for war that parliament had voted the necessary monies for the Gordon relief expedition and that, as a result of a number of factors, including the desirability of making a show of force to the natives along the Nile, the river route had been chosen over the desert route. A camel corps (an idea developed by Wolseley himself) would be formed which would march along the river bank. The majority of the soldiers and their voluminous supplies would, however, go up the river in small boats.

On the afternoon of 22 August Wolseley met Hartington's private secretary, who was on his way "to Devonshire House to advise Huntington to insist on my being... sent. He asked me what I thought of this. I replied, I fully concurred, and that were I the ruler here, I should certainly have sent myself to Egypt for this expedition, but that clearly... I could not... tender such advice myself, and that moreover, I could not imagine this Govt. adopting any such heroic policy in this matter."[15]

On 26 August, Hartington further telegraphed to Cairo that since Stephenson continued to believe that the Nile route was impracticable, the government had decided (despite the Duke of Cambridge's misgivings) "to send Lord Wolseley to take temporarily the Chief Command in Egypt" and, at the same time, of the Gordon relief expedition. On 31 August Wolseley left London and on 9 September arrived in Cairo with several of his staff, which, not surprisingly, was to include Redvers Buller and William Butler. There was again a scramble to serve under Wolseley and his "Ring"; young officers in England, finding soldiering at home dull and offering little opportunity for distinguished service, employed every device and used all their influence to be appointed to the expedition, which, to some, appeared to be about the equivalent of an elaborate regatta in the land of the pharaohs. It certainly promised more adventure and amusement than garrison duty in Victoria's peaceful England.

At the very moment when Wolseley was assuming his new and pressing tasks in Cairo, a sense of yet greater urgency was created by the murder of Gordon's aide, Colonel Stewart. He had been told by Gordon that he could perform no further useful services in the besieged town. Accompanied by the French consul and the only other Englishman in Khartoum, the correspondent of *The Times*, he embarked upon a small steamer with messages for Baring in Cairo and with Gordon's cypher which Gordon had decided—for reasons only known to himself—should be carried to safety rather than burned. Stewart and his companions were murdered upon landing from their steamer which had become stranded on a rock below Berber. When the news of this tragedy reached Cairo, questions began to be asked. What must be the true position of Gordon in Khartoum if Stewart could be so easily murdered in an area far down the Nile toward the Egyptian border?

Except for the Austrian consul with whom he had quarreled, Gordon was now the sole European remaining in Khartoum. He was alone with his Christian faith, his rigid military sense of honour, and his journal into which he now began to pour his daily confidences. The stage was now well set for a drama such as the British Empire had never before seen. The prologue was over. The tragedy had begun.

6

The Voyageurs to Egypt!

When Allah made the Sudan, he laughed.

AN ARAB PROVERB

During the few weeks that Wolseley had between his appointment to Egypt and the day of his arrival in Cairo, he was absorbed in the innumerable details that a rapid ascent of the Nile would entail. The logistics of the operation were staggering; the force had to be entirely self-reliant and its success would depend upon meeting a rigid deadline. It could count upon very little in the way of supplies from the country through which it would pass. However, in the midst of all his preparations, Wolseley played the Canadian card he had been husbanding for just such an eventuality. He immediately asked the Colonial Office to send to the governor general of Canada, Lord Lansdowne,[1] the following cypher telegram:

It is proposed to endeavour to engage 300 good voyageurs from Caughnawaga, Saint Regis, and Manitoba as steersmen in boats for Nile expedition—engagement for 6 months with passage to & from Egypt.

Will pay of 40 dollars a month with suit of clothes and rations free be sufficient?

If this could be done, perhaps you would permit Lord Melgund to undertake charge of these voyageurs to Egypt, and priest could be attached to party receiving Captain's pay & allowances.... The voyageurs should arrive at Liverpool not later than the 1st of October, but if possible by the 15th of September.

Three officers of Canadian Militia might accompany party.[2]

This message of 20 August 1884 bore the indelible stamp of Wolseley; he knew the value of the Iroquois from Caughnawaga; the esteem in which the *voyageurs* held their priests; the desirability of having Canadians commanding Canadians. He had not forgotten the lessons of his expedition to the Red River.

When Lord Lansdowne received this telegram, he was in summer residence at the Citadel in Quebec City. He immediately asked his secretary, Major Lord Melgund (the veteran of the Battle of Tel-el-Kebir and a future governor general), to go to the prime minister to discuss the request from London. While "Rollo" was preparing to travel to Rivière du Loup where Sir John A. Macdonald was spending August at his summer house, Lansdowne sent in advance to the prime minister the following telegram which incorporated the text of the Colonial Office message:

> There should I imagine be no difficulty in obtaining the services of the necessary voyageurs. Whether the inducements are sufficient I do not know, but these could be increased if necessary.
>
> I have told Melgund that his engagements to me shall certainly not stand in his way.... Wolseley has a high opinion of him and this project has evidently arisen with Wolseley, and is founded on his Red River experiences.
>
> I have told Melgund to go to you at once, and to ask you first whether you see any objection to the scheme, and then for your advice as to the best means of carrying it out. He should I apprehend not lose a moment in putting himself in communication with the agents for these Indian settlements.[3]

Before Melgund could begin to make any preparations for the recruitment and despatch of the *voyageurs* whom Wolseley so much admired, it was of course essential that the views of the prime minister of the seventeen-year-old confederation be obtained. Macdonald was prompt in his concurrence, stipulating only that it should be made very clear that the men recruited were to be considered to be in the employ of the British government, not the Canadian. The realities of the Canadian political scene led the prime minister to take great care to avoid any controversy about whether his government was supporting an imperial adventure. At the same time, Macdonald did not wish to appear to be placing obstacles in the way of British recruitment of Canadian boatmen for the rescue of Gordon. He was unwilling to risk alienating either Canadian imperialists or Canadian liberals. This compromising attitude, so typical of Macdonald, was subsequently reflected in the arrangements made for the despatch of the contingent. The Canadian government was never directly involved; the plans were made entirely by the governor general's staff under Melgund or by private persons assisting him. When the British request for the boatmen was made public, such Toronto newspapers as the *News* and the *World* criticized the Canadian government for its acquiescence in facilitating the recruitment of the *voya-*

geurs. But Macdonald's caution was rewarded; their criticism was muted and struck no responsive chord. Even opposition newspapers such as the Ottawa *Free Press* replied to Macdonald's critics. On 12 October 1884 it commented, "We are so far a part of one immense empire and the interest of the part should be that of the whole. The Empire does not ask this part to fight in the Sudan, but it says:—'You have skilled labour which we lack. Lend us that labour and so save the lives of British soldiers.'" The whole project was, the *Free Press* explained, really a business transaction: so many *voyageurs* for so many dollars.

And yet it was not really *voyageurs* whom the British got. When Wolseley had led the Red River expedition in 1870, true *voyageurs* of the fur trade were very scarce. By 1884, *les vrais hommes du nord*, whose courage and skill British officers like Isaac Brock had praised so highly seventy-five years earlier, had in fact all but disappeared. Expert rivermen of a different type were, however, readily available.

During the winter in the woods of Quebec and Ontario, men felled trees and stacked logs on the river banks. In the spring, when the ice broke, and thereafter all summer long, they drove rafts of logs down the swollen rivers to the waiting sawmills. The great rafts that were a common sight on the Ottawa, the Gatineau, the Saguenay, and other Canadian rivers were a hard school where the devil-may-care "shanty-men" learned the ways of turbulent water. Familiarity with the wild water of Canadian rivers bred a class of men who were as open as the great blue sky overhead and as boisterous as the logs that danced beneath their feet in the fast-flowing rivers. It was danger-ous work, especially when a "shantyman" could not swim—and many of them never learned—but riding herd on the tumbling, pitching logs was also work which led to a contempt for danger and a disdain for all who did not know the wild freedom of the Canadian backwoods. Further west, in Mani-toba, the railway had not yet completely replaced the network of lakes and rivers as the principal highway for the transport of goods. There the last of the real boatmen plied their dying trade. It was, then, the "shantymen" of the eastern rivers and the boatmen of the western rivers rather than the old fur-trading *voyageurs* to whom the British government offered forty dollars a month to exercise their unique skills half-way around the world.[4] Melgund later summed up the situation well when he wrote, "The bona fide voyageurs have in many districts now become extinct. The country which fourteen years ago supplied the water transport of the Red River Expedition is now intersected by railroads and, except in the remote Northwest, long canoe journies are no longer necessary."[5] This was, however, no drawback, as Lord Lansdowne noted in his confidential reply to the first Colonial Office tele-gram. There were other skilled rivermen readily available: "the freighting business formerly carried on . . . has greatly declined of late and the best class of men now obtainable as river boatmen and pilots is to be found amongst the raftsmen engaged in the Lumber Trade. . . . They are excessively hardy and unequalled in their knowledge of river navigation—they are full of resource and able to turn their hands to almost any employment."[6]

To recruit such men, Melgund's first task in Ottawa was publicity. Since there was so little time to contact the boatmen (who will henceforth be called *voyageurs* with the above caveat in mind), he wisely requested the help of agents of the great lumber kings, men like J. T. Lambert, a timber broker in Ottawa who knew the trade intimately. At the same time, with Macdonald's approval, Melgund sent off telegrams and letters to the Canadian government's Indian agents and inserted in various newspaper advertisements headed "IMPORTANT TO BOATMEN" giving the terms of the British offer of employment on the Nile. A former British army supply officer, Deputy-Commissary-General M. B. Irvine, who had retired in Canada after serving under Wolseley both on the Red River and in West Africa, also offered his services in organizing the despatch of the *voyageurs*. Melgund's own small staff at Government House, with the help of Lambert and Irvine, went into action with the governor general's admonition in mind: "Be as civil as you can to the [Canadian] Militia Dept, they will perhaps be a little huffed at the whole thing not going through their hands."[7]

Lansdowne's apprehensions about the attitude of the Canadian militia authorities proved unnecessary. The minister of militia, Adolphe Caron,[8] co-operated with the governor general's office in a variety of ways, particularly in the selection of the three Canadian militia officers to lead the *voyageurs*. These three officers must, Caron stressed, be in complete sympathy with the simple, hardy men whom they would command. Caron, a French Canadian himself, well knew the tough and independent nature of woodsmen from Quebec. Wolseley had expressed the wish that militia officers might be secured who had served under him on the Red River expedition. His wish was partly fulfilled. By 27 August, the thirty-seven-year-old veteran of the Fenian Raids and the Red River expedition, Frederick Charles Denison, had agreed to set aside his flourishing law practice in Toronto and his promising career in municipal politics to take command of the contingent, Melgund having previously declined the appointment because of the impending birth of his first child.

The newly appointed commanding officer was the second son of Colonel George Taylor Denison of Toronto. In 1866 when he was a nineteen-year-old law student at Osgoode Hall, he and his older brother, George,[9] had served as lieutenants during the Fenian Raids on the Niagara frontier. During the subsequent years of peace, Denison, after having been called to the bar of Ontario in 1870, was promoted captain and eventually brevet major in the smartest militia unit in Toronto, the Governor General's Body Guard. Upon his return to Toronto from his service as an aide-de-camp to Wolseley on the Red River expedition, he had commanded the guard from 1872 until 1876 when George had succeeded him.

Frederick Denison was a more reserved and gentle man than his somewhat flamboyant older brother, who was a leading figure in imperial movements in Canada and a close collaborator with Sir John A. Macdonald and the Conservative party. George and his busy moustache achieved a certain fame in the byways of Canadian politics, but he never enjoyed the popularity of his more conciliatory brother. It is hard to imagine the reactionary George displaying the tact and understanding that enabled Frederick to be such a successful leader of the tough and often obstinate *voyageurs*. Frederick Denison had a fine, sensitive face, but he could be firm when firmness was required. Otherwise, it was his invariably kindly and considerate disposition that won the affection of such a motley group as the *voyageurs*, many of whom were naturally suspicious of an English-speaking patrician Torontonian.

It was obvious from the beginning that, given the fact that many of the volunteer boatmen were French Canadian, it would be desirable if at least one of the three militia officers appointed to the contingent was also. Captain Telmont Aumond, a gruff, ursine officer in the prestigious Ottawa militia unit, the Governor General's Foot Guards, obtained leave of absence from his employment with the Department of Marine and Fisheries to go with the contingent to Egypt. Aumond's father was a prominent lumberman on the Ottawa and Gatineau Rivers. It was there that his son had first learned the skills of a riverman.

The third officer authorized by the War Office to accompany the contingent was Captain Alexander C. MacRae of the Seventh Battalion, Fusiliers, of London, Ontario. MacRae was similar to Aumond in that he was a "rough, hard-looking fellow" who had considerable knowledge of river work. Moreover, MacRae, like Denison, had served under Wolseley on the Red River expedition fourteen years before. Of MacRae and Aumond, Melgund noted, "I am glad that we have got Aumond (but such a bear you never saw); we certainly have succeeded in sending two of the toughest customers but I believe they are both well suited to the work."[10]

Denison, Aumond, and MacRae were the three Canadian militia officers selected to lead the boatmen. Upon the recommendation of Militia Minister Caron, Surgeon Major John Louis Hubert Neilson, a regular force officer, was appointed to look after the contingent's physical well-being. Neilson, a Laval graduate with a taste for adventure, had served as a medical officer on the Red River expedition and, under the auspices of the International Red Cross, in Serbia during the Russo-Turkish War of 1877 (in which Melgund had also participated). A bilingual officer, Neilson was appointed correspondent for the Gordon relief expedition by both the Toronto *Star* and the Trois Rivières *Nouvelliste*. Like Denison, he kept a diary (in English) of his experiences. His is a more factual account than Denison's somewhat rambling journal. It suffers in comparison from the fact that he made no attempt to describe his own feelings and the people and events he encountered in the way Denison did.[11]

The spiritual welfare of the predominantly Roman Catholic *voyageurs* was entrusted to an enormous French-Canadian priest with a bushy black beard, Arthur Bouchard,[12] who had been recommended to Lansdowne by Caron. Born in Rivière Ouelle, Quebec, in 1845, Bouchard had been trained as a tailor, but he never lost his desire to become a missionary, despite his ill-health as a young man. Eventually he achieved both his goal and robust health. He was ordained as a priest in 1878 at the age of thirty-three, after having studied in Baltimore, London, and Verona. A hardy and simple man, Bouchard arrived in Cairo in early 1879 to undergo further training for missionary work in the Sudan where he spent the following two years (he arrived in Khartoum in November 1879, shortly before Gordon's departure). During 1882 and 1883, Bouchard had been travelling in Europe and Canada raising money for his mission in the Sudan. Speaking good Arabic and well acquainted with the Sudan, the devout but worldly Bouchard was instrumental in helping to prepare the *voyageurs* for what lay ahead of them. With his "taille de cuirassier, barbe de sapeur, bati comme un monitor, coeur d'agneau,"[13] he was just the man for the job and was soon very popular with his new parishioners.

The War Office had anticipated that only three militia officers would accompany the Canadian contingent. Two more, however, managed to work themselves into the group in which they eventually served as officers. Another veteran of the 1870 Red River expedition, Lieutenant-Colonel William Nassau Kennedy of Newcastle, Ontario, had decided to settle in Winnipeg. There, at Melgund's request, he took the leading part in the recruitment of Manitoban boatmen.[14] Kennedy was a prominent local lawyer and politician and, like his brothers and his sons after him, was also an enthusiastic militia-man—so much so that he allowed his militia comrades to influence his choice of boatmen. He enlisted two officers and several men of the 90th Battalion (including one of his brothers) and no less than eight fellow lawyers, despite the fact that they knew little or nothing of boatwork. Kennedy in turn induced Melgund to include him among the Manitoba *voyageurs*, initially in what was for him the somewhat humble status of a foreman. Upon arrival in Egypt, Kennedy was, however, appointed to the post of paymaster of the whole contingent. His presence among the *voyageurs* necessitated the immediate promotion of Denison, still a major, to lieutenant-colonel so that he would not be outranked by one of his men.

Kennedy was not the only militia officer who was determined to accompany the *voyageurs*. One of Denison's younger brothers, Egerton, a captain in a militia battalion of the South Staffordshire Regiment of the British army, had an even more difficult time in achieving his ambition to participate in the Gordon relief expedition. Egerton was denied a place in the contingent because he clearly had very little experience as a boatman, but at his own expense, he travelled to Egypt where Wolseley appointed him to join his fellow Canadians, and he soon proved himself a skilful apprentice. Finally, Surgeon-Major Neilson obtained permission to take with him his volatile and imaginative hospital sergeant from "B" Battery of the Regiment of Canadian Artillery, Gaston P. Labat, who subsequently wrote an amusing little book about his experiences, *Les Voyageurs Canadiens à l'Expédition du Sudan, ou Quatre-vingt-dix Jours avec les Crocodiles.*

These were the commissioned and non-commissioned militia officers who accompanied the *voyageurs.* But there were many other army officers in Canada, some in the small permanent force, others in the militia, and still others in retirement who longed to participate in the great adventure of attempting to rescue "Chinese" Gordon. Denison came from Toronto to Ottawa to help Melgund make arrangements for the recruitment of the *voyageurs* and upon arrival told the *Free Press* that he had begun to receive applications from men across Canada and in the United States to join the contingent or to serve in Egypt in any other capacity. Indicative of the general military enthusiasm which swept over English-speaking Canada in the autumn of 1884 were the offers of service that Lansdowne and Macdonald continued to receive not only from individuals but also from whole militia units who volunteered *en masse* to go to the Sudan. These volunteers, hungry for adventure in distant lands, were to importune Ottawa and London throughout the campaign. Only one was successful in his application. From as far distant as Kingston, Ontario, Major James Frederick Wilson of "A" Battery of the Regiment of Canadian Artillery had sensed the way things were going in the Sudan in the late spring of 1884. When the expedition to Khartoum was officially announced, he had immediately applied for permission to accompany it "for the purpose of acquiring a practical experience of the actual operations of war on active service."[15] As it had done two years earlier in the case of Lieutenant Joseph Hébert, the Canadian Government recommended "Cupid" Wilson's request to the War Office so that one of the permanent force officers could gain more experience in the field. The War Office again agreed, on the explicit understanding that all Wilson's expenses would be borne by Ottawa.

It was not, however, militiamen or other volunteers whom the War Office wanted. British professional soldiers did not generally welcome the help of "colonials" in the thin red line, although in this case they were willing to pay the price to get the skilled boatmen they urgently needed. Perhaps too Wolseley's well-known admiration for Canadian militia officers was sufficiently recognized in Whitehall to ensure that at least some of the Canadian militia who had volunteered would be accepted along with that absolute necessity, the *voyageurs*. One week after the original request for three hundred *voyageurs* was received in Ottawa, an additional two hundred were requested. Another week passed, and after the most energetic and determined efforts by Melgund and his small staff, a total of almost four hundred boatmen had been recruited. All were given a thorough medical examination and issued with a complete set of work clothes (the officers wore their militia uniforms). For those who wished it, arrangements were made for three-quarters of their wages to be paid direct to their families in Canada. Of the total of 386 who finally sailed from Canada, 159 were from the Ottawa area, 92 from Manitoba, 56 from Caughnawaga, and the remainder from elsewhere in Quebec and Ontario, mainly Trois Rivières and Peterborough. A number of boatmen had been recruited at the Lakehead, but they could not arrive in Quebec in time for the sailing. About one-half of the *voyageurs* spoke English and the other half French. Some were illiterate. More than one hundred were Indians or métis. One of the *voyageurs* later described with some surprise the odd collection of men who were his fellow passengers on the ship carrying them to Alexandria.

> We have on board all sort and conditions of men, as respects nationality, creed, character, and usual occupation, and a student of human behaviour would here have an abundant field of labour. We have English, French Canadians, half-breeds, and some Englishmen in the Winnipeg detachment who had not been long in Canada. The body comprises bank clerks, store clerks, mechanics, and labourers, and of apparent cut-throats and professional drunkards we have a few.[16]

In short, with the addition of the militia officers and a French-Canadian priest, the contingent reflected the varied nature of the Canadian frontier in the late nineteenth century.

A British steamer, the 2,500-ton *Ocean King*, was chartered by the War Office to carry the party from Montreal to Alexandria. Dr. Neilson was despatched in advance to Montreal to supervise the outfitting of the ship, availing himself of the assistance of the British Army Board of Survey in Montreal whenever necessary. Arrangements were made by the diligent Melgund for the men to be given additional food aboard the ship because, "while at the shanties, no limit is placed to [the woodman's] consumption of food, and he eats when he likes and as much as he likes, his chief food being salt pork and beans." The true *mangeurs de lard* among the *voyageurs* were not going to be deprived of their favourite food, even in mid-Atlantic. Food was also provided for the mind as well as for the body: an evangelical group in Montreal gave each man a Bible.

The recruitment and despatch of the Canadian contingent was an extraordinary feat of rapid organization and improvisation. From the moment when Lord Lansdowne first received the Colonial Office telegram to the sailing of the *Ocean King*, only twenty-four days had passed. Melgund had shown remarkable efficiency. In addition to conducting a voluminous and rapid correspondence concerning the recruitment of the boatmen in various localities, "Rollo" himself travelled to Montreal and Trois Rivières to interview suitable applicants. Melgund had a talent for the details of administration, and he performed his quasi-military duties with flexibility and despatch. The subtleties of Canadian parliamentary procedures and party politics which were sometimes to prove bothersome when Melgund was governor general during the Boer War did not hinder his efforts in 1884. His experience in recruiting and despatching the volunteers was in fact to prove useful when Canada decided to send troops to South Africa.

On 13 September 1884, almost two hundred of the boatmen entrained in Ottawa for Montreal. The Ottawa *Free Press* of the same date described the enthusiastic send-off that a large number of Ottawans gave to their fellow citizens destined for the Sudan. After being photographed on Parliament Hill, the *voyageurs*, dressed in their rumpled suits and broad-rimmed hats, and with the brass band of the Governor General's Foot Guards at their head, marched down Wellington Street to the Broad Street station of the Canadian Pacific Railway. At the station, a large farewell dinner had been prepared for the men, who were famous for their appetites. Other appetites also soon showed themselves: two of the foremen had to take a later train to Montreal because, as the *Free Press* noted, "they were busy this afternoon hunting up about a dozen of the men who missed the [first] train, owing to their having imbibed too freely." The exhausted Melgund observed, "it was decidedly what they call a 'cheery crowd' and I don't think that I ever had such a rough journey, as on that day from here [Ottawa] to Montreal." In Hull, just across the river from Ottawa, the train stopped briefly and some of the *voyageurs* quickly availed themselves of the unexpected opportunity to obtain yet more beer or whiskey. In Montreal the men were confined overnight to the *Ocean King* pending its departure early the next morning for Trois Rivières and Quebec City. The independent-minded *voyageurs* were not, however, to be so easily restrained. A number of them, as soon as their companions and the ship's crew were asleep, bypassed the guarded gangway and swung themselves down the ship's lines to the dock. Montreal relatives and friends of the *voyageurs* suddenly received unexpected visitors in the middle of the night. That was, of course, a good reason for celebrating. The result was that two of the boatmen missed the morning sailing of the *Ocean King* from

Montreal and the army had to send them by train to Quebec City to rejoin their ship.

The graphic description provided by the Ottawa *Free Press* of the departure from Ottawa was equalled by the Quebec *Morning Chronicle's* account of the departure of the *Ocean King* from Quebec City on September 15.[17] Shortly before the ship sailed, Lord Lansdowne, who had throughout taken an active interest in the arrangements made for the welfare of the volunteers, visited the ship with Lady Lansdowne, Militia Minister Caron, and Lord Melgund. In the Citadel at Quebec, he had already had several long talks with Father Bouchard about the Sudan. Lansdowne had, therefore, a good idea of the terrain the Canadian boatmen would face. When he arrived at the dock, the *voyageurs* were formed in line on the upper deck of the *Ocean King* to be inspected by him. Lord Lansdowne visited the officers' and men's quarters and presented both English and French books and magazines and table games before ascending to the bridge of the ship. From there, in simple terms in both English and French, he attempted to explain to the men why exactly they were going to the Sudan.

One of Lansdowne's staff later wrote,

He gave an admirable address to the British [sic] boatmen; it was kindly, encouraging, full of sound and patriotic sentiment, and it was delivered in the strictest gubernatorial style, without gesture or motion. He then turned around to the French Canadians. His speech was in substance much the same, though the sentences were shorter and terser; but in less than two minutes he spoke with all the animation of a born Frenchman, with all the gesticulation and vivacity of the race, and the staidness of his demeanour entirely disappeared. The genius of the French language had taken possession of him, and he concluded an impassioned oration in the most approved French style, both as regards language and movements.[18]

Some boatmen had only the vaguest or no idea at all where the Sudan was or who "Chinese" Gordon was. And, with the rough nature of the boatmen in mind, Lansdowne called upon them to behave themselves.

That you will acquit yourselves creditably, that you will do the work for which you are specially engaged as no other men in the world could do it, that you will show yourselves hardy, skilful, enduring I have no doubt. But I want you to do even more than this and to remember that you carry with you the reputation of your own country, and that when you return next year you must bring that reputation back without blot or blemish. To do this you must be not only bold in the presence of danger and skilful in the face of difficulties, but steady, well-conducted and obedient to discipline from the moment you leave these shores until the day when you return to them again. You are not going to serve as soldiers, but you must show the soldiers that a civilian can upon occasion display many of the best qualities of a soldier.

It was, perhaps, as well for Lansdowne's high hopes for the "soldierly" conduct of the *voyageurs* that he had not witnessed a scene in Montreal the evening before, an unedifying scene that Sergeant Labat had recorded before the *Ocean King* sailed down the river to Trois Rivières and Quebec City to collect the remainder of the Quebec boatmen.

> Samedi soir quand presque tous les voyageurs étaient à bord, une squaw apparut voulant voir son homme. Celui-ci l'avant aperçue, franchit le bord du pont et le voila dans les bras de sa moitié. Je vous assure que cette moitié était une totalité complète, taille de Chine, labougru et pesant au bas mot plus de 200 livres. Les voilas donc s'embrassant comme Daphnis et Chloe, ces deux enfants de nos forêts, quand, pour mettre fin à cette attendrissement, on oblige à notre homme à remonter à bord. Comme il résistait, elle aussi..... Enfin, dans une dernière étreinte pas trop rapprochée ou les levres étaient aux levres, les mains du mari disparurent dans le corset de la squaw, et, cherche à prendre. ..... quoi?.... shocking?.... patatas, une fausse manoeuvre s'étant produite on entendit un bruit de verre cassé et une bouteille de whisky vint s'aplatir sur le pavement. La squaw se met à pleurer, lui aussi, à fendre larme et je crois qu'on peut trouver l'origine de l'expression "larmes de crocodiles."[19]

Father Bouchard was pessimistic about the possibilities of rescuing Gordon and regarded the great expedition as a futile gamble which risked the lives of other men without any assurance that it could save Gordon's. The only sure way of holding the Sudan was, he believed, to build a railroad from the Red Sea coast to Berber and then go up the Nile to Khartoum— but this, as Bouchard's biographer, Father Têtu later noted, would have taken far too long to be of any help in the rescue of Gordon.

> Le Père Bouchard n'avait aucune confiance dans cette expédition qui venait comme la moutarde après diner. Que de fois il m'en parla dans

ce sens! Et il s'en ouvrit clairement auprès du gouverneur et des officiers
...il était convaincu qu'il était trop tard, et que Gordon serait trahi
par eux et tué, ou livré vivant au Mahdi. Sa répugnance était si grande
que, d'après moi, le sacrifice qu'il fit en acceptant le titre d'aumônier,
fut le plus grand de sa vie, et je puis en parler avec connaissance de
cause.[20]

The physical appearance of the *voyageurs* themselves did little, apparently,
to reassure Bouchard or three other priests who had come down to the dock
in Quebec City to see him off. Father Têtu, who was one of them, was especially startled by the rough appearance of the *voyageurs*.

> Je dois à la vérité de dire que je ne fus pas très enthousiasmé, ni très fier,
> à la vue des trois cents voyageurs qui étaient sur le pont et qui allaient
> représenter le pays en Egypte. Quel assemblage étrange! Pas d'uni-
> formes—des habits de toutes couleurs—des figures hâlées, quelques-
> unes aux traits durs et féroces—ca et là les sinistres visages des Iroquois
> de Caughnawaga—un demi-silence—l'air ennuyé de gens qui attendent;
> tout cela avait un aspect terrible et funèbre que je n'oublierai jamais.[21]

Unknown to the gloomy Father Têtu, recent encounters with squaws
and whiskey bottles accounted in part for the funereal appearance of the
voyageurs when the *Ocean King* sailed from Quebec City at noon on 15
September. If the men looked unprepossessing to Têtu while the ship was
still at the dock, he was fortunately not to see them during the rough two-
day passage down the Gulf of St. Lawrence when many combatted the
combined effects of hangovers and seasickness. The steamer put in for coal
at Sydney, Nova Scotia, in the early hours of the morning of 18 September.
After a stowaway had been put ashore and while the ship was coaling, Denison
took his men for a march along the shore. They soon showed that they were
not such a gloomy group as Têtu had thought them to be. Many had never
seen the ocean before, and the warm, early autumn weather induced them
to try swimming in the strange water that tasted of salt. Others amused themselves by attempting to catch lobsters or to dig oysters from the sand. A few,
however, were unsatisfied with such simple pleasures and were soon reeling
drunkenly about the streets of the quiet little Nova Scotian town. "One young
man entered a schoolhouse and delivered a speech to the children, attempted
to 'mash' the teacher, and concluded by excusing himself for being drunk.
He next entered the courthouse and addressed the magistrate and told him
that he had come to wish him goodbye. A constable endeavoured to put him

out. He resented this injustice and laid the constable prostrate on the ground."22 That night, thirty of the *voyageurs*, having found their afternoon exercises insufficient to satisfy their restless and exuberant natures, broke ship to join in sampling the nocturnal diversions of Sydney. Three boatmen, apparently having second thoughts about going to Egypt, did not return in the morning, but Denison was able to recruit another in Sydney to replace one of them—and the contingent thereby gained its one Nova Scotian and one of its best boatmen. The French Canadians in particular had been interested in the French frigate *Flor* in Sydney harbour and welcomed the French admiral and some of his officers aboard the *Ocean King*. After inspecting the two long lines of boatmen drawn up on the dirty coaling wharf, the French admiral had in turn invited the Canadian officers to visit his ship the next day. The invitation had to be declined. The early morning of 19 September found the *Ocean King* outward bound from Sydney, steaming eastward toward its next coaling stop, Gibraltar.

The *voyageurs* had been recruited and despatched, taking with them 386 paddles and two birch-bark canoes (one for Wolseley and one for Denison), but what of the boats they were to take up the Nile and of the route they were to follow? Colonel Sir William Butler, the Red River veteran and one of the "Canadians" in Wolseley's "Ring," who had acted as liaison between the War Office and the Colonial Office in the recruitment of the *voyageurs*, had also been ordered by Wolseley to organize the construction of the boats required to carry the expedition to Khartoum. In addition to being a resourceful and energetic officer, Butler was a prolific writer. He later described in detail in *The Campaign of the Cataracts* how he fulfilled his urgent task.

The list of conditions that the boats had to meet was formidable: they had to be able to carry twelve fully equipped soldiers and their supplies for one hundred days (to be used only south of Korti); they had to be strong enough to withstand the punishment of rapids and rocks, yet light enough to be carried short distances across obstacles such as sand-bars; and they had to be capable of being rowed, poled, towed, or sailed. Finally, they could draw only two feet of water with a four-ton load and were to be equipped with twelve oars, two masts, two large lug sails, and a removable rudder. For a single boat to possess all these characteristics seemed to some impossible, but Butler set about with his usual energy in discovering exactly what kind of boat might conceivably possess them all. He soon found that the standard Royal Navy whaler, if somewhat enlarged and otherwise modified, was probably what he wanted. After testing a loaded whaler in Portsmouth dockyard, Butler had a thirty-foot long and six-and-one-half-foot wide prototype hastily built. He found to his delight that it met all his requirements. Once satisfied that he had the boat he wanted, Butler sent urgent enquiries to boatbuilders throughout England and Scotland. The Admiralty had assured him that it would take at least two to three months to build four hundred such boats. But Butler was not to be deterred; the orders he had received from Wolseley were clear.

Can you build . . . 400 boats capable of carrying 4,000 men, with provisions for three and a half months, over the cataracts between Wadi Halfa and Dongola? Can you deliver these 400 boats, together with their sails, oars, masts, poles and outfits complete, at the head of the Second Cataract, beyond Wadi Halfa, on the Nile, in time to enable troops to reach Khartoum if necessary, during the winter season, and return from Khartoum before the Sudan summer is upon them?

You will have not only to build these boats, but to ship them from England, land them at Alexandria, carry them by train 350 miles to Assiout, thence by river 400 miles to Assouan, thence up the First Cataract, and on to Wadi Halfa, 220 miles further. From Wadi Halfa they will have to be taken by train to the head of the Second Cataract, and there, at a place called Sarras, thirty miles beyond Wadi Halfa, they will be delivered to the soldiers who are to work them to Dongola.

The answer from various boatyards to Butler's queries was a confident affirmative. Late on 12 August, orders to construct the boats were finally approved by the War Office. At forty-seven boatyards a total of eight hundred enlarged whalers began to be built at a cost of £275 each. Within ten weeks all eight hundred boats, complete with oars, sails and towlines, had been despatched to Alexandria, neatly stacked aboard nineteen steamers. The first whaler arrived at Alexandria on 22 September, while the *Ocean King* was still in mid-Atlantic. The last was unloaded on 18 October, eleven days after the arrival of the *Ocean King*. All the whalers were carefully placed on straw pallets on open rail carriages and sent southward without delay. Colonel Butler had reason to congratulate himself on his timing; it could hardly have been better. Procrastination and delay might be characteristics of Gladstone's government whenever it tried to decide what to do about the Sudan, but there was never any doubt in the minds of Wolseley or Butler about what had to be done to get the expedition under way.

Butler could also congratulate himself on the design of his boats. Critics were later to contend that they were too light or that their rudders were improperly secured, and certainly various pieces of gear became dispersed on the rail trip south. But the men who came to know the modified whalers intimately praised the design of the boats. "We had all come to the conclusion that the boats and outfits were well devised for the service," one of the Canadian foremen, Louis Jackson, later wrote.

We had tried them now in various ways; we had sailed against a swift current with a beam wind, where a flat bottom would have had to be towed with lines, and the more this towing could be avoided, the better it was on account of the fearful track along the shore. The boats were sufficiently strong for all necessary handling and in case of accident, they were light enough to be brought ashore and turned over for repairs without extra help.

... Many of my men had been portaging on the Ottawa for different lumber firms and all agreed with me, that whilst the Nile river boats would have been of no use on the Ottawa, they could not be improved upon for the Nile service on account of the nature of the river. For the ascent of the river as well as the cataracts, the sailing qualities of the boats were all important, and when towed by line, the keel would give a chance to shoot out into the current to get around rocks, where a flat-bottomed boat would have followed the line broadside and fetched up against the rock.[23]

While Butler was engaged in arranging the construction of the boats and Melgund was occupied with the recruitment of the *voyageurs*, troopships full of British soldiers and the necessary stores to feed them in the wilderness of the Sudan had been arriving in Alexandria. Over 1,600,000 tins of bully beef (mostly from Chicago), 1,359,400 pounds of ship's biscuit, 16,656 tins of condensed milk, 30,000 gallons of rum, and 1,000 bottles of champagne (a Victorian comfort for the sick) were shipped from Britain, to be supplemented with those very few foodstuffs that could be obtained in Egypt itself. The rapid procurement of supplies in Britain and in Egypt presented problems, but they were nothing compared to the problem that their transportation up the Nile posed. The skill of the *voyageurs* in handling boats had been noted by British officers who had served in Canada; other officers—including Wolseley and many of the "Ring"—also recalled how well West Africans had manoeuvred their boats through the surf on the Gold Coast. They too might be able to help in the despatch of the supplies southward, and, moreover, they were accustomed to the climate. Hence two British officers were given a bizarre assignment. They were despatched to West Africa with the steamer *Shelley* to recruit the agile and skilful boatmen known as *kroomen*, whom Wolseley had first seen on the Gold Coast in 1873 when he and his Red River companions, Redvers Buller and John McNeill, had defeated King Koffee. When the *Shelley* arrived off Monrovia, the president of Liberia refused to cooperate in any "war-like scheme," but elsewhere along the West African coast, 266 of the short, muscular *kroomen* volunteered readily for a shilling a day and a sailor's uniform. The names of the illiterate *kroomen* were too difficult for the two British recruiting officers to enter on the pay-sheets so the black boatmen happily took such names as "Smart All Day," "Jack Upside Down," and, unlikely as it seems, "Black Man's Trouble."

With the very model of a modern major-general at its head and with such a varied cast as English noblemen, North American Indian *voyageurs*, West African *kroomen*, Aden Arabs, and Egyptian *fellaheen* and such properties as champagne and pickles all destined for the Nile, the Sudan expedition included many of the essential ingredients of a Gilbert and Sullivan operetta. The addition of Messrs. Thomas Cook to this already motley cast should, perhaps, have been the final touch for a Victorian satirist. The thought of Gordon besieged in Khartoum was, however, sufficient to stop any tendency to engage in light satire.

Messrs. Thomas Cook did enter the scene as the curtain was first going up. The reputation for efficiency and dependability that the abstemious Thomas Cook and his son, John, had already earned for themselves among that new English phenomenon, the tourist, had been so well established by 1882 that the War Office had provided tickets from Cook's for both Wolseley and the Duke of Connaught when they had set out for Egypt to quell Arabi's revolt. Cook's Nile steamers had for several years been carrying tourists in comfort and fashionable elegance to view ancient Egyptian monuments. Following the suppression of Arabi's revolt in 1882, John Cook voluntarily placed his steamers at the service of the British army so that wounded soldiers might be carried in comfort to Cairo. His steamers had also carried British soldiers suffering from that most prevalent Egyptian disease, typhoid, on convalescent excursions up the Nile. Even Gordon had taken one of Cook's river steamers on one stage of his last journey to Khartoum.

Given John Cook's knowledge of transport problems on the Nile, it is not surprising that he was asked by the War Office to join in the planning of the Gordon relief expedition. Cook attended meeting after meeting at the War Office, finally offering the services of his company to carry the whole force as far as Wadi Halfa.[24] He originally contracted to transport six thousand soldiers and ten thousand tons of stores by rail from Alexandria to Assiout and thence by boat to Wadi Halfa. But before the end of the expedition, he had in fact carried eleven thousand British and seven thousand Egyptian troops and one hundred and thirty thousand tons of supplies in his river steamers between Assiout and Wadi Halfa. The eight hundred whalers, some carrying soldiers, were towed up this easiest stage of the river route by Cook's steamers. With awnings spread over their heads, and with sleeves rolled up and their pipes aglow, the soldiers wished that they could make the trip all the way up to Khartoum with as little effort. Not all the initial arrangements were, however, so successful. Cook had also been contracted by Wolseley's chief of staff, Redvers Buller, to supply twelve thousand tons of coal for the use of steamers on the Nile. This amount, originally suggested by the Admiralty, proved in the event to be one-fifth of the total required. Because of misunderstandings about what orders had been given and how much coal was actually needed, a hiatus in the supply of coal later caused a major disruption in the flow of men and supplies.

On 9 September, Wolseley established his headquarters temporarily at a palace in Cairo put at his disposal by the Khedive, while several members of his "Ring" moved into Shepheard's Hotel. They had immediately set about establishing the required base organization for the supply of the expedition. One month later, the Canadian *voyageurs* arrived in Cairo, after a voyage which Denison had described later in a letter to Melgund from Gibraltar: "We have had splendid weather and made better time than expected. Everything has gone smoothly—except a growl one day by one gang, about soup being burnt. It amounted to nothing. The other men were satisfied."[25] One of them long afterward recalled with pleasure the unlimited amount of "plum duff" that had been provided for them. The only untoward event on the quiet voyage across the Atlantic was the death of a Manitoban Indian, Richard Henderson, from what Dr. Neilson described as a brain disease. Hospital Sergeant Labat's diagnosis was less sophisticated. He believed that Henderson had died of an acute case of the disorder which was to afflict several of the *voyageurs*: homesickness. "[Il] a été pris de nostalgie, mal du pays, deux jours après le départ. Très superstitieux, il voulait revenir chez lui voir sa femme et ses enfants."[26] In a simple but moving ceremony in mid-Atlantic, Henderson's body, sewn in canvas, was buried at sea.

When, ten days out of Sydney, the *Ocean King* had arrived in Gibraltar to take on five hundred tons of coal, Lord Lansdowne's table games and books had begun to bore the *voyageurs* (especially those who were illiterate). The tugs-of-war to keep in shape, the card games played for apples, and the nightly sing-songs on the upper decks no longer held much attraction. The *Ocean King* possessed a piano and several of the *voyageurs* had brought flutes, fiddles, and banjoes, but even their music had begun to pall. Cape St. Vincent on the Portuguese coast had brought the men running to the rails to cheer their first sight of land. Gibraltar was a welcome diversion for them since, generally, they were unaccustomed to such a long period of inactivity or to finding within themselves resources for their own amusement. Having been given shore leave in Gibraltar until 7:00 P.M., while Denison was sightseeing and enjoying the unexpected honour of dining with the governor, a number of the *voyageurs* had returned to their ship "under the influence of liquor, as might be expected."

Several did not return that night at all, Denison noted in his journal with, perhaps, some pride in the prowess of his men. Two powerful Indian brothers, Alfred and Joseph Ayotte, "gave a lot of trouble being drunk and quarrelsome; six water-police assisted by four or five civilians tried to arrest them but failed." Gaston Labat was also impressed by the strength of the brothers Ayotte: "Vous le savez, ces grands enfants gâtés aiment le gaudriole, à se battre, à rire, à chanter, et c'est ce que deux de nos forts gaillards ont fait, lors de notre passage à Gibraltar, en mettant la police en deroute et en s'écriant: 'nous avons vaincu Gibraltar!' "[27] In accordance with the authority allowed him by the terms of the men's contracts, Denison had fined the two brothers seven dollars each for their misbehaviour in Gibraltar. And once the *Ocean King* was out into the calm Mediterranean, making its way along the Algerian coast toward Alexandria, the bilingual Dr. Neilson had delivered the men a simple and sensible lecture on the virtues of abstention.

> Presque tous les dangers réels que nous aurons à recontrer se résument dans un seul mot: l'Intempérance! N'allez pas croire que je vais vous faire un sermon de tempérance; ce serait impiéter sur le terrain de notre éloquent et dévoué aumonier. Je ne puis non plus poser comme un apôtre de tempérance, mais je suis convaincu d'une chose: c'est que la plus grande modération dans l'usage des boissons spiriteuses est nécessaire en tout temps, et si cette modération est nécessaire dans un pays salubre comme le nôtre à plus forte raison est-il de la plus grande urgence d'être tempérant dans des régions chaude et d'une lubrité douteuse, comme celle du Nil.[28]

Denison, however, was taking no chances of the excesses of Sydney and Gibraltar recurring. By the time the *voyageurs* arrived in Alexandria, he had learned a lesson. The first thing he did ashore was to request from the British army an armed guard to be placed on the *Ocean King* to prevent any of his men from landing. Denison need not have worried. By then the *voyageurs* had had their fun and were now ready for work. With only a few exceptions, all were well-behaved throughout the remainder of their employment. They seldom drank more than the muddy water of the Nile and their occasional rum ration.

On 8 October, the day following the arrival of the *Ocean King* in Alexandria, Major Wilson of the Regiment of Canadian Artillery arrived from England aboard the troopship *Anglian*. He was immediately appointed to the First Battery of the First Brigade of the Southern Division, Royal Artillery. As a result, he became automatically a member of the Desert Column since his artillery was later assigned to support the Camel Corps.

The Canadians had arrived on the Nile: Denison with his *voyageurs* and "Cupid" Wilson with his orders to join the Southern Division. But these four hundred Canadians were not the only ones seeking adventure in Egypt; before the hot, trying campaign to save Gordon was over, several more Canadians, in addition to those Englishmen of Wolseley's "Ring" who had served in Canada, were to appear in a number of different and sometimes unexpected roles.

7

Up the Nile

When years ago I 'listed lads,
To serve our Gracious Queen,
The sergeant made me understand
I was a Royal Marine.
He said we sometimes served in ships
and sometimes on the shore;
But did not say I should wear spurs,
Or be in the Camel Corps!

SERGEANT H. EAGLE,
ROYAL MARINES.

Like the British soldiers who had preceded them, both "Cupid" Wilson and the *voyageurs* found the first stage of their long ascent of the Nile unexpectedly enjoyable. Their 550-mile journey to Wadi Halfa behind the Khedive's yacht, *Ferooz*, which towed forty whalers, was such an effortless way to travel that Denison was even able to go ashore briefly to view a number of ancient ruins and to purchase fresh meat, vegetables, and dates for his men. In Alexandria, the *voyageurs* had been issued rubber ground-sheets and blankets which they spread out on the crowded decks of the little steamer and the barges when the temperature dropped sharply at night. During the day, they guarded their eyes against the glare of the bright sun and the unwanted attentions of clouds of flies by wearing the blue-tinted glasses presented to them by a Montreal optometrist. Many, being simple and unschooled men, were uninterested in ancient ruins, but they were often diverted by the people along the river banks. As the Canadians moved southward, the natives whom they encountered became to them ever more bizarre. Such a riverside sight as "a pasha or some Egyptian swell...mounted on his horse with a white umbrella over his head and followed fifty yards behind by a native cavalryman or policeman with his carbine at the advance" interested the *voyageurs* greatly. The boatmen were rough and boisterous, yet they were also prudish. The appearance of almost naked Egyptian girls along the banks of the river astonished them. They were shocked by what they considered their indecency. "The maidens wore no covering except a lace breech clout. Captain Denison succeeded in purchasing one of these articles of apparel from a maiden for which he paid the munificent sum of twenty-five cents.

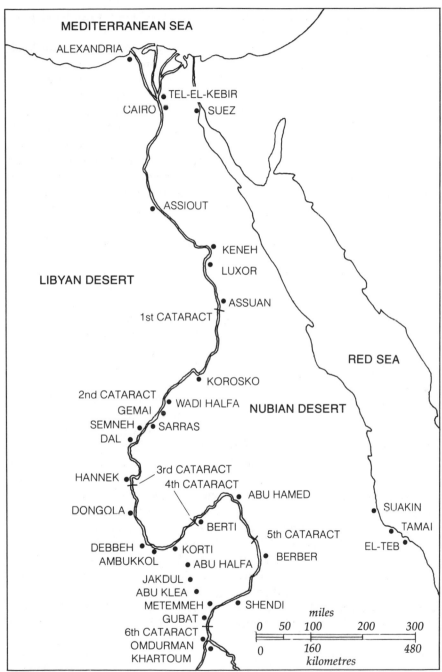

The Nile River

The girl took the money first, undid the string around her waist, handed the clout to the Captain, and ran off at a fast pace."[1]

On the Nile itself, they encountered British troops also headed for Wadi Halfa with increasing frequency. Old friends from earlier campaigns exchanged surprised greetings. But few meetings were quite so unexpected as that between two Torontonians, Frederick Denison and Lieutenant Edmund Barker Van Koughnet of the Royal Navy. Three years Denison's junior, Van Koughnet was the son of a former chancellor, commissioner of crown lands, and minister of agriculture of Ontario. He had entered the Royal Navy as a cadet in 1863 at the age of fourteen. By October 1884, Van Koughnet had served as a midshipman on the Great Lakes during the Fenian Raids (when he saved two boys from drowning) and as a sub-lieutenant and lieutenant in the flagships of the North American and West Indies, Channel, and Mediterranean fleets. On the Nile, he had his own command, a minute gunboat, the *Sadieh*. Van Koughnet, who had not distinguished himself as a student during his midshipman days (he was awarded only third-class certificates), had proven his courage in small boat raids in the Zulu Wars, where he had been severely wounded. Always eager for adventure and action in any corner of the world, promotion for him had nevertheless been slow during his twenty-one years in the Royal Navy. It was not until he had again exhibited great courage further up the Nile in early 1885 that Van Koughnet was finally promoted Commander.[2]

After passing their fellow Canadian and his river gunboat, the *voyageurs* arrived at Wadi Halfa on the afternoon of 26 October. Wolseley welcomed them both that day and the next by riding to their camp and chatting with them. He noted in his journal that they were "a rough-looking lot, but I hope I shall get plenty of work out of them. They won't funk this river at all events."[3] Wadi Halfa—inevitably dubbed "Bloody Halfway" by the British troops—was normally a small, dusty market town of sunbaked brick and palm trees. During the autumn of 1884 it was fast becoming the major military headquarters that it was to remain for the next fifteen years. To Butler, Wadi Halfa looked as if "the goods station of a London terminus, a couple of battalion of infantry, the War Office, and a considerable portion of the Woolich Arsenal had been all thoroughly shaken together, and then cast forth on the desert."[4] Here Wolseley, along with many of the British troops, had arrived three weeks before the Canadians. Since his arrival from Cairo, he had been engaged in making preparations for the ascent of the increasingly difficult stretches that lay ahead. He never had a wholly efficient staff to assist him—a staff organized on systematic lines was an innovation yet untried in the British army—and his own "Ring" was beginning to show signs of wear. Most of its members were now so senior in the army that they were reluctant to take orders from each other and tended to be prima donnas. Most decisions, including minor ones, had to be taken by Wolseley personally.

Even such questions as what to do about the boats as they arrived from Cairo were addressed to him. Delays inevitably arose from a system of command which placed such burdens on the commander-in-chief.

At Wadi Halfa, Wolseley's time and that of his former Red River companions, Buller, Butler, and Alleyne, was fully occupied with supervising the unscrambling of boat gear and other supplies which were arriving in a state of great confusion. Butler quickly established an extensive boatyard for the repair and the refitting of the whalers (not an easy task since each boat had twenty-six different pieces of gear, and in most cases, the rudder made by one boat-builder would not readily fit another's). Wolseley's attention and that of his staff was also taken by planning the next stage of the advance southward. Yet they made time to welcome warmly the *voyageurs* and especially such Red River comrades as Denison, Neilsen, Kennedy, and MacRae. Among the Canadian foremen, Butler immediately recognized an outspoken Indian chief from Manitoba whom he had not seen for fourteen years. It soon became evident that Chief William Prince had strong feelings about some of his fellow Canadians who had come to Egypt to serve their Queen. He had marked a number of incompetents in the contingent even before seeing them at work on the river.

Fourteen years earlier this same William Prince had been the best Indian in my canoe when we forced our way up the rapids of the Winnipeg to meet the advance of the Red River Expedition through the wilderness of the North-west. And here today, on the Nile above the Second Cataract, stood William Prince, now chief of his tribe, grown more massive of frame and less agile of gait, but still keen of eye and steady of hand as when I last saw him standing bowman in a bark canoe among the whirling waters whose echoes were lost in the endless pinewoods of the Great Lone Land.

Seated in my tent in old Indian fashion, crosslegged on the ground, Prince and his companions soon found themselves at home in this strange land, for dry and arid as these deserts were, there were drops of whiskey and plugs of tobacco to be found in them, and these are keys to unlock the tongue of a Redman, just as potent in the sands of Nubia as in the pine-islands or prairies of the North.

"How many Indians had come from Winnipeg?"

"About a dozen; but had longer time and fuller notice been given, fifty or even a hundred would have come."

"Were the voyageurs, taking them all together, up to the old North 'West mark?"

"No; but there were a good proportion among them able boatmen. The Iroquois and French Canadians were nearly all first-class men;

there were also several excellent boatmen from the Ottawa, but there were some 'Deadbeats' who knew nothing of the work."[5]

Wadi Halfa was proving to be a place both for meeting old friends and for making new ones. Denison first met there the boisterous naval officer who had distinguished himself by his daring during the bombardment of Alexandria two years before. Captain Lord Charles Beresford had used his friendship with the Prince of Wales and his influence in the fashionable world of London to secure his appointment as naval aide-de-camp to Wolseley. But once in Egypt he soon proved to be the energetic officer needed to command the nine miles of rapids—or Second Cataract—stretching southward from Wadi Halfa. Beresford, ever resourceful, supervised and exhorted the troops and *voyageurs* from the back of a little white donkey whom he had named "County Waterford" because, he explained, "the second time I contested him, I lost my seat" (a reference to his unsuccessful attempt in 1876 to be re-elected member of parliament for Waterford).[6] It was Beresford who succeed in dragging several small steamers through the wild torrent of water, first using four thousand Egyptians and later fifteen hundred cursing British troops to do so. Getting the steamers through was worth any effort. They were invaluable in helping to carry supplies and troops south from Wadi Halfa toward Dongola.

Once in Wadi Halfa, the *voyageurs* had, in a sense, reached their destination. It was at that dusty town that their work began. Until Wadi Halfa, steamers and the railway had been available to provide a quick passage up the river. The *voyageurs* now found themselves approximately 800 of the 1,600 miles from Alexandria to Khartoum. So far, everything was "all Sir Garnet." But now their scenic tour of the milk-coffee Nile was over. There were no Mahdists for many miles ahead. But there was incessant toil and turbulent water. Steamers could no longer pull the whalers in the increasingly dangerous river. Some of the Iroquois from Montreal left immediately to take boatloads of soldiers and supplies over the next hundred miles south of "Bloody Halfway." The other *voyageurs* stayed in a tent camp near the town where Denison established temporary headquarters. From there, they took the heavily laden whalers through the Second Cataract, working thirteen and fourteen hours a day and, in the best traditions of the *mangeurs de lard*, eating every evening as much as possible of whatever rations were issued them. For many of the soldiers, it was the first time they had handled oars.

Six at oars, one at helm, and one in bow, the latter to keep a sharp eye for dangers and warn the helmsman, especially for sunken rocks hard to discover until actually hit by them; he was furnished with a long pole to push us away from rocks, or to push us off in case we got lodged on them. When the crews... having received instructions, took their places, each man with a long, single oar, and pushed off from the bank the fun began. Only a few of us had ever held an oar... we dipped oars; a general splash, no concert of action; no rhythm. Suddenly the head rower caught a crab [mishandled his oar] and turned a back somersault into the lap of the man behind it; it was the head pin in a bowling-alley, over went the whole crew, heels up.[7]

But the soldiers learned quickly, and such mistakes became increasingly less frequent. At Wadi Halfa, Father Bouchard rejoined his fellow Canadians after having remained behind in Cairo to report to his bishop on his work in raising funds for the mission and to obtain permission to continue as chaplain to the contingent. The *voyageurs* were delighted to see Bouchard again. He was both a good priest and a good companion, and his command of Arabic was most useful.

Nous avions encore une journée de marche pour atteindre Wadi Halfa, lorsque nous sommes accostés par le steamer de la malle, sur lequel est M. l'abbé Bouchard, notre aumônier. Le bon père, qui nous avait laissés au Caire pour rendre compte de ses deux années d'absence à son évêque, nous apporte des nouvelles du pays. Il a en mains plusieurs lettres qu'il distribue à qui de droit. Le soir, il met pied à terre pour serrer la main à tous les canadiens, par qui il est adoré. Nos évêques ne pouvaient jamais nous mettre entre meilleures mains. A part son ministère, il a un chic épatant pour faire venir à lui non seulement les petits mais les hommes les plus rebelles. Vous pensez bien que parmi un composé de voyageurs, hommes de chantiers, draveurs, sauteurs de rapides comme celui-ci, il s'en trouve qui ne sont pas de la croix de Saint-Louis. J'en ai rencontré plusieurs qui, après une entrevue avec ce bon missionnaire, s'écriaient le coeur plein de joie: "Cà c'est un bon père!"

A part ce rôle, il remplit aussi celui d'interprète, car l'abbé Bouchard parle très bien la langue du pays qu'il a parcouru, comme apôtre de la Négritie, pendant plusiers années. Combien de fois n'a-t-il pas été de la plus grande utilité à nos officiers dans mille circonstances imprévues qui se recontrent et qui se recontreront souvent dans cette expédition, c'est au point qu'il est devenu indispensable et qu'il est considéré parmi nous comme un envoyé de la Providence.[8]

The speed of the expedition increased perceptibly following the arrival of the *voyageurs* at Wadi Halfa. Experienced hands took over from the amateur fumblings of the British troops and sharp eyes that knew what to look for in the rushing water were now guiding the expedition in its ascent of the rapids. One of the *voyageurs* wrote home with pride,

> Si vous aviez vu nos canadiens, vous en auriez été réellement orgueilleux; les officiers en charge en sont ébahis. ... A l'heure où je vous écris, toutes les chaloupes qui étaient rendues à Assouan sont montées, et je suis certain qu'il y en a plusieurs qui sont déjà rendues à Dongola. Le colonel Butler, qui se trouve commandant de notre campement, disait hier que c'était extraordinaire de voir la rapidité avec laquelle marche l'expédition depuis que les canadiens sont arrivés; et nous sommes d'autant plus surpris de ce compliment que nous trouvons que l'ouvrage ne nous a pas forcés. Il nous a seulement procuré un délassement.[9]

This was the reaction of an experienced and able boatman to the first section of Nile rapids that he encountered. The reaction of those who had falsely claimed to be *voyageurs* was quite different. Butler has left a memorable picture of one "shantyman" who felt only rage and frustration in an encounter with Nile rapids.

> The attitude of one huge tree-cutter from the backwoods I well remember in this Ambigole Cataract. He had got his boat fast aground at stem and stern. Recklessly and with unskilful strength he laboured at his pole, shouting to the men on the track-line to haul away, while he relieved his over-burdened feelings by repeatedly kicking the ribs of his boat with heavy hob-nailed boots. All his efforts were useless, he was trying to drag the keel with its three-ton load straight over a ledge of rock. It would seem as though he had exhausted the upper portion of his body in fruitless curses and imprecations upon cataracts in general and Ambigole in particular, which for the most part the roar of the Ambigole mercifully drowned; but that the lower man—and there was a good deal of that—had still sufficient vitality left to viciously kick at the unoffending boat timbers.[10]

Near Wadi Halfa Denison tested for the first time the small birchbark canoe that he had brought from Canada. He soon realized it was a much more satisfactory means of transport than the Egyptian ships-of-the-desert which he had tried to use along the river bank. Camels, Denison had found, were generally "brutes and gave me any amount of trouble." The canoe was to prove very useful on the quick trips of inspection and trouble-shooting which Denison was constantly undertaking.

Within ten days of their arrival at Wadi Halfa, the *voyageurs* had taken the boats over their first real hurdle by a combination of towing, rowing, and sailing. The second cataract had not proven very difficult. Now the Canadians were needed further up the river at the next stretch of rapids. They were divided into several groups, working and living for considerable periods with individual regiments or other units to which they were assigned. In these self-contained groups, the expedition moved slowly up the river as November passed.

The long day on the river began at first light. It ended at sunset when the few minutes of dusk—day changes quickly into night in North Africa—were often spent both by soldiers and by *voyageurs* repairing ragged clothes not designed to withstand the constant wear of boats and sand. Between dawn and dusk there was a long and weary day of work on the river, a day of rowing, poling, or pulling on a rope, a day of hazard on the swift-flowing river. In a lecture that he delivered several times after his return to Canada, Denison described a typical day as the *voyageurs* settled into the routine of their new tasks.

As a usual thing six men pulled. The voyageur took the rudder, some-times the bow. When the boat came to a strong current, the men would pull their best, and with a good way on would get up; but if they failed and were carried back, I have seen them make the attempt a second and third time, straining every nerve and then succeed. If it was impossible to row up, all the crew but the bowman and the man at the rudder would disembark, get out their tracking line, put it over their shoulders, and walk along the bank, tracking the boat, until they reached smooth water again. When they came to a bad rapid, instead of having one crew on the rope, 3, 4 or 5 crews, according to the rush of water, would be put on. This was avoided as much as possible, as it took five times as long. When it became necessary to place 30 or 40 men on the line, it was generally necessary also to unload the arms, and perhaps part of the load. In these cases a voyageur was put in the bow, another in the stern. Great care had to be exercised to see that there was not any slack rope, so that on the Nile you would hear the words from morning until night, "Pull up the slack," "Haul away." When the men were on the line and all was ready the word would be given, "shove off." If there was too much slack rope, the current would catch the boat, running her out into the stream broadside on, and sometimes filling the boat. She would turn over, throwing the voyageurs into the water, unless they were smart enough to climb over one side as she went under at the other, and then cling to the bottom, until taken off.[11]

After a day on the river, few of the Canadians looked for any diversion beyond that afforded by a pipe of tobacco (occasionally rum and lime juice were also issued). One or two found amusement in attempting to ride camels. On the last day of October, several of the Canadians celebrated a North American festival, despite their weariness and the fact that they were in the midst of the Egyptian desert. "Hallowe'en Night was observed...as best we could. As there were no cabbages to steal, the boys capsized a few tents and stole and concealed several blankets."[12]

The soldiers and the *voyageurs* were working hard, fully aware that Gordon's life and the safety of the Egyptian garrison at Khartoum depended entirely on their progress. On 16 November a messenger managed to pass through the Mahdist lines with a brief note from Gordon dated 4 November stating that Khartoum could hold out "for forty days with ease: after that it will be difficult." Forty days was not long. Twelve of the forty days had already passed by the time the cryptic note reached Wolseley. The expedition still had many hundreds of miles of increasingly difficult river to ascend. Wolseley's force, large and powerfully armed so that it could face almost any number of the Mahdi's warriors, must, if Gordon's estimate were accurate, reach its distant destination not later than the middle of December. It was clearly going to be a very close thing at best. The British soldiers were themselves gradually becoming experienced boatmen, but the current of the great river was strong and the terrain increasingly difficult. Progress could not be swift. The only time when the current could be of any help to the *voyageurs* was on those rare occasions when they wanted to go down the river instead of up it. On one such occasion, during the latter half of November, Denison and a number of his men covered the one hundred miles between Dal and Wadi Halfa in thirty-six hours, a journey which had taken them fifteen days when going against the current. They had safely transported the South Staffordshire Regiment up the river; now it was the turn of the Black Watch. Denison himself and some of his best *voyageurs* were working almost incessantly, helping the troops over the most difficult stretches of the river, but despite their efforts and Wolseley's worried exhortations, the progress of the expedition was not encouraging. The drama of its ascent of the Nile was being followed with intense interest throughout the Empire, but no amount of anxiety felt in London or Toronto could help the soldiers over the formidable natural obstacles that lay across their path to Khartoum. Increasingly serious delays began to occur. Down the Nile nearer to Cairo the flow of men and supplies had faltered temporarily because of the lack of coal for the steamers. Buller, the chief of staff, had badly underestimated how much coal Messrs. Thomas Cook should have been contracted to provide. This was later to be recognized as a major error. For the first time, the hitherto steady stream of soldiers, food, and equipment flowing up the river faltered. From 25 October to 10 November, the passage of troops and supplies between Assuan and Wadi Halfa stopped completely.

Through the rapids between Wadi Halfa and Dal, however, the rate of progress was not dependent on coal but rather upon the determination of the British soldiers and their Canadian guides. Day after day under the burning sun they worked their way up the Nile but

Sometimes when the wind failed altogether, or was so adverse as to render towing absolutely unpracticable, the halt was necessarily called quite early in the afternoon. Then was Thomas Atkins in his element. He bathed in some shallow part of the stream, took his tea comfortably and at his ease reclining on the bank, and then, attired in his favourite off-duty undress, lounged about the bank enjoying the inevitable pipe and the jokes and conversation of his friends. Comfort in the costume to the British soldier is represented as follows. His jacket and shirt are replaced by his great coat, the cuffs of which are turned back. His trousers, unbraced, are rolled up to his knees. His boots are unlaced, his pipe, of course, upside down, and his helmet is put on wrongside before. Has he been able to obtain some particularly uncouth head-dress—such as an old and mangy rabbit or rat skin cap, a battered tarboosch [sic], or broken-down and brimless felt hat—he dons it with pride and satisfaction, provided always it be thoroughly disreputable—for otherwise where would be the merit—but failing this he is content with the helmet worn as I have described. In this attire, and with a convenient post or tree to lean against, or with a rail or a bank to sit on, he enjoys the assertion in his dress of his momentary freedom from restraint, and feels that he has for the time being retired into private life where care cannot reach him till the next bugle call.[13]

The opportunities for even such quiet enjoyment as this were few. Often a short walk after a simple dinner of bully beef and dates was the only recreation before a deep sleep in the cool desert air. On one such walk a *voyageur* from Montreal wandered one evening a little way inland from his camp on the river bank. At a small oasis he chanced upon, he saw a bedouin sitting on the ground. As he drew nearer, the *voyageur*, to his astonishment, heard the words of a song adopted by French Canadians exiled following the Rebellion of 1837:

> Un canadien errant,
> Banni de ses foyers,
> Parcourait en pleurant,
> Les pays étrangers. . . .

The "Arab" sitting near the well proved to be a former French-Canadian sailor who had, years before, deserted his ship in Alexandria. For the sheer love of adventure, he had joined a caravan setting out across the desert towards the Red Sea. Bedouin robbers had attacked the caravan, captured him, and kept him in their tribe. The sailor from Quebec eventually became so enamoured of the bedouin life that he adopted it by choice and thereafter never attempted to escape.

By day, the expedition continued to move slowly up the river. As November passed, the urgency to press forward became as relentless as the hot sun overhead. The worried and harassed commander-in-chief began to cast about for new ways to hasten his mission of rescue. Someone would have to be sent to the two miles of thundering cataract at Dal with full powers to do all that he could to accelerate the passage of the expedition through the channel chosen by Colonel Butler on the advice of several *voyageurs*. Lord Charles Beresford was still fully occupied with hurrying the remaining boats —each with almost four tons of cargo—over the second cataract, so Wolseley sent Colonel Burnaby. Burnaby was an excellent choice. In addition to his knowledge of the Sudan gained from his 1875 visit to Gordon and his recent unofficial service against the dervishes on the Red Sea coast, Burnaby also knew something of the land and the attitudes that were native to the *voyageurs*. During the summer of 1883, the restless colonel had visited Montreal and Quebec and had seen the "shantymen" at work on their own rivers. But even Burnaby's wide experience, his resource, and his great energy proved to be of only limited avail in getting the expedition over the obstacles at Dal. As he wrote to his wife,

> Each boat weighs eleven hundredweight, and her stores three and a half tons, so this will give you an idea of the labour. I passed eleven boats through the cataract the first day, seventeen the next, thirty-four yesterday, and hope to do forty more today. Our work is to spur on all officers and men, and see that they work to their uttermost. This I think they do, and it will be very difficult for me to get more out of

them. It does not do to overspur a willing horse.... A strong north wind is blowing today which helps us much with the boats. I do hope it will continue, as some four hundred and fifty more have to pass through the cataract very shortly.[14]

For the volunteers among the soldiers, the passage through the rapids was a harrowing one. Sergeant Gordon of the Black Watch volunteered to make three trips in emptied whalers (the supplies being portaged by camels).

Nothing less than the level-headedness and surpassing skill of the voyageurs could have guided us. Many were the hairbreadth escapes from death; for once cast overboard would have meant doom sealed; not only a watery grave but even if we could float, a zigzag journey thereto with bangs and slams against rocks, a course over which one would have no more control than an insect.[15]

The officers, the soldiers, and the *voyageurs* were all willingly working to their utmost, but Gordon's deadline of 15 December arrived and passed and the whalers were still many miles north of Khartoum, moving in a seemingly endless line up the river past Dal. Now, with time clearly running out, all possible innovations were introduced to quicken and further the progress of the expedition. Improvisation had from the beginning been characteristic of Wolseley's hastily organized force. It was never more so than during the last weeks of December 1884. Much to the subsequent annoyance of Queen Victoria, who believed that her soldiers would always exert themselves to the utmost from a sense of duty and not for money, Wolseley offered a prize of £100 to the regiment that made the best time between Wadi Halfa and Korti, the site selected for the advance base. The Royal Irish Rifles won the prize by covering the distance in thirty-seven days. Another innovation was more simple: at Butler's insistence, the boats were lightened of five hundred pounds of supplies and their progress was thereby accelerated. A third important change was that the *voyageurs* were divided into small independent groups and stationed permanently at the worst rapids. Hitherto they had accompanied specific units over long stretches of the Nile. Now they remained at fixed points where they learned to know intimately the peculiarities of a particular stretch of the river. The new arrangement proved most successful. In the words of the official historian of the expedition,

It greatly economized the skilled labour of the Canadians by using them only where they were specifically wanted, with the result that at bad places, it was always possible to put two, and frequently more, voyageurs in each boat. It saved the delay which had previously occurred ... when the voyageurs were coming [back down the river] their labour was lost to the expedition. The second system was greatly preferred by the men themselves, as they were far more comfortable in fixed camps and with regular hours of work, than when perpetually on the move and never sleeping two nights in the same place. ... most important, was the result that the voyageurs knew the cataracts much better, and their knowledge kept pace with the changes in the water produced by the fall of the Nile. These changes were so rapid and considerable, that the whole aspect of a cataract would alter in a week. Under the trip system, a voyageur's previous experience was of no use to him when he got back to the same place on the river. In the intervening fortnight or three weeks, the water and the channels had completely changed. Under the fixed station system, his knowledge of a cataract increased every day.[16]

Despite the acceleration resulting from these several innovations, Christmas Day found one of the leading infantry regiments, the Gordon Highlanders, no farther south than the rapids of Dal. The expedition was proving distressingly slow, and Wolseley now gave up any hope of being in Khartoum by 1 February. There was, nevertheless, a short respite to celebrate Christmas. Fred Burnaby and Lord Charles Beresford helped to demolish a plum pudding which James Alleyne had brought with him all the way from England and had carried in his personal supplies for more than three months. Denison, however, fared more simply further up the river; his journal for 25 December 1884 recorded, "My Christmas dinner was stewed bully beef and biscuit, some lime juice and dates for dessert." The *voyageurs*, always hungry, celebrated Christmas in the best fashion they could wherever they found themselves. One of the oldest among them, Foreman Alexis de Coteau, aged sixty-four, spent Christmas Day with Colonel Butler, who was delighted to have the old *voyageur* from Trois Rivières with him once again.

That at that time of life [de Coteau] should have been ready to leave his little frame house on the St. Lawrence and come all this long way to fight the battle of this expedition with the cataracts of the tropic Nile, was a striking instance of the pluck and hardy spirit of his race. ... I gave this old veteran of a thousand cataracts an extra issue of grog, and began to question him about his old life. For forty years he had set out from Montreal in the spring, said his prayers in the little church of St. Anne, where the great Ottawa River falls into the still mightier St. Lawrence, and then held his way for months into the wilderness, through pine-forest, over rapid, up rivers and down rivers, across lakes, over a hundred portages, until at last the broad waters of Lake Winnipeg opened before the laden canoes.

"Ah! those were the good days, monsieur, and those were fine rivers —not like this river—this Nile."

"Why, Coteau, what is there in this river that is different from others?"

"Different, monsieur,—everything is different. Here you can see no rock until you strike it; then you put your pole down on one side, and, lo! there is no bottom at ten feet. Ah! it is a bad, bad river!"[17]

New Year's Eve was marked by the sober Denison falling into the Nile for a second time, on this occasion near Hannek. His boat had already capsized once. Overturned boats were becoming a common occurrence. Denison was luckier than the five of his *voyageurs* who had already drowned. Two Iroquois from Caughnawaga, Louis Capitaine and John Morris, had been the first fatalities. They were soon followed by George Fletcher of Winnipeg, John Faulkener of Peterborough, and William Doyle of Ottawa. Before the end of December, two other *voyageurs* from Ottawa had also died: Michael Brennan of dysentery and Simon Bigeault of smallpox. Early in the new year, 1885, A. M. Armstrong of Winnipeg succumbed to typhoid fever. The deaths among the *voyageurs* reflected the toll of the expedition as a whole. It began to mount rapidly through disease and drowning. There would have been even more deaths from drowning if the large wooden biscuit boxes—which did not keep the biscuit very well—had not served as admirable life-buoys.

Denison had, however, more to think about as the new year began than his ducking or even the rapid rate at which the fatality list of the expedition was growing. The *voyageurs* had been engaged for six months from 9 September 1884. Hence, according to their contracts, they had to be back in Canada not later than 9 March 1885. Many had made clear from the beginning that they wanted to resume their logging work when spring returned to the Canadian woods. The inducements to stay in the Sudan were, nevertheless, made yet more attractive. An additional twenty dollars per month for a total wage of sixty dollars was a strong temptation to men accustomed to earning less than one-half that in logging. As a further inducement, the men were offered a second issue of work clothes and a return journey to Canada via London instead of direct from Alexandria. But during January, only eighty-nine of the then surviving 377 boatmen volunteered to stay on for a maximum of another six months. Some, as already noted, wanted to resume their logging. Others were simply afraid of the reputation of the hot Sudanese summer. Yet others, Denison himself no longer wanted. In particular, he refused to offer re-engagement to those among the Winnipeg gangs who were not genuine rivermen.

In early January, however, there were several more weeks of work before any Canadian, however eager to return home, could leave the sweltering gorges and dangerous rapids of the Nile. The river route was taking longer than had been expected. But Wolseley had chosen the route and now he could do nothing more than to continue to push the main body of his troops forward as rapidly as possible. At his advanced headquarters at Korti, Wolseley received one further message from his old friend Charlie Gordon. An Arab had managed to slip through the Mahdist forces just ahead of the expedition.

That this last message from Gordon reached Wolseley at all was largely a result of the clandestine efforts of Major Herbert Kitchener. After having distinguished himself in the bombardment of Alexandria, Kitchener had been appointed to the Egyptian army in February 1883, upon its re-organization following the defeat of Arabi. In May 1884, he had been ordered to attempt to open secret lines of communication between the Egyptian-Sudanese border and Khartoum.[18] For the next several months, at considerable risk, Kitchener had travelled in Arab dress through the no-man's land separating the Anglo-Egyptian and Mahdist forces. Carrying a vial of poison with him as a last resort against capture, he succeeded in gathering valuable information about the disposition of the Mahdi's forces and in exchanging a few messages with Gordon. One part of the final communication from Gordon to reach Wolseley was written on a minute piece of paper, no bigger than a postage stamp, which had been sewn into the clothing of the messenger. It contained the following cryptic message: "Khartoum all right. 14.12.84. C. G. Gordon." Such information could be of no value to the Mahdi if it fell into his hands. A longer message was concealed in the strands of the harness of the Arab's camel. This longer message was not encouraging. Khartoum was clearly in its last extremity.

We are besieged on three sides. Fighting goes on day and night. Enemy cannot take us except by starving us out. Do not scatter your troops. Enemy are numerous. Bring plenty of troops if you can. Our troops in Khartoum are suffering from lack of provisions. Food we still have is little—some grain and biscuit. We want you to come quickly. You should come by Metemma or Berber. Make by these two roads. Do not leave Berber in your rear; keep enemy in front, and when you have taken Berber, send me word from Berber.[19]

Obviously something had to be done in the greatest haste if Gordon was yet to be saved. His message was already sixteen days old when it was finally received by Wolseley, who then made a decision which he was subsequently criticized for not having made earlier.

Part of Wolseley's large force consisted of a Camel Corps composed of eleven hundred of his "finest men" from the smart cavalry regiments, from senior infantry regiments (mainly the Guards), and from the Royal Navy and Royal Marines. This unorthodox force of "camelry"—organized despite the strenuous objections of the Duke of Cambridge—had made its way southward along the banks of the Nile, replenishing its supplies from depots which had been established on the river bank by the steamers and whalers. A small naval detachment under the command of Lord Beresford accompanied this desert force, ready to man two of Gordon's four armoured steamers known to be waiting further up the Nile near Metemmeh.[20] As Wolseley had studied his maps of the Nile between Korti and Khartoum, he had conceived the bold idea of sending, if the need arose, approximately twenty-four hundred soldiers and sailors (including his élite Camel Corps) as a flying column across the one hundred and seventy-five miles of desert to Metemmeh. The Nile between Wadi Halfa and Khartoum forms something like a giant S. It was across the lower of these two curves that the Camel Corps was to march, thus avoiding the longer journey around the great bend in the river. Meanwhile, the remaining troops would continue their much longer journey by boat up four hundred miles of winding and turbulent river to the same destination. There they would be able to replenish, in a modest way, the supplies of the desert force. On 2 January 1885, Wolseley informed Baring of the reasons for his decision to divide his force in two:

> Gordon's message...compels measures that will postpone my arrival at Khartoum.... He warns me not to leave Berber in my rear, so I must move by water and take it before I march upon Khartoum. Meanwhile, I shall have established post at Metemma, by men and stores sent across the desert. I shall be able to communicate with Gordon by steam, learn exact position, and, if he is *in extremis* before infantry arrive by river, to push forward by camel corps to help him at all hazards.[21]

The decision to split his force rendered Wolseley's need for a large number of *voyageurs* less pressing. Much of their work had now been completed. Some of the most difficult rapids had been overcome. An advance headquarters, complete with pay and other administrative offices and a base hospital, had now been established at Korti. From there the final advance on Khartoum could be directed and supplied. Furthermore, the infantry-men on the river would no longer be required to carry with them so much heavy equipment. The desire of most of the *voyageurs* to return to Canada coincided with the beginning of that phase when they were no longer needed to the degree they had been when the expedition, still new to the river, was passing through the major cataracts. Arrangements were made, in accordance with their contracts, for all those who had not volunteered for re-engagement to leave for Cairo in late January, under the command of Captains Telmont Aumond and Egerton Denison. Father Bouchard accompanied the boatmen as far as Cairo. On their way down the Nile—a trip quickly made in com-parison with their laborious ascent—the Canadians stopped at Wadi Halfa long enough to participate in a garrison sports day during which, Egerton Denison observed happily, "Our fellows took everything worth taking."[22] The rapid return journey to Cairo was marred only by an unexpected acci-dent. Two of the Canadians, Leon Pilon and William O'Rourke, both of Ottawa, were killed beneath the wheels of their train when they fell off it between Assiout and Cairo.

At Cairo itself the *voyageurs* enjoyed themselves greatly. Despite the multitude of problems which constantly beset him, Wolseley had not for-gotten the Canadians whom he had brought half-way around the world to help him. Under the supervision of a British officer, Major E. T. H. Hutton (a member of "Wolseley's gang" who, later, as a major-general, commanded the Canadian militia),[23] they were taken for a carriage tour of Cairo. At the base of the pyramids, they were reviewed by the commander of the British garrison in Lower Egypt, General Stephenson. Accompanied by fifty English ladies from Cairo, the general inspected the *voyageurs* in what must have been one of the oddest military reviews in history. With the pyramids as a backdrop, the Canadians, some of Indian, some of English, and some of French descent, some in white pith-helmets, others in floppy felt hats, and all in their rough grey work clothes presented an intriguing spectacle to the fashionable ladies of Cairo as the fashionable ladies did to the *voyageurs*. After the review by the pyramids, there was little time left to sample the flesh-pots of Cairo, many and famous though they were. However, some of his companions, Sergeant Labat was pleased to see, had worked remarkably quickly in the brief time remaining before their train left for Alexandria.

Le moment du départ approchant, j'aperçois quelques-uns de nos Voyageurs qui se rendent à la station. Ils s'y rendent en compagnie de quelques tendres Egyptiennes dont ils ont su toucher le coeur. Galanterie française!
Ces dames les accompagnent en fumant des cigarettes. J'en aperçois

une qui fume le cigare. Horreur! à quand la chique? La machine chauffe; elle nous attend; les curieux aussi. Une vieille dame, la femme d'un ministre protestant très probablement, à en juger par le costume, gesticule, s'extasie, salue de son mouchoir au passage des Voyageurs.

"*Hurrah boys!*" s'écrie la bonne dame. Tout le monde la regardait, et malgré les exhortations de son mari qui lui disait, "Don't excite [yourself] Kate!" Elle s'enflammait, s'enthousiasmait et nous sommes partis aux cris de la vieille qui criait: "Hurrah! for the Canadian boys!"[24]

A final review by a general, a tour of the pyramids, cigar-smoking Egyptian women, and a farewell cheer from a protestant missionary's wife: it had been a busy day for the *voyageurs*. After they had each been presented with a pipe and two plugs of tobacco, "all the men spoke highly of the way they were treated in Cairo."[25]

Sergeant Labat did not give all his time in Cairo to enjoying the tours that Major Hutton had arranged. He later recalled, while talking of the deaths among the *voyageurs*, that he had attempted to visit the grave of Lieutenant Hébert who had died in Cairo over two years before:

Puisque je parle de morts, laissez-moi vous dire en terminant que je viens de voir le chapelain, et le chirurgien qui ont assisté le regrette Major Hébert, de la Batterie B. Ils m'en ont fait un éloge cordial et conservent un souvenir si touchant que c'est un honneur pour le Canada. C'est pour cela que je suis heureux de vous le dire en attendant que je puisse accomplir sur sa tombe le pélerinage que mon coeur s'est promis....

J'ajoute ici un alinéa pour faire savoir au lecteur que n'ayant pu, moi-même accomplir ce désir de mon coeur à mon retour au Caire, c'est Monseigneur l'Evêque du Caire, accompagné du R. P. Bouchard, qui ont accompli cette sainte mission, en déposant sur la tombe d'Hébert une couronne d'immortelles "*au nom des frères d'armes canadiens de cet excellent garçon.*"[26]

The *voyageurs* had been delighted by the way the British authorities in Cairo had welcomed them. They were much less pleased with their accommodation and meagre fare aboard the British troopship *Poonah*, which carried them from Alexandria to Queenston, Ireland, via Malta. They found the troopship's fare so bad that they elected one of their own number to act as chef to supervise the cooking of their food in the *Poonah*'s galley. After arriving at Queenston on 18 February, seven *voyageurs* chose to remain in Ireland. The remaining 260, burdened with spears, shields, cockatoos, and even monkeys, sailed on the S. S. *Hanoverian* on 20 February. One of the seven who left the contingent in Ireland was Captain Egerton Denison, who crossed the Irish Channel to undertake militia training at Lichfield. Captain Telmont Aumond, returning to his duties in Ottawa with the Department of Marine and Fisheries, was the only remaining officer to accompany the *voyageurs* on what must have been a most difficult trans-Atlantic crossing. The winter weather presented problems, but they were in no way comparable to those resulting from the fact that the Canadians were "drunk all the time from Queenston to Halifax."[27] They certainly were still in a happy mood when they landed in Halifax at two o'clock on the morning of 4 March. "When the boatmen had got all their goods and chattels from the vessel and dumped them indiscriminately on the floor, in costumes that rival a modern drama in variety, with white helmets, coarse and dirty clothing, Turkish, Sudanese, and Egyptian turbans of every possible color and shape, blue, white, and green blouse, deep dyed, sun-burnt cheeks and shaggy hair, and unshaven faces their appearance was nothing, if not unique. To talk with real Canadians was so profound a pleasure that they gathered here and there in little knots, the sturdy *voyageurs* laughingly related their experiences in the land of the Pharaohs to eager throngs."[28] It would be pleasant to think that the Ottawa members had been sober enough to listen to a speech of welcome by Melgund (who had never lost his interest in their welfare) at a dinner given in their honour on 6 March, the evening before they dispersed to their homes and lumber camps. The dinner in the Ottawa armouries was only one mark of welcome which an enthusiastic Ottawa bestowed on its returning boatmen. The streets had been lined with cheering spectators as the *voyageurs* marched from the Canadian Pacific Railway station to the drill hall. An enterprising local photographer offered a graphic memento of exploits of heroes. He had prepared large portraits of Wolseley and Gordon and imaginative composite photographs of them with some of the *voyageurs*.

It comprises a pictorial illustration of the celebrated Contingent, who so nobly left home and friends, on the 18th of September, 1884, to lend their valuable aid to Her Most Gracious Majesty, in subduing the rebellion in the Sudan. The Contingent have accomplished a most essential work in the difficult and perilous task of ascending the raging cataracts of the Nile. Several valuable lives were lost in the undertaking but their loss was their country's gain, inasmuch as a work was accomplished to which their aid was vitally necessary. To memorialize such an achievement, as heroic and self-sacrificing, as it was romantic, is well calculated to inspire patriotic emotions, and the chivalric enterprise itself will, in the ages to come, form an attractive page in the annals of a great nation.

In surveying the picture, the eye is first attracted to the three groups of *voyageurs*. In the centre are the two renowned heroes of the expedition, the lamented Gordon and General Wolseley. In the line immediately below these are the portraits of the three organizers of the Contingent, Lord Melgund in the centre, Captain Costin on his left and J. T. Lambert on his right. In the same line are two representations of the Lachine Rapids, serving to exemplify what our hardy boatmen are accustomed to do at home while in the line immediately below are presented illustrations of their work on the Nile, together with pictures of the three officers of the corps, Col. Denison, Captain Aumond and Captain McRae. In the upper line, to the left hand corner, is the portrait of Col. Kennedy, who represents Manitoba, and in the other corner that of Dr. Neilson. In the same line are represented two groups of steamboat captains, who formed part of the expedition, those to the left being from the Ottawa, and to the right from Manitoba. The representations constitute a tout ensemble gotten up in first-class style, well worthy of being kept as a souvenir of the Contingent, some of whom will soon be receiving the greetings of their friends in Ottawa.

The *voyageurs* had participated in a uniquely Victorian expedition. They returned to be greeted by the uniquely Victorian prose of an editorial in the Ottawa *Free Press* of 7 March. The *voyageurs* themselves tended to talk in exaggerated terms about their own feats both in the woods of Canada and on the famous river of Egypt. They were, therefore, probably pleased to be welcomed home in similarly inflated terms: "Hurrah stout hearts, well and bravely have you done your duty, though at times it has been hard and perilous, cheerfully and fearlessly have you faced the danger, and overcome it! Welcome home, an honour to your cherished country which proudly salutes you and totally delights to honour you." The prose may be florid, but it was accurate. The Canadian boatmen had shown in a unique fashion that Canada was indeed becoming a nation. They had participated with honour as a Canadian contingent in the scramble to save Gordon, on the outcome of which the whole world had set its eyes. And still in the Sudan were dozens of their comrades who had re-enlisted, various other Canadians who had found their way by one means or another into the expedition, and the "Canadians" of Wolseley's "Ring," all ensuring that the young nation of Canada would share in the dramatic dénouement of the adventure.

8

The Journey's End

The sand in the desert is sodden red,
Red with the wreck of the square that broke;
The Gatling's jammed and the Colonel dead,
And the regiment blind with dust and smoke.

SIR HENRY NEWBOLT
VITAI LAMPADA

Wolseley's decision to split his force into a Desert Column and a River Column was sensible, if somewhat tardy in the circumstances. But unfortunately for Wolseley's best laid plans, there were insufficient camels to carry out the daring desert march as he had originally conceived it. Administrative confusion and faulty staff work had resulted in not enough of the beasts or even of saddles being purchased to carry all the men and their supplies from Korti to Metemmeh in one stage. The need for camels had from the beginning been underestimated and their availability overestimated. Moreover, the general ignorance about how to handle camels resulted in many of the limited number available becoming sore or lame. This shortage of camels, as the shortage of coal had done before, caused a major delay and further hardship for the troops. All the camels that could be pressed into service were gathered at Korti to be sent with half the Desert Column to the oasis of Jakdul, the half-way point on the way to Metemmeh, the Column's immediate destination on the Nile. When eleven hundred soldiers and two hundred natives were establishing a supply base at Jakdul, the camels were driven the ninety miles back to Korti to bring the other half of Brigadier-General Sir Herbert Stewart's flying column across the desert.[1] Kitchener, who had for some time had been living among Arabs near Jakdul, helped command the supply dump while Stewart returned to Korti to bring up the remainder of his force. Stewart brought with him on his second trip Colonel Sir Charles Wilson, chief of staff to General Stephenson, a survey officer and a Middle Eastern expert, who was to take thirty red-coated soldiers on two of Gordon's steamers up to Khartoum for the purpose of reviewing the situation with Gordon.[2] Wolseley would await his report before making any final dispositions for the general advance on Khartoum. The sight of the red-coated soldiers who were to accompany Wilson would, some fondly hoped, convince the Mahdi that in fact the arrival of the famous British army, of which so much had been rumoured, was imminent. This news alone might induce him to raise the siege of Khartoum.

It was not until two o'clock on the afternoon of 14 January that Stewart was ready to lead his now complete force from Jakdul across the ninety miles of the second stage of its journey to Metemmeh. It had taken twelve days to implement the urgent plan which Wolseley had hoped might be carried out in six. What had been intended as a dash across the desert had become a ponderous procession. Moreover, Kitchener's agents had already reported that a large number of the dervishes were to be withdrawn from the siege of Khartoum to oppose the British advance near Metemmeh. This would be the first time that the expedition had come into conflict with the Mahdi's followers. No one could be confident of the result.

"I don't like unnecessary slaughter," Brigadier-General Stewart had said before leaving Korti, "but I'm afraid that we shall have to kill five hundred or so of the poor devils before we can establish ourselves in Metemmeh."[3] The young brigadier-general underestimated the numbers his soldiers would have to kill before they could reach the Nile safely. Near the wells of Abu Klea on 17 January, twenty miles from Metemmeh, the first real battle of the expedition was fought. About fourteen thousand dervishes suddenly arose from the desert scrub or appeared from nearby wadis and attacked Stewart's column, formed into a square to receive their fanatical attack. Although many of the reckless Mahdists were armed with rifles taken from Hicks's army the year before, some barefoot warriors were armed only with long spears or, particularly young boys, with no more than sticks. It was in circumstances such as these that the courage of the Mahdists never failed to evoke the admiration of British soldiers. Redvers Buller later wrote, "I never saw finer fellows than these Arabs; they came on, spear and sword in hand, right on to our guns."[4] Largely because advance British scouts and pickets were still seeking the safety of the square, it was not fully formed when it received the brunt of the dervishes' wild charge. Their incredible courage in pressing home their attack resulted in a great mass of dervishes breaking, for a few confused and dangerous moments, through the left rear corner of the British square. For enemy infantry to break a British square was a rare feat. It was the nearest a British force in the Sudan came to annihilation. As Winston Churchill has noted, the Battle of Abu Klea was "the most savage and bloody action ever fought in the Soudan by British troops."[5] At least two of the officers died from the excited firing of their men during the first confused minutes of the attack. Other soldiers were killed when their rifles jammed or the steel of their bayonets proved to be below the required temper and bent on impact. In the dust, smoke, and noise, with brown and white bodies tumbling over each other in a frantic melee, the confusion was great. But the overall superiority of the weapons and discipline of the British in the end secured them the victory. The famous square had once again proved effective against troops without artillery and machine guns. Fanatical courage could not match cold discipline and superior arms. Soon eleven hundred dervishes lay dead outside the square as the remainder withdrew into the nearby hills. Inside the square were the corpses of seventy-four British, among them the tall, heavy figure of the redoubtable Colonel Fred Burnaby. "A spear had inflicted a terrible wound on the right side of his neck and throat, and his skull had been cleft by a blow from a two-handed sword," but he had fought to his last breath with "the wild strokes of a proud man dying hard."[6]

Although Stewart had clearly won the Battle of Abu Klea, the way to the Nile was still contested. The Mahdists regrouped themselves in the nearby hills, and on 19 January, a second but smaller battle was fought in the riparian scrub near Abu Kru. It was a short, vicious struggle. As it began, Stewart himself received a wound that was eventually to prove fatal. Near him fell dead a Canadian, St. Leger Herbert, a thirty-four-year-old Oxford graduate whom the London *Morning Post* had engaged as a correspondent to cover the expedition and whom Stewart also employed as his secretary. Herbert, a sort of gentleman soldier of fortune, was not one to hang back in battle. After killing several dervishes, he suddenly dropped with a bullet through his head. "Poor St. Leger Herbert," Wolseley recorded in his journal, "A braver soul never lived."[7]

The son of a retired Royal Navy commander, St. Leger Herbert had been sent to England from his home in Kingston, Ontario (where he was born in 1850), to prepare himself to follow in his father's nautical footsteps. However, his quick intelligence and a perceptive if somewhat facile style of writing carried him to Oxford where he graduated in 1874. The following year, Herbert returned to the new Dominion of Canada where he spent the next three years serving as a secretary to Lord Dufferin, the governor general, and as a jack-of-all-trades in the embryonic Canadian public service. Upon leaving Canada, Dufferin recommended Herbert to Wolseley, who employed him as his secretary while high commissioner in Cyprus. (It was there that Herbert and Kitchener first met, the latter being engaged in carrying out a topographical survey.) Wolseley retained Herbert as his secretary at his next post as high commissioner in Natal and the Transvaal. There Herbert continued to act as correspondent for the *Times*, a practice that he had begun in Cyprus. He was, however, more than an amanuensis and a newspaper correspondent. He was also an amateur soldier. Working for "England's only general," he saw action against the Zulus, was decorated for his services in South Africa, and served in the Mounted Infantry at Tel-el-Kebir. This combination of journalistic skill, military courage and experience, and close friendship with Wolseley and his "Ring" had been reason enough for the *Morning Post* to employ Herbert as their correspondent with the Gordon relief expedition. For the most part Wolseley despised war correspondents as vulgar scribblers. But Herbert "was a gentleman, as brave as a lion, and admitted to the intimacy of the best in the Army, not because he was a buffoon and professional jester ... but because he was socially their equal."[8]

After Herbert and the other dead of the two fierce battles had been buried, the officers of the Desert Column began to realize that they were in a situation which had not been anticipated. With Burnaby killed in one battle and Stewart mortally wounded in the other (he did not die until 14 February), the command of the battered Desert Column devolved on Colonel Sir Charles Wilson, who had served mainly in intelligence and survey appointments. He was accompanying the column for the purpose of conferring with Gordon about the situation at Khartoum and the best means of extracting the garrison since it was clear that Gordon would not leave without his Egyptian troops and Sudanese followers. Wolseley had never foreseen Wilson filling any other role: if Stewart were killed, he had envisaged that Burnaby would succeed to the command. Now Wilson was left to lead, for the first time, troops into combat.

Wilson's initial acts were decisive enough. He ordered the Desert Column toward the Nile on 21 January, two days after it had fought its second battle. It had been badly weakened by its forced marches, the inadequacy of its supplies and its two battles, but a tremendous fillip was given to its morale by the sight of Gordon's small, rat-infested steamers awaiting it on the Nile. At last it seemed that a final dash could be made to rescue Gordon.

The natural concomitant of the Desert Column, which had now reached the Nile, was the River Column. Shortly after Wolseley had first ordered the despatch of the Desert Column overland to Metemmeh, he had ordered the River Column of approximately three thousand men to continue the advance up the Nile. Berber was its immediate target. After having taken Berber, the River Column was to "use every endeavour to forward as many soldiers as possible to the [Desert Column] which will have proceeded by land to Khartoum."[9] While reaching his decision to split his force, Wolseley had kept in mind Gordon's injunction not to leave that conglomeration of low mud huts known as Berber in Mahdist hands. The long-term safety of the Desert Column could only be assured if its rear and the river supply route were secured by the River Column's occupation of Berber. In turn, the safety of the River Column would depend largely upon the skill of the Canadian boatmen who were to guide it through the worst stretch of rapids that had yet been encountered.

On 21 January, the day the Desert Column finally completed its long march to the Nile at Metemmeh, Frederick Denison arrived at Korti. From there he was ordered to proceed immediately another thirty miles further south to join the River Column led by Major-General William Earle[10] and Colonels Butler and Alleyne. In addition to Denison, sixty-seven of the eighty-nine *voyageurs* who had volunteered for further service in the Sudan were also ordered to assist the River Column in its advance on Berber. Surgeon Major Neilson was serving in the tent hospital at Dal, while Captain MacRae, until he fell sick with sunstroke, commanded those few *voyageurs* still helping to bring supplies up the river to Korti. When Denison joined the River Column, it was entering a challenging stretch of the Nile. Rapids in deep gorges made navigation exceptionally difficult. Moreover, as the official history of the campaign later noted, the terrain was particularly advantageous to the dervishes. "Instead of rolling plains, so favourable to long-range fire, and so fatal to an enemy whose strength lies in the impetuous charge of his spearmen are here found cramped and tortuous passages, down which a company could scarcely march in line. The rocky ground is almost impassable for cavalry. On every side extended rugged ridges, behind any one of which thousands of Arabs might be concealed, ready to spring out on a column, with a minimum of exposure to themselves in the open."[11]

However, the immediate problem as the column began its arduous journey around the great bend of the Nile to Berber was not the enemy but the river itself. The stretch from Hamdab to Abu Hamed was the most turbulent that the *voyageurs* had yet worked. Progress was painfully slow as they and the British soldiers hauled and poled their boats through the treacherous rapids. There was little time for rest, and, in any case, there was no safety on the banks of the river—crocodiles alone prevented any respite there. Anyone injured in the rapids or wounded in action had to be carried with the column in the lice-infested, crowded boats. It was in this way that one of the Indian *voyageurs*, as the result of an accident, made part of the journey under the care of a fellow Canadian, Surgeon Henry Anthony de Lom, who was attached to the Gordon Highlanders.[12] Although born in England, de Lom had been brought to Canada as a young boy. He had received his schooling in Ontario and was one of the first graduates of the University of Toronto medical school. After further studies at St. Thomas Hospital in London, he joined the British army in August 1883. Eighteen months later he found himself treating fellow Canadians on the Nile.

The River Column was not only self-contained from a medical point of view; it also had to be self-reliant for its food and other supplies. As it laboriously made its way toward the Mahdist troops reported to be blocking the way to Berber, the column began to consume stores which had been carried with such difficulty in whalers all the way from Wadi Halfa. But when Denison opened the first case of supplies in his boat, he found that it no longer contained what it once had. "I opened the box of jam and found only eighteen tins out of thirty-four—or sixteen have been stolen." At the risk of imprisonment, or, worse still, of endangering the lives of their fellows, some British as well as Egyptian troops had been pilfering stores from the beginning of the expedition.

Complaints about faulty packing, spoilage, and theft of stores were, however soon replaced as the leading topic of conversation by rumours about the approach of the Mahdists. By 30 January, the dervishes were just ahead. "The Mounted Infantry made a reconnaissance today," Denison noted in his journal that evening,

> and were seen by the enemy, exchanged shots and lost one camel shot. Some 10,000 men were discovered near "Berti Island" about 6 miles off, and one brass gun, about 1 in 20 armed with rifle. One deserter came in to camp and gave himself up. Every precaution against surprise is taken by the General. Some men are always under arms. At night they sleep with their accoutrements on and arms beside them in square, so that as they stand up they are ready at once for action. They are not allowed to put on their coats not even the officers, so that when the reveille sounds an hour before daylight, they have to stand to their arms shivering for an hour.

Each morning, in the half-light of dawn, the soldiers were especially vigilant for that was the hour the dervishes preferred for attack. Yet days passed and nothing happened as the column of boats made its way slowly and laboriously up the river. The enemy was all around, but they still did not take the offensive. Among the British troops, morale was high. The force was compact and most of the men in it were in excellent condition and now skilled in the handling of boats as a result of their experience further down the river. They moved up the Nile as rapidly as any such large force possibly could. However, on the afternoon of 5 February, the column suddenly stopped its arduous progress. It was not the enemy ahead who halted the advance, but the arrival of a messenger from the Desert Column. A number of rumours (or "shaves" as Denison, employing British army slang, called them) then went around the camp. One rumour had it that Gordon had left Khartoum, while another suggested that the Mahdi had surrendered to him. It became obvious that something crucial had happened, but no one seemed certain of what exactly it was. All that Denison knew, as the sixth, seventh, and eighth day of February passed, was that the now immobile River Column, perched on the banks of the narrow confines of the Upper Nile valley, was "waiting for orders."

What had happened, known only to General Earle and his two senior officers, William Butler and Henry Brackenbury, was that Khartoum had fallen and Gordon was dead.

One of the foremen of the *voyageurs*, Alexander McLaurin, had been commissioned by the Ottawa *Free Press* to report on the progress of the expedition. "The expedition so far is not so successful as anticipated," he had written bitterly and with some prescience as early as 1 December,

It is a most costly one I assure you. The boats in the first place are not calculated to stand the usage they are compelled to receive and to bear the enormous amount of stores. They carry as many as four tons besides eight to twelve men and luggage. This load is enough to sink or strain an ordinary boat in still water. I have been over one hundred miles up from here by boat, and every day I could see boats drawn up on shore undergoing repairs, if not entirely abandoned. Again you can see box after box floating down the current to destruction. Hundreds have been lost and hundreds more will follow, as it cannot easily be avoided. The top-heavy loads in going through rough places tip the boats, if not entirely upset them. The result is your boat, if she is not entirely ruined beyond repair, is much lighter than when you started. It is enough to make the projector of the Nile Expedition blush to see the great loss both of life and property, and ought to make him devise some other and more satisfactory way of releasing Chinese Gordon. If we succeed as well as we have since we started, we may possibly reach Khartoum about Christmas 1885 [i.e. in another twelve months] and pay a tribute to the great by a few English tears. Then to march back heavy with the thoughts of how General Gordon must have felt when the last crust was eaten; when he gave the last look towards the north for succour which never came; when the last fierce fight was fought, for one more day of life, which their famine-stricken arms failed to gain, and then the sad death with none of the great English there.[13]

McLaurin erred on the side of pessimism as far as his date for the fall of Khartoum was concerned, but he saw clearly enough what Gordon's end was to be.

Gordon himself cannot have been surprised at his fate. Three months before, he had noted in his diary,[14] "We are a wonderful people; it was never our Government which made us a great nation; our Government has been ever the drag on our wheels. It is, of course, on the cards that Kartoum [*sic*] is taken under the nose of the Expeditionary Force, which will be *just too late.*"

The nose under which Khartoum was taken belonged to Colonel Sir Charles Wilson. The disaster might possibly have been averted if Herbert Stewart or Fred Burnaby had continued to be available to lead the Desert Column. Both were energetic, determined men who would probably have adopted a bolder approach to the task of getting through to Khartoum without delay. Wilson, who had never before been in action, was not the best man to lead a fighting force into the besieged city. However, despite being cut off from communication with Wolseley (the lack of reliable communications was a major oversight and frequent hindrance to the whole expedition),

Wilson had decided to press on with the original plan for reaching Khartoum. Aside from this one decisive act, Wilson thereafter showed less firmness than the situation required. He constantly sought advice from his fellow officers. No army can be effectively led by a sort of cabinet. In this way, Wilson allowed himself to be convinced, probably by Beresford, that he should use Gordon's two steamers, the *Bordein* and *Telawiyeh*, to reconnoitre the river near Metemmeh rather than set out immediately for Khartoum. With more time available, such a move might have been wise. Possibly Beresford, with a boil on his posterior so painful that he could barely walk, wanted two or three days to recuperate in the hope that he would not miss the excitement.[15] In any case, Wilson probably felt a strong sense of responsibility for ensuring as best he could the safety of the men he was leaving behind on the river bank while he took the two steamers to Khartoum. Whatever the real reason for Wilson's vacillation, when joined with the hundred and one other delays, major and minor, that had already occurred along the way from Cairo to Korti, it cost Gordon his life.[16]

Thirty-six hours before Gordon was killed, Wilson and thirty soldiers had finally started for Khartoum (Beresford was still so unwell as to be unable to accompany them). Despite the heat of well over 37°C, the soldiers carried red serge coats (borrowed from the Guards) intended to frighten the Mahdi. Gordon himself had written in his diary on 13 December, "All that is absolutely necessary is, for fifty of the Expeditionary Force to get on board a steamer and come up . . . and thus let their presence be felt; this is not asking much, but it must happen *at once*; or it will (as usual) be too late."[17] At the moment of Gordon's death during the late afternoon of 25 January, Wilson's two steamers were still about fifty miles north of Khartoum, slowly making their way southward through the rapids. On the 26th, one of the steamers grounded on a rock in the treacherous channel of the Sixth Cataract and was only floated free with great difficulty. More hours had been lost. On the morning of the 28th, Gordon's fifty-second birthday, Wilson's little force steamed around a bend in a flat stretch of the river and finally saw through the haze of the heat its goal. But Wilson and his men did not see the Egyptian flag which they knew Gordon had always flown over his white-washed palace. Two natives had already shouted from the bank further down the Nile that the governor general was dead.

Now for the first time, Wilson had to admit to himself that it was probably so. The expedition had arrived hours too late. Whatever his first melancholy thoughts, they were cut short by the heavy fire that his small flotilla began to receive from the Mahdi's troops near Khartoum and from warriors near the town of Omdurman on the opposite shore. This heavy crossfire was the final proof needed to convince Wilson that Khartoum had, indeed, fallen to the enemy. There was nothing more to do but to put his two steamers about and, with the bad news, run the gauntlet back to the Desert Column's camp near Metemmeh. As Wilson was doing so, four thousand corpses were being piled together in the streets of Khartoum and Gordon's severed head was being exhibited on the fork of a small tree in the dervish camp. The "Anti-Mahdi," for whose rescue an elaborate expedition costing a total of several hundred lives and several million pounds had been organized, had been killed by a dervish spear as he calmly descended the steps of his palace to meet the onrush of the fanatics after they had finally broken through the disheartened, sickly, and starving troops defending the walls of Khartoum.

Wilson was in an unenviable position as he put his two steamers around to head back down the Nile. Nature joined with the bullets of the dervishes to endanger his passage. As every school-boy geographer knows, the Nile is a river which follows a more or less regular pattern of rising and falling. In some places the annual variation in the depth of the water is as much as thirty feet. The level of the Nile begins to fall every September. By January 1885, it was dropping rapidly. The rocks in the rapids through which the two steamers had to pass on their return from Khartoum were, therefore, especially dangerous. On the morning of 29 January, after Wilson had satisfied himself that Khartoum had indeed fallen four days earlier, the *Bordein* and the *Telahawiyeh* started northward. During the afternoon, the *Telahawiyeh* struck a rock and quickly sank, but the men and guns aboard were safely transferred to the other of Gordon's paddle-wheel "penny-steamers." Surprisingly, further descent down the river of the *Bordein* was unopposed by the Mahdi's troops. But on the afternoon of 31 January, she also struck a rock, tearing a great gash in her side. The most cursory inspection showed that she could go no further. The position of Wilson's small force was now extremely hazardous. It was immobilized on an island deep in the enemy's territory. Forty miles still separated it from the safety of the Desert Column's camp. However, Wilson remained cool. He quickly decided to send in the *Bordein's* boat a young infantry officer, Edward Stuart-Wortley,[18] to seek the help of Beresford. Stuart-Wortley and a mixed crew of British and Sudanese soldiers rowed most of that night and the next day to reach Metemmeh.

On the afternoon of 1 February, having learned of Gordon's death and Wilson's dilemma from the exhausted Stuart-Wortley, Beresford first despatched the sad news to Wolseley. Then he set out at once with Lieutenant Van Koughnet in one of Gordon's remaining steamers to attempt the rescue of Wilson's party. Van Koughnet, who had relinquished command of his minute gun-boat further down the Nile, had just arrived in Metemmeh from the supply base at Jakdul. Except for Beresford himself and a sub-lieutenant, he was the only naval officer in the camp. During the daylight run up the forty miles of Nile which separated Metemmeh and Wilson's island, Beresford's steamer had to pass through the heavy fire of a Mahdist outpost on the river bank, an outpost Stuart-Wortley had safely slipped by during the night. In the exchange of fire between the dervishes on the shore and the soldiers and sailors sheltered behind sand-bags stacked along the steamer's decks, Van Koughnet was severely wounded in the leg. Another shot hit the steamer's boiler. Repairs to the machinery were effected with great ingenuity, and, finally, the island was reached and Wilson and his stranded soldiers were quickly taken aboard. Beresford then turned the small steamer about and ran with the current to Metemmeh and safety.

The death of his old friend had come as a great shock to Wolseley. "What an ending to all our labour, and all our bright hopes, is this!!"[19] While realizing that it would have many implications for him and all those involved in the relief expedition, Wolseley's first thoughts were for the safety and well-being of his Desert Column. In his view, Wilson was not the type of forceful, vigorous officer needed to command it. Buller, however, was. During the long haul up the river Wolseley had had cause to regret the obstinacy and pride of his chief of staff. And Buller had clashed with other members of the "Ring" (who, like him, were no longer simply young men joining in a common effort to reach the top). But Wolseley never questioned Buller's fighting qualities. The newly appointed commander of the Desert Column left Korti immediately for Metemmeh. On 11 February, one week after Wilson and his men had arrived back among their comrades of the Desert Column, Buller assumed his new command. The commander-in-chief—or "Sirdar"—of the Egyptian army, Major-General Sir Evelyn Wood, was in turn ordered to Korti with his aide-de-camp, Lieutenant Reginald Wingate, to replace Buller as Wolseley's chief of staff.[20] This appointment Wolseley regarded with misgivings. To his journal, he confided his waspish opinion of Wood: "he will not be able to take in posterity by whom he will be found out and rated as a very second-rate general and an unpatriotic & selfish public servant, whose two most remarkable traits were extreme vanity and unbounded self-seeking."[21]

Upon assuming command of the Desert Column, Buller found it in a sad state. Its long march across the sands and its enforced sojourn beside the Nile while Wilson was making his vain effort to succour Gordon had greatly reduced the reserves of food for both soldiers and camels (only twelve days rations remained); ammunition was low and the clothing of some of the soldiers was ragged and their boots in shreds; many of the surviving camels were lame or sick; and morale had sagged at the news of Gordon's death. Worse still was the information that thousands of the Mahdi's followers, greatly encouraged by the fall of Khartoum, were advancing on Metemmeh. Buller quickly decided that his extended force was in no condition to oppose them. He thereupon withdrew the column in the direction of Korti, leaving the banks of the Nile on 14 February.[22] The long odyssey of the Desert

Column was ending. Its return march was an extraordinary feat of endurance. An account of it later moved the great Prussian General von Moltke to remark, "They were not soldiers but heroes."

Upon learning of Gordon's death, Wolseley had immediately telegraphed to Cairo and London. In his message of 4 February to Hartington, he observed, "It is now for the Government to decide what policy they wish me to pursue, as the fall of Khartoum leaves me without instructions, the object of my mission to this country being no longer possible.... If you wish, I could still advance on Khartoum and could defeat the Mahdi; but operation under present conditions is much more difficult than before, and owing to the lateness of the season, would be somewhat hazardous, for our serious enemy would be the hot weather, not the Mahdi."[23] On receipt of Wolseley's telegram, Gladstone's cabinet met immediately, but as usual when it addressed itself to Egyptian affairs, it could not make up its collective mind.

At the same time as the government had despatched the Gordon relief expedition, it had pursued its vain attempts to induce the French to agree to financial arrangements for Egypt which might permit Britain to achieve its declared policy of withdrawing from the country. With Gordon's death, it became yet more difficult for the Liberals to reach a decision about the future of Egypt and the Sudan. They now had to face a hostile public crying loudly for revenge. Queen Victoria, made ill by the report of Gordon's death, summarized the feelings of the country when she telegraphed openly to the prime minister, "The news from Khartoum are frightful, and to think that all this might have been prevented and many precious lives saved by earlier action is too frightful." To one of Gladstone's ministers, "She spoke strongly against the Govt., mainly against *Mr. G.* for the delay of the expedition, for not having done their best to save Gordon, etc."[24] Gladstone could not ignore the widespread cry for vengeance. But he did not like it at all. "Chinese" Gordon dead was as much an enigmatic nuisance to Gladstone as he had been alive. Gladstone felt no sympathy for the almost hysterical public demand for vengeance. A cousin of Baring, the future foreign secretary Viscount Grey, was a young member of parliament when, on 18 February, the prime minister spoke about the failure to rescue Gordon. Grey recorded in his diary the following day,

Gladstone's manner and speech last night shows up one of the great flaws of his character most painfully.... With all his enthusiasm for a principle and a cause, he has come to identify himself with that cause. He is angry with the cause or the principle if it fails, because he can't bear to allow himself to fail. So now he is half angry with himself for having let Gordon go out, half angry with Gordon's fanatical chivalry for so putting his plans about by staying at Khartoum and getting killed.

He won't confess to the first feeling and he daren't utter the second. Yet he had to say something, and the result was a sullen and embarrassed refusal to apologize for himself or even to give credit to the merits of Gordon, our Army and the Colonies... left all the eulogy of Gordon, troops and Colonies, one bright spot amid the awful gloom, to be set forth by Sir Stafford Northcote, his opponent.[25]

What the general public thought of Gladstone's handling of the Sudan debacle was soon summed up in a popular music hall song which reversed the "G.O.M."—the "Grand Old Man"—to become the "M.O.G.": the "Murderer of Gordon."

> The M.O.G., when his life ebbs out,
> Will ride in a fiery chariot,
> And sit in state
> On a red-hot plate
> Between Pilate and Judas Iscariot.

With the sentiments of this jingle, Wolseley fully agreed. He had for years despised Gladstone and all others whom he considered "Little Englanders." But amidst the frustration at the failure of his expedition and knowledge that the many enemies he had made during his public career would eagerly seize on it as an opportunity to denigrate him, Wolseley redoubled, in the privacy of his own journal, his almost daily denunciation of the Grand Old Man and all who supported him.

I pity myself and those who urged Mr. Gladstone to prepare for the relief of *Khartoum* early last spring, but as for the main body of the English taxpayer I have *no* pity for him: he has in his utter folly set up for himself the most contemptible of idols, the G.O.M., and he persists in believing in him; let him therefore pay for his folly: possibly it be a warning to future generations. If God punishes men in the world, and if *we* are judges of right & wrong, he will send down this old hypocrite in shame to his grave & with the outcries of the nation he has misgoverned ringing in his ears, as he dies despised & hated by every good Englishman.[26]

However much Gladstone mistrusted the popular jingoism and the desire for revenge, he could not, for political reasons, afford to ignore the outcry. He must appear to do something. Moreover, if the Mahdist forces did advance northwards now (as they had so often declared to be their intention), the border of Egypt would itself be threatened. Gladstone's cabinet thereupon decided that Wolseley's force should undertake a task for which it had never been intended. It should be used to stop a Mahdist advance on Egypt by forever vanquishing the dervishes at either Berber or at Khartoum itself, if necessary. In short, the government had finally decided "to smash up the Mahdi." The details of how exactly this great undertaking was to be accomplished were left to Wolseley to decide. Whatever the final shape of his plan, it was certain that there would be a role for the "Canadians" of his "Ring" and that the Canadian imperial adventurers still serving in Egypt and the Sudan would play their role in the next stage of this incredible saga.

9

Advance and Retreat

We've fought with many men acrost the seas,
An' some of 'em was brave an' some was not;
The Paythan an' the Zulu an' Burmese;
But the Fuzzy was the finest o' the lot....
So 'ere's *to* you, Fuzzy-Wuzzy, at your 'ome in the Soudan;
You're a pore benighted 'eathen but a first-class
        fightin' man.

RUDYARD KIPLING
"FUZZY-WUZZY (SOUDAN EXPEDITIONARY FORCE)"

The British government's decision to "smash up the Mahdi" meant the establishment of defensive lines which could be held without difficulty during the hot summer months in preparation for the attack that Wolseley now concluded could be made on Khartoum only during the relatively cooler months of autumn. For the now-ragged Desert Column, Wolseley's decision meant retreat to the headquarters at Korti. There it could be reorganized.

But all this—including the news of Gordon's death—was unknown to the men of the River Column, except to Earle, Brackenbury, and Butler. All that the men knew was that they were to advance farther up the Nile. From the proposed summer quarters at Berber Wolseley could direct an attempt, if necessary in co-operation with a reorganized Desert Column, to open communications with the Red Sea coast so that the whole army could be re-equipped for an autumn offensive against Khartoum. The River Column accordingly resumed its advance. The day after Earle learned of the fall of Khartoum, the column set off for Berber, through a valley of hot, black cliffs and dangerous rapids, the worst yet encountered. Further north, the river had often been bordered by desert; now it passed through narrow, rocky gorges.

Officers and men had greatly profited by their prolonged struggle with the Nile cataracts below Dongola. The whalers were no longer manned by untutored crews.... Experience had taught the troops how to manage their boats in broken water, and how to get the fullest advantage out of the means of propulsion at their disposal. But even so, and although the men were in admirable condition for performing severe and continuous labour, the constant succession of rapids and the intricate channels of rushing water through a wilderness of rocks, taxed their capabilities and their endurance to the utmost. In spite of the strenuous exertions of the troops, progress was slow, and as the river was falling, advance became more and more difficult from day to day. But up to the present time the struggle had been merely against nature. Although it was known that a hostile force was in the broken rocky country to the front, and although traces of the enemy showed that resistance had been contemplated at more than one point between Hamdab and Berti, the Mahdieh had shirked a conflict.[1]

General Earle's force soon found, however, that the Mahdists, elated by their conquest at Khartoum and reinforced by recent arrivals from the southern Sudan, no longer shirked a conflict. On the second day of the resumed progress up the Nile, advance scouts signalled to the boats that, near a small village called Kirbekan, a force of approximately two thousand Mahdists were forming themselves along a ridge three hundred feet high that ran down to the river's edge. Hitherto, the dervishes had withdrawn as the column had moved up the river; now it was clear that they were going to make a stand. The column could not reach either Abu Hamed or Berber as long as the enemy controlled the rocky ridge. The dervishes would have to be dislodged—if necessary with the bayonet.

On 10 February the Battle of Kirbekan, the first and only battle of the River Column, took place. Once it was beyond doubt that the dervishes intended to oppose any further advance, Earle ordered the column to stop, beach its boats, and prepare to fight. Although clearly the dervishes already enjoyed an advantage in their loose clothing which blended so well with the stones and sand, the soldiers actually doffed their khaki uniforms (introduced by Wolseley on the Indian army model) and donned their tight-fitting red-coats to do battle, one of the last times British troops ever did so. The bagpipes of the Black Watch were soon heard over the roar of the rushing water as the column was deployed for a bayonet attack on the ridge. Most of the *voyageurs*, non-combatants who had remained unarmed throughout the campaign, stayed near the boats and their precious supplies. But Denison, an ardent militia officer, was determined not to miss a chance to see action. He was attached to Colonel Alleyne's column of 150 men from the South Staffordshire Regiment. His description of the battle, hurriedly noted in his diary, was both cryptic and modest:

We reached the hill and had our guns and men in position by 8:30. The enemy commenced firing upon us at once, which we began to return [fire] at 9. Shortly after this we heard the main column firing as they turned their position and got to the rear of the 3rd position. We kept up a steady fire until noon, very heavy from 11:30 to 12 for at this time the main column had charged the heights and some of the Mahdi men retreated across our front and across the river. We shot a number in the water and while landing on island. The 42 [the Black Watch] and 38 [the South Staffordshire Regiment] made a gallant assault. Col. Eyre and Col. Covenay were shot, 14 men killed and 50 or 60 wounded. General Earle was shot after it was practically all over, a little after noon, and all the firing was over at 1 p.m. The enemy loss is said to be 300 or 400.

Another *voyageur* was more expansive. Foreman Alexander McLaurin of Ottawa described the column's only battle in considerable detail and gave an account of Denison's role in it.

The voyageurs were not permitted to leave the Zareba [the defensive square], but a few managed to get away and went up and saw the fight. Lieutenant-Colonel Denison stood beside the cannon and assisted materially in sending some splendid shots into the enemy's rank. Eighteen shell and six shrapnel were hurled into their ranks, doing great damage. As soon as the battle was over, the voyageurs rushed out of the Zareba and made for the battleground, where they reached in time to see the wind-up of the fight. They secured many valuable mementos in the shape of guns, knives and swords, etc.[2]

The result of the battle was the same as that of all such encounters between well-armed, disciplined British troops and the poorly armed, fanatical spearmen: about six hundred dervishes were killed at the cost of fifteen British. However, one of the British dead was the popular Major-General Earle. Immediately following his victory, he had looked into a hut of straw and mud near the battlefield and had been promptly shot dead by a Mahdist lurking inside. The command of the River Column thereupon devolved upon Brigadier-General Henry Brackenbury, one of the most prominent and least-liked of "Wolseley's Gang."[3] An ugly man with a yellow face, a red nose, and a black moustache, Brackenbury had made himself immensely unpopular among reactionary officers by his brilliant efforts to forward the Cardwell army reforms. It was at the War Office that Wolseley had first met Brackenbury, and he realized that the then young captain would make a superb staff officer. Subsequently, in West and South Africa and in Cyprus, "Brack"—his nickname was as much inspired by the disgusting way in which he cleared his throat as by a desire to shorten his cumbersome surname— had more than justified Wolseley's confidence in him. Upon assuming command of the River Column, he showed himself to be a resourceful leader in the field as well as a scholarly theorist and desk officer.

Although it had cost the column its leader and two of its colonels, the Battle of Kirbekan opened the way toward the village of Abu Hamed. On 13 February, the column was given the devastating news that Khartoum had fallen and that Gordon was dead, but they were told at the same time that the advance on Abu Hamed would proceed in order to secure the town before a final autumn attack on Khartoum. During the following days, the skill with which the *voyageurs* took the whalers through the rapids won the praise of the new commander and of the officers serving under him. Tangible evidence that the column was approaching Abu Hamed was provided by the wreck of the steamer in which Gordon's aide, Stewart, had been travelling when he had been murdered near the small town six months earlier. By the morning of 24 February, Brackenbury's force in its 215 boats was within twenty-five miles of Abu Hamed. It then stopped. A messenger from Wolseley had reached the column just before it moved off. Unknown to the soldiers, they had now reached the farthermost point of their advance. Wolseley had decided that Brackenbury's force would also have to be recalled to Korti. His idea of establishing an advance base at Berber where contact could be made with the Red Sea coast had to be given up for the time being. The success of such an operation would have depended upon the ability of the Desert Column to join the River Column in a combined offensive against Berber, especially if opposition proved stubborn. It was now clear that the Desert Column, after two battles and its long march to Metemmeh and back, could no longer guarantee the River Column that support. Having come so far, the soldiers and *voyageurs* of the River Column were staggered by the sudden order to turn back down the river. "The swearing that ensued was almost powerful enough to dam the Nile."[4]

Yet their ordeal on the Nile was far from over. Great obstacles still confronted them. "The phase of the operations now beginning witnessed the voyageurs' supreme test and their greatest triumph. Once the column began to withdraw, it was imperative that it get out of the enemy's country as quickly as possible. It was going to run the rapids, and in these circumstances the skill of the Canadian rivermen became more important to it than ever before. For nine eventful days the safety of the expedition depended entirely upon Denison's men."[5]

With Denison in one of the leading boats, the River Column turned around and started down the Nile on the morning of 26 February, at a rate of progress which stood in sharp contrast to its laborious ascent. Because the column

Plate 18. Whalers being hauled through the Second Cataract by an elaborate system of ropes.

Plate 19. Towing a steamer through one of the Nile rapids. It was on such river boats as these that the eight Manitoba and Ottawa wheelsmen served.

Plate 20. A sketch by Melton Prior, the special artist of the *Illustrated London News*, of whalers being towed through the Second Cataract. In the foreground is a group of *voyageurs* tracking one of the whalers.

Plate 21. A rare day of good sailing on the Nile between Sarras and Dal, with *voyageurs* in the bows of the whalers.

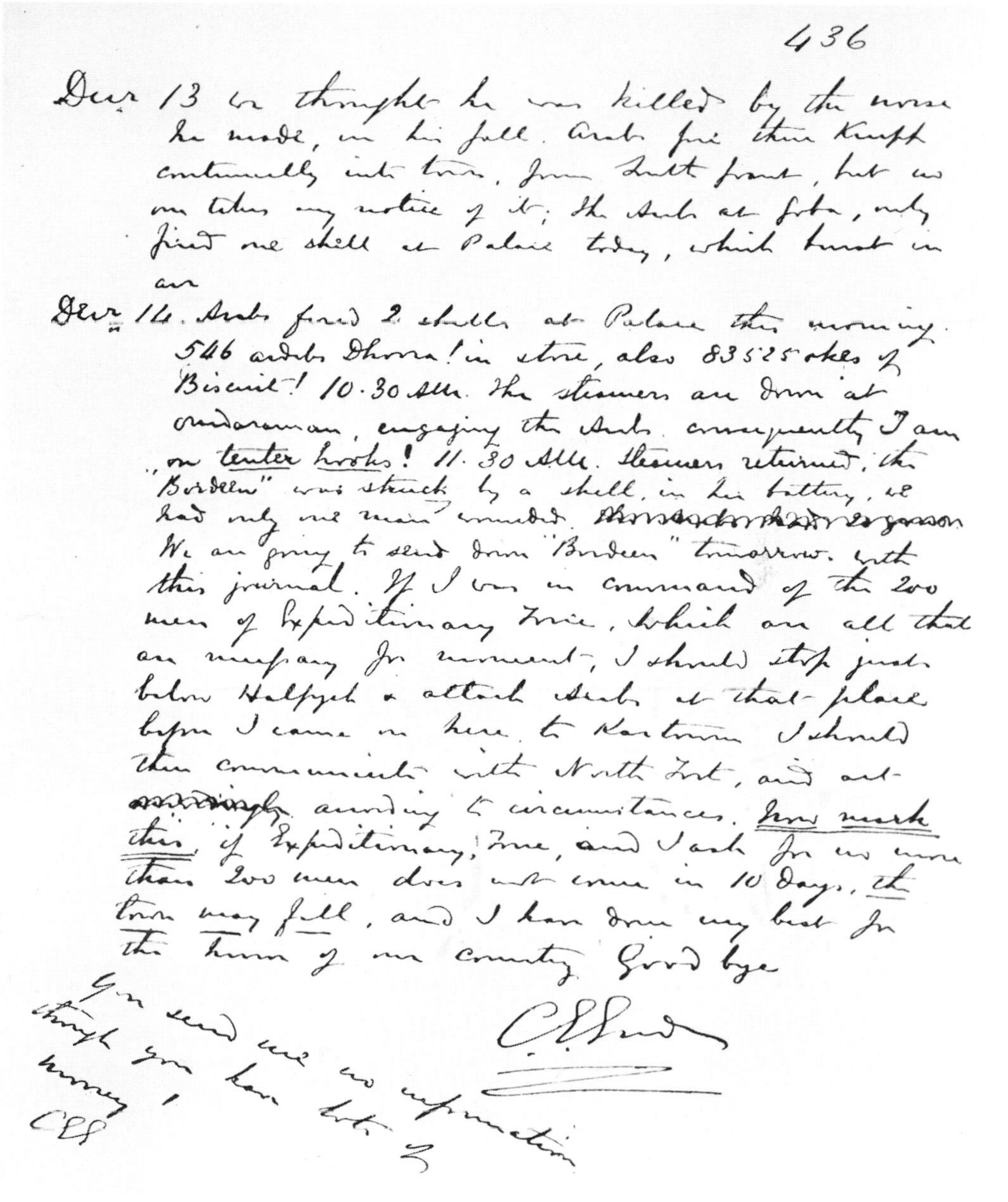

Dec 13 or thought he was killed by the horse he made, in his fall. Arabs fire their Krupp continually into town, from Bult front, but we on takes any notice of it; the Arabs at Goba, only fired one shell at Palace today, which burst in air

Dec 14. Arabs fired 2 shells at Palace this morning. 546 ardebs Dhoora! in store, also 83,525 okes of Biscuit! 10.30 A.M. the steamers are down at Omdurman, engaging the Arabs. consequently I am on tenter hooks! 11.30 A.M. steamers returned. the "Bordeen" was struck by a shell, in his battery, we had only one man wounded. We are going to send down "Bordeen" tomorrow, with this journal. If I was in command of the 200 men of Expeditionary Force, which are all that are necessary for moment, I should stop just below Halfyeh & attack Arabs at that place before I came on here to Kartoum. I should then communicate with North Fort, and act according to circumstances. Now mark this, if Expeditionary Force, and I ask for no more than 200 men does not come in 10 days, the town may fall, and I have done my best for the honour of our country. Good bye

C. E. Gordon

You send me no information though you have lots of money! C.E.G.

Plate 22. Page 436 of Gordon's *Journal*; the final entry of 14 December 1844 which concludes. "*Now mark this* if... no more than 200 men does (*sic*) not come in 10 days, *the town may fall*, and I have done my best for the honour of my country Good bye C. G. Gordon"

Plate 23. "Gordon's Last Stand: Khartoum
January 26, 1885" from the painting
by George W. Joy.

Plate 24. "Too late!" Sir Charles Wilson's arrival within sight of Khartoum." The *Bordein* and *Telahawiyeh* returning the Mahdists' fire as Wilson's small force approached the captured capital of the Sudan on 28 January 1885.

Plate 25. Herbert Horatio Kitchener of Khartoum.

Plate 26. Percy Girouard, the French-Canadian military engineer who built the railway which enabled Kitchener to capture Khartoum.

Plate 27. A sketch by a Royal Engineer Officer of the railway advancing across the desert.

Plate 28. On Girouard's railway: "Pushing on to the Front: Moving Camp on the Halfa to Abu Hamed section." The work crews were self-contained, carrying with them all necessary supplies and equipment.

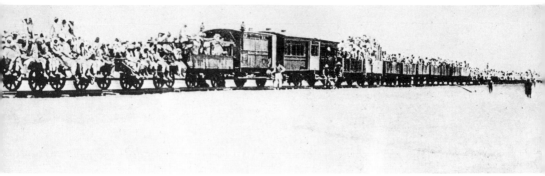

Plate 29. A work party on the way to the railhead as the Sudan railway was being extended across the desert in 1897–1898.

Plate 30. "Two miles a day in the Nubian desert, Sudan railway."

Plate 31. Lieutenant Percy Girouard of the Royal Engineers and several of his fellow officers with a sheikh in the desert. Girouard is on the right of the British officers.

Plate 32. The charge of the 21st Lancers at Omduran (in which Winston Churchill participated):
the bloody dénouement of the Sudan conquest made possible by Girouard's railway.
A detail from a painting by R. Caton Woodville.

was now moving with the current, its descent was, of course, swift. Yet there were even more dangers than in the ascent. Brackenbury therefore issued an order stating, "The Brigadier-General Commanding has to remind the troops that the descent of this swift river will require even greater care than its ascent. All will depend upon the vigilance of the men in the bows, and the coolness and resource of the men steering." The *voyageurs* were the only ones who had the necessary coolness and resource to meet the challenges that certain sections of the river presented. Another order was accordingly issued: "In difficult rapids special arrangements will be made for taking each boat through with Canadian pilots."[6] During the next eight days, the work alternated between the British soldiers who rowed the boats through the slack sections of the river and the Canadians who steered them through the plunging rapids. The Nile was narrow and treacherous, its level falling constantly and rocks appearing which were hidden less than a fortnight earlier when the column had ascended the same stretch. The skill of the boatmen was, however, always more than the equal of the river. One section that had taken thirty days to ascend took only nine to descend. The Canadians carried the column through the stifling gorges and over the flat stretches, shimmering with heat, without major mishap. In the most treacherous of the cataracts, the *voyageurs* took the boats down one by one, walking back along the shore to bring down another.[7] At one such rapid, Brackenbury was as impressed by the skill of the Canadian boatmen as Wolseley had been fifteen years before on the Slave River in Manitoba.

The voyageurs walked to see the shoot, before attempting to pass it. They said it was bad, but practicable. To me it seemed as bad as bad could be. The channel turned to the left, and then sharply at right angles to the right. Just at this turn, two great rocks stood out in mid-stream. It was necessary to pass between them. The least error in steering would be fatal. To make the turn too soon would bring the boat on to the right-hand rock; to wait too long would sweep her on to the lefthand rock. Sitting under the shadow of a great rock, I watched this triumph of skill over a difficulty that to anyone unaccustomed to such work would have seemed insuperable. Boat after boat came down at lightning-speed, the men giving way with might and main to give steering power; the bowmen standing cool and collected and watching the water, and only using the oar should the steersman seem to need help; the steersman bringing round the boat with marvellous judgment at the right moment. Now and then an error of half a second brought a boat on to the edge of the left-hand rock, and she rose and fell like a horse jumping a fence. But in the day's work only one boat of the Gordons and one of the Staffords were wrecked.

At a lower rapid, one boat overturned and two wounded soldiers carried in it drowned in the swift river. Denison noted tersely in his diary, as if in way of explanation, that "They had no voyageur in their boat." The two soldiers drowned were the only casualties suffered by the River Column on the Nile itself, although nine boats were lost and thirteen damaged. The survivors of a trying ordeal, unique in the varied history of Victoria's army, arrived back at the base camp at Korti on 8 March. The column had defeated both the enemy in battle and the Nile at its worst. In a book which he later wrote about its adventures, "Brack" recorded the pride he felt as he led it back to safety, triumphant and intact.

Near the forward supply base at Korti, the River Column established its last camp and awaited orders from Wolseley. There the force, which had overcome the worst that the Nile had to offer, held its first and last review. Brackenbury invited Denison to accompany him as he inspected on horseback more than twenty-five hundred men. After the review, Denison watched the return from Metemmeh of one section of the Desert Column, men from some of the crack regiments of the British army, from the Royal Marines, and the Royal Navy. They were the cream of the cream, but they returned with their appearance—although not their courage—sadly ravaged by the desert. The River Column had been dressed in a motley and ragged collection of uniforms and work clothes, but their appearance was nevertheless better than that of the men who had crossed the desert. "They seemed very much worn out, many without boots. The horses all showed their ribs and a number have died. Nearly all the Camel Corps are dismounted, their animals having died, and they are coming in footsore." Three Canadians returned with the Desert Column: "Cupid" Wilson, major in the Regiment of Canadian Artillery (whom Denison was on hand to greet on his return from the arduous march), Edmund Van Koughnet, commander (since 4 February) in the Royal Navy; and war correspondent Alexander MacDonald.

A native of Quebec, MacDonald had spent part of his youth travelling in the wilds of western Canada and the United States. An inveterate traveller and writer, he later published a number of books while pursuing his career as a journalist in Britain. He served on the Nile expedition as a correspondent for a syndicate of five British newspapers and later based a book on his experiences: *Too Late for Gordon and Khartoum*. MacDonald was not a man to ignore the popular demand for adventure stories; thirteen years later, at the time of the Sudan expedition of 1898, he added a second book to the rapidly mounting literature about the Gordon relief expedition, *Why Gordon Perished*.[8] .

MacDonald later confirmed Denison's impression of the sorry state of the Desert Column when it arrived back to Korti. An ardent naturalist, he was appalled at the way in which the camels had been mistreated. He held Wolseley responsible. Eight years after the event, MacDonald still could write bitterly about the cruelty to the camels. Travelling in Armenia, he noted how well camels in the mountains of Ararat were cared for compared with those on the Nile Expedition. The Armenian camels "carried a load of about 400 lb., so securely and well placed on their backs that we cannot remember having seen one of them with holes that were, alas! so often noticed in the backs of the camels Lord Wolseley sent with us . . . across the . . . Desert. How much better it would have been if he had then acted on the experience of those accustomed to use the camel, than in his impetuosity, and thinking that he had discovered something new in natural history, treating his camels as if they could work *ad libitum*, without food, water, or rest or even without proper baggage saddles. The consequences were that the . . . Desert was strewn with the bodies of the poor brutes, who had carried their heavy burdens until they had succumbed under the improper treatment."[9]

The adventures of both the Desert and River Columns were over. So, in fact, were those of the remaining *voyageurs*, although they did not yet know it. It soon became clear that the British had no intention of asking them to observe the terms of their renewed contracts and remain in the Sudan from March until September unless they themselves wanted to do so. The British authorities did, however, want Canadian boatmen to return to participate in the projected autumn campaign to "smash up the Mahdi," again to help in taking boatloads of soldiers and supplies over the route they now knew well. Denison saw both Wolseley and Buller soon after his arrival at Korti. He was requested to bring from Canada four or five hundred *voyageurs* for the proposed autumn campaign. "They did not want any tinkers or tailors"[10] such as had been included in the Winnipeg contingent, but obviously both Wolseley and Buller believed that the safety of the force to be organized to destroy the power of the Mahdi once and for all would depend partly upon the assistance of Canadian boatmen. Denison was gratified with this tangible indication of the esteem with which Wolseley regarded the contribution his *voyageurs* had made to the expedition. He was also pleased with the way in which his men had been welcomed back to Korti.

Our arrival on the 8th inst. . . . was the signal of great stir and bustle, we were heartily received by everyone and question after question was asked and as readily answered by everyone as to the river route and its success. At 3:30 p.m. we were ordered to parade before General Wolseley which we did and had the pleasure of hearing that great warrior speak and highly compliment the Canadians for the very valuable services tendered, which went to make the expedition so successful. He said he therefore hoped to see us and many more Canadians in the autumn camp again, and though our agreement called for six months longer service he would not place any pressure on us, but those who wished to remain at their present salary could do so, but any or all could go home to Canada just as they might decide.

All of the remaining *voyageurs* elected to return to Canada before the beginning of the dreaded Sudanese summer, leaving the option open of returning to Egypt in the autumn for the proposed campaign.

On 13 March, Denison and his boatmen began their long journey down the Nile to Cairo. Upon parting from Wolseley, Denison promised that he would return in the autumn to join in retaking Khartoum. Denison did not yet know of pressures that were already working against such an adventure. In London, following the news of Gordon's death, the Liberals had barely managed to survive a vote of censure on their Sudan policy (although Lord Salisbury, the Leader of the Opposition, was careful not to commit the Conservative party irrevocably to attempt the reconquest of the Sudan). But the initial resentment at Gladstone's handling of the Sudan problem, the popular desire to see the "M.O.G." roasted on a red-hot plate, soon gave way to a more mellow sorrow at the passing of Gordon:

> Too late! Too late to save him.
> In vain, in vain, they tried.
> His life was England's glory,
> His death was England's pride.

Even amidst the popular agitation, Gladstone never foreswore his intention to evacuate the Sudan. From the beginning, he had been sucked into the bog of Sudanese problems against his better judgment. Now he was determined to have done with the barren and barbarous land that had caused him so much trouble.

Public passions have a way of cooling rapidly unless they are constantly fed. Soon a variety of domestic issues and, above all, the continuing problem of Ireland began to drive Gordon from the forefront of the electorate's mind. And before long a military reason for withdrawing Wolseley's force from the Sudan presented itself. At Korti on 11 March Denison had recorded in his diary the news that "Gladstone has demanded that the Russians withdraw their troops from the Afghan frontier." Growing tensions in the Middle East with expansionist Russia offered the Liberals a good occasion to withdraw Wolseley's force from the Sudan so that it might be ready for service in Afghanistan if it were needed. No one in Gladstone's cabinet wanted to tempt Russia by enlarging Britain's already extensive involvement in Africa and thereby further weakening the forces available for service.

Wolseley himself did not learn of what amounted to a decision to withdraw from the Sudan until after he had established a defensive front at Korti and departed for Cairo. There he would escape the hardships of the hot season and be able to maintain better control of the British forces both on the Red Sea coast and on the Nile. On 14 April, three days after Wolseley had arrived in the Egyptian capital, he received final instructions to evacuate the Sudan and to establish a permanent line of defence near the Sudanese-Egyptian border south of Wadi Halfa. There was no longer any question—if there ever had been—of an autumn campaign to "smash up the Mahdi."

Soon the Hussars, the Guards, the Highlanders, the *kroomen*, and all the other participants in the vain effort to rescue Gordon were joining the *voyageurs* in the descent of the river, gradually evacuating one post after another, posts that they had established with such toil six months earlier. Stores which had required many weeks of work to bring up the Nile were burned or thrown into the river in as many minutes. The great camp at Korti was dismantled and all the troops withdrawn, and by July Dongola was evacuated. The retreat was completed without opposition from the dervishes, and permanent defences were established near Wadi Halfa. The control of the upper Nile was left to the Mahdi. On 7 July, after briefly visiting the Red Sea coast, Wolseley sailed for England. The last Nile expedition regiment to leave Egypt, the Gordon Highlanders (with Surgeon de Lom still accompanying them), embarked at Alexandria on 9 September. The futile campaign to save Gordon was at an end, one year after it had first been organized. Except for a narrow strip along the Red Sea coast, the Sudan was now completely in the hands of the Mahdi.

As the Liberal government—and the Conservative one under Lord Salisbury which had succeeded it on 24 June—were reaching the decision to withdraw from the Sudan and Wolseley and his staff were carrying it out, Denison, Kennedy, and the remaining *voyageurs* made their way down the Nile, Denison reaching Cairo on 13 April, two days after Wolseley. The descent of the river by the *voyageurs* was quick. They covered thirty to fifty miles a day on stretches of the river that had taken them weeks to ascend. They still assumed that they would in a few months be seeing those same stretches of river for a third time. Even when Denison reached the relative civilization of Wadi Halfa and had left the desolation of the upper Nile far behind him, he was still under the impression that Canadian *voyageurs* would again make the arduous ascent of the Nile in the autumn. In the meantime, however, he would visit both London and his large family in Toronto. When, on 3 April, he learned that "the Canadian Government had sent up 5,000 troops to suppress an insurrection by Riel, who is joined by some Indians," his thoughts turned increasingly to home and to the earlier expedition against Riel in which he himself had participated. The Northwest Rebellion had begun. Suddenly "Cupid" Wilson, still serving with the other gunners of what had been the Desert Column, was ordered back to Canada to command the artillery detachment being sent to Manitoba. Frederick Denison's older brother George also accompanied General Middleton, and Lord Melgund went as chief of staff. Hospital Sergeant Labat, like Major Wilson, returned to Canada in time to participate in the campaign. Several of the first group of *voyageurs* to return also found employment for their unique skills in the expedition. The Canadian boatmen were becoming one element in a larger imperial "fire brigade" which was drawn upon for service in varied colonial wars during the latter half of the nineteenth century.

For Denison, however, there was still ahead more than a month of service in Egypt. On 8 April, at Wadi Halfa, he boarded one of Thomas Cook's steamers. Its modest comforts were especially welcome. As he noted in his diary, Denison had begun to feel distinctly "seedy." So seedy in fact that at Luxor, Kennedy, rather than Denison took the men to see the ancient ruins. The next day one of the *voyageurs*, Daniel McLean of Winnipeg, had to be left at Assiout fatally ill with typhoid, the disease that had already killed so many more British soldiers than the spears or bullets of the dervishes. On 10 April, Philip Leonard of Winnipeg died at Dal of typhoid fever and six days later McLean died. The number of Canadians buried in British army cemeteries along the Nile now numbered eleven.

By the time the *voyageurs'* train had pulled into the Cairo station on 13 April and Denison had reached Shepheard's Hotel, that cool oasis of so many travellers in the Middle East, it had become apparent that what was making him feel ill was nothing less than typhoid fever. Through the good offices of the British army in Cairo, the *voyageurs* were taken to see the pyramids but Denison himself was carried off immediately to the garrison hospital. Two days later, most of his fellow Canadians sailed for England where they were issued individual tickets to return to Canada when they pleased. A few days later, Surgeon Major Neilson, after having supervised a field hospital at Dal, and Captain MacRae, after recovering from sunstroke, brought up the rear. By the middle of April, only Denison and Father Bouchard were left in Egypt.

On 17 April 1885, two days after most of his companions had embarked for England, Denison's journal abruptly stops. Almost one month later, he revived it with the note, "I have been nearly a month in the Citadel Hospital. Just after I entered I was delirious for some days. Ever since I have been getting stronger and for the last four or five days have been allowed carriage exercise, which I have taken advantage of in driving about Cairo." Exactly one month after he had entered the garrison hospital, he boarded the P. & O. liner *Siam*, outward bound for England. The sea journey was to be a period of convalescence, but before sailing, Denison mustered the necessary energy to buy a "chair and some candy (Turkish delight) for my children." Now aware that there would be no autumn campaign, he wondered whether he would ever see Egypt again.

After a brief stop at Marseilles, the *Siam* reached Plymouth on 27 May. There one of Denison's brothers, John, a lieutenant in the Royal Navy aboard the battleship H.M.S. *Iron Duke*, was awaiting him with an invitation to spend two nights aboard his ship. Denison was to see his younger brother again during his visit to England and, later, to follow his naval career with interest and pride. John, six years younger than Frederick, had entered the Royal Navy in 1867 at the age of fourteen and subsequently served in the flagship at Halifax as midshipman and sub-lieutenant. He had been in *Iron Duke* only a few weeks when his brother passed through Plymouth on his way to London.[11]

The first few days after his arrival in London on the afternoon of 29 May, Denison spent as most tourists do when they first arrive in that great city; despite a lingering weakness from his severe illness, he hurried about, gazing first at Westminster Abbey, then Buckingham Palace, Hyde Park, and St. James Palace. Soon Egerton Denison, who had come to England with the first contingent of *voyageurs* to leave Egypt, and yet another brother, Septimus,[12] joined Denison in his London sightseeing before the two younger brothers travelled northward to undergo militia training with their regiment, the South Staffordshires. Lieutenant John Denison arrived in London from Plymouth to complete the reunion of the four brothers. On 6 June, the Queen's official birthday, Denison was invited to a state dinner at Devonshire House, the palatial residence of Lord Hartington. After being presented to Hartington and the crusty old commander-in-chief, the Duke of Cambridge,[13] he was widely complimented on the conduct of the *voyageurs* on the Nile. Among the guests, Denison met a fellow Canadian who was a senior civil servant in the War Office. Arthur Lawrence Haliburton (later Baron Haliburton) had been born in Nova Scotia in 1832, a son of Thomas Chandler Haliburton, the creator of Sam Slick. Having served in the Commissariat Department of the British army, Haliburton rose to be director of supplies and transport at the War Office at the time of the Nile expedition and had thus been intimately connected with its complicated planning and organization.[14]

Denison ended his fortnight in England by completing some reports for Colonel Alleyne, who had been in charge of river transport, and by visiting Egerton and Septimus in their barracks at Lichfield and John in his battleship at Portsmouth. It was the last time that Frederick Denison was to see Egerton. After completing his militia training at Lichfield, Egerton, in search of more adventure, volunteered for military service on the Gold Coast. Soon after his arrival at Accra, disease overtook him (as it did so many British soldiers serving in West Africa). He was immediately sent to England and Canada but died *en route* on the S.S. *Vancouver* on 8 July 1886 when the ship was in the Gulf of St. Lawrence. He was twenty-five years old.

Frederick Denison also never saw again his Nile companion, Lieutenant-Colonel William Kennedy of Winnipeg. Kennedy had volunteered to remain with the expedition and had journeyed down the river to Cairo with Denison. Like him, Kennedy had passed through villages where the dread disease of smallpox as well as typhoid had recently been reported. Perhaps it was in one of them that he contracted smallpox, which had already killed John Sherlock of Peterborough. In any case, while Denison lay delirious with typhoid in the Cairo garrison hospital, Kennedy led the remaining *voyageurs* to England, *en route* to Canada. In London, both Kennedy and a *voyageur* were found to have smallpox, and on 3 May Kennedy suddenly died. Two days later, in the presence of many of his comrades from the Nile, he was buried with military honours in Highgate Cemetery (not far from where, two years before, a grave had been dug for Karl Marx). This outbreak of smallpox among the *voyageurs* prevented Queen Victoria from inspecting them at Windsor Castle as had been planned. Instead, the Queen sent a message stating "how greatly pleased she had been by the reports received of the energy and devotion they had shown in the arduous duties performed by them on the Nile." As a yet more tangible mark of gratitude, the War Office hired a guide to take the Dominion visitors to "some places of interest and amusement" in London before the majority of them sailed for Montreal on 15 May 1885.

Father Bouchard spent from early February to late March in Cairo. There the bishop of his missionary order, realizing that there was now no hope for an early return to Khartoum, agreed that Bouchard should go home to Canada to undertake parish work in his native province of Quebec until his return to the Sudan became feasible. After having visited Rome, Verona, Paris, and London (where he called upon the family of a British soldier who had died in his arms in the military hospital at Dal), Bouchard was assigned to the parish of Sainte Julie, Quebec, in late May 1885.[15]

William Kennedy had been dead four weeks when Frederick Denison arrived in London from Cairo. Egerton Denison was still safely drilling on the barrack square at Lichfield. One death had already happened; the other had not yet occurred. What filled Denison's mind as he boarded his steamer for Canada on 11 June were happier thoughts of seeing his family again after a separation of ten months. His excited anticipation is reflected in the increasingly cryptic notations in his journal as he crossed the Atlantic. His impatience mounted upon his steamer's arrival at Quebec City: "The baggage was examined & all passed by 8 or 9, but the special train did not get away until 11:15 a.m. It was very tiresome waiting." But on 22 June all was well: "I reached Toronto sharp on time. Henry got aboard the train at Yonge

St. Hettie and Lotta, Tom Delamere, Oliver, Frank, Geo., and Oliver, my nephew met me. I found all well at home."

For months afterward, Denison was in great demand as a speaker, but with his return to Toronto, his military adventures had ended. In recognition of his outstanding services on the Nile, he was made C.M.G., was mentioned in despatches, and, along with the other prominent officers of the expedition, was included by name in thanks voted by the British parliament. Denison continued in public life in Canada. In 1887, while pursuing his career as a lawyer, he became the member of parliament for Toronto West. Nine years later, he died of cancer, age forty-nine.

Denison was the last of the *voyageurs* to return to Canada (other than those few who had elected to remain in the British Isles), but a small and self-contained group of riverboat pilots had returned only shortly before him.

On the same day as the *Ocean King* had sailed from Sydney, Nova Scotia, outward bound for Alexandria, Lord Lansdowne had received another request from the War Office: "Can you obtain eight good men thoroughly accustomed to working and steering sternwheel steamers in rapids for service on the Nile? Pay the same for *voyageurs* unless you recommend higher."[16] As early as April 1884, anticipating the need for a river expedition to save Gordon, Wolseley had written to the former Confederate General Beauregard for details about sternwheelers similar to those he had seen on the Mississippi during the American Civil War. As soon as the Nile expedition was sanctioned, the War Office had placed the order for two prefabricated sternwheelers and had asked Lansdowne for assistance in finding experienced riverboat pilots in Canada. With the same energy that he had shown in recruiting the *voyageurs*, upon receipt of the War Office telegram, Melgund had immediately begun to cast about for wheelsmen experienced in sternwheelers. Ten days later, he had telegraphed London: "Can get men accustomed to sternwheel steamers from Winnipeg but very good men to be had from Ottawa and St. Lawrence thoroughly accustomed to work steamers up and down rapids—these are not sternwheel steamers but good men would find no difficulty in working sternwheel boats. All ask 150 dollar a month." The War Office had agreed to pay the men what they had asked and accepted the applications of four wheelsmen from the Ottawa River: Captains William M. Jones, John A. Williamson, James McKeever, and Thomas Anson Cummings, and four from Manitoba: Captains William Robinson, J. Weber, R. A. Russell, and John S. Seeger. The latter three were citizens of the United States, men who worked on the river steamers on the Mississippi during the winter and on various Canadian lakes and rivers during the summer.

For all eight wheelsmen, the expedition was to prove never more than uncomfortable at worst. For the most part, it was an amusing excursion to an ancient and romantic land. After having been certified qualified wheelsmen by the Department of Marine in Ottawa, the eight volunteers were formally engaged by Lambert on 8 October at $150 per month. They set out immediately to take a steamer from New York to London. The quickest way from London, which they left on 20 October, to the Mediterranean was across the continent. They passed quickly by train down the Rhine to Trieste, but they broke their journey to spend a day in Vienna. Thirty-four-year-old Captain Thomas Cummings described for his wife at home in Grenville, in the Ottawa Valley, how

> Captain [sic] hired a rig and a pilot to show us around Vienna. . . . It is one of the finest cities in the world. We went to see the Treasury. There we saw the country's wealth. Diamonds in thousands and all sizes of rubies and precious stones worth millions and 100's of millions. Then to Bell Vidure Pallace [sic] to see the paintings. It is something past describing. I can't begin to tell you of the paintings we saw there, some 400 years old. Then we went to St. Stephens Church tower. We had to go up 456 steps to get to the top of the tower. Then we saw over the city. There is as much difference between it and Montreal as Montreal and Grenville.[17]

The eight wheelsmen arrived in Alexandria on 30 October, delighted with their trans-European journey.

Two months later, on 10 January 1885, from Wadi Halfa, Captain William Robinson, manager of the Northwest Transportation Company of Winnipeg,[18] wrote to a friend, the deputy minister of Marine and Fisheries in Ottawa, describing their experiences. In Alexandria on 1 November 1884 they had found one of their two flatbottomed sternwheelers (the *Water Lily* and *Lotus*) being assembled from parts brought from the Yarrow shipyards in Scotland. As soon as the two sternwheelers were finished, Robinson and three of his colleagues began their new work.

> On the 12th we were ordered to be at the dock where the men were finishing the stern-wheel boat, and we were there most of the time till the 13th when we were ordered to take the Steamer over to the Canal, and the same day she had her trial trip, with a lunch on board and the usual ceremony. The 14th she was loaded. The 15th at 7 a.m. we started for Cairo. We took two barges in tow, loaded with Railway plant, and proceeded to Assouan and Wady Halfa. We were told that ours was the fastest trip that ever was made with a Steamer while encumbered with a tow. We made the good time by running by night as it is not

customary to run at night in this country. Distance from Alexandria to Wady Halfa 1,000 miles. I had the position of Captain and Russell was mate while Segers and Webber were pilots, but there was a Military Captain put over me. He was a nice gentleman but he knew no more about running a Steamer than I would know about making a watch, however I was careful to obey orders although sometimes it was against my own judgment. After a short time he told me that my calculations were always correct and that it was a pity I should be burdened by men who did not understand River Navigation and he said he would recommend that I be given full charge as it was the only way to get the benefit of [illegible] and so he left us and I have been Captain on the *Water Lily* every since.[19]

Robinson and his seven companions remained throughout their employment much further north on the river than Denison and the *voyageurs*: their steamers were generally employed ferrying supplies between Assuan and Wadi Halfa. In his letter to the deputy minister, Robinson not only took the time to describe—somewhat immodestly—the great satisfaction that he and his fellow Manitobans were giving but also added that the Nile was "a fine river as far as Wady Halfa, but there is very little good land in Egypt. The country is nearly all sand and rocks, with temples strewn in all directions." Robinson clearly did not think much of Egypt, ancient or modern, but British army officers exceeded his expectations. Those he met were unexpectedly pleasant and not so arrogant as he had anticipated. "I have a better opinion of Englishmen than I had before I left Winnipeg. I hope the same feeling may remain in my breast till I see sweet Canada again."[20] By the end of January 1885, most of the supplies for Wolseley's force had passed "Bloody Halfway," and although the wheelsmen later served a little further south on the river, their principal work was over. By the end of March, shortly after the return of most of the *voyageurs* to Canada, all eight wheelsmen also returned home.[21]

10

Canada and the Nile Expedition

But w'ere's de war? I can't mak' out, don't see no fight at all!
She's not'in but une Grand Piqnique, dat's las'in all de fall!
Mebee de neeger king he's scare, an' skip anoder place,
An' pour la Reine Victoriaw! I never see de face.

W. H. DRUMMOND
"MAXIME LABELLE"

When Lord Melgund had first set about organizing the *voyageurs* to go to the Nile, the British general commanding the militia in Canada had told him that he was wasting his time. The War Office "might get as good men on Portsmouth beach."[1] Major-General Middleton was the first, but not the only detractor of the rivermen. The germ of subsequent criticism and trouble was implied in a message Lord Lansdowne sent to the Colonial Office on 25 August 1884. "The men employed under Lord Wolseley at the time of the Red River Expedition were...somewhat hurriedly collected, and amongst them were a considerable number of white men who represented themselves to be voyageurs but who had in reality no experience of River navigation, their object being to obtain a passage to the North West at the public cost. These men...gave a good deal of trouble, and had in several cases to be dismissed, while those taken from the Indian settlements, and who were *bona fide* voyageurs acquitted themselves creditably." The London *Post* had described some of the *voyageurs* of the Red River expedition as "photographers, cooks, bank cashiers, a biscuit maker (10 years ago an Etonian dandy)—all out for a holiday."

It is both common and questionable to say that history repeats itself, but in the case of the Red River and Nile expeditions, the adage seems valid. The haste with which the Gordon relief expedition was organized in London had repercussions in Canada in the recruitment of the boatmen. As had been the case in the Red River expedition fourteen years earlier, there was no time to screen the volunteers effectively. Again there was no time to test their skills before signing them on. Novices again offered their services as experienced boatmen simply to obtain a passage to adventure—this time in Egypt—at public expense. As early as 5 September 1884, at least one anonymous observer in Winnipeg had publicly questioned whether some of the Manitoba contingent were really the men whom Wolseley required. Signing himself "Red River Expedition" in a letter in the Winnipeg *Daily Times*, he contended that they were "not the class of men required for the work to be done...[was it] necessary to send to Canada to get men of the class many in the Manitoba contingent belong to?... How will our men look beside the river drivers from the Ottawa—the descendents of the couriers du bois [*sic*] in Quebec?"

It was these *soi-disant* boatmen from Manitoba who, for a short while, gave the *voyageurs* a bad name. From among them came most of the "tinkers and tailors" whom Wolseley later said he did not want again. It was they and the lawyers, the office clerks, and the school teachers who, especially during the early weeks of the campaign, showed such gross incompetence that several British war correspondents had sent reports to their newspapers that the *voyageurs* as a whole were proving worthless. Here, the reporters thought, was colourful material to please their editors. If the number of incompetents was inflated, the copy was that much better. For example, the London *Morning Post* printed a tendentious story about the *voyageurs* on 13 November, which its correspondent had filed from Wadi Halfa even before the Canadians had arrived there:

> I alluded in a recent telegram to the unruly conduct of the Canadian *Voyageurs*. They hardly promise well to be a success. Each man carried a bottle of spirits, many were drunk and were fighting with each other, brandishing their knives, and did not pay the slightest attention to their officers and these, of course, knew nothing of their men, many of whom were not *Voyageurs* at all but simply "trippers"—clerks and others who have got employed on the job just for the sake of the high pay.

Alexander MacDonald, the Canadian who was a war correspondent for a syndicate of five English newspapers, later attributed such distorted stories to the sheer laziness of some of his colleagues.

> Colonel Kennedy, as well as the doctor and the other officers of the Voyageurs, expressed their strong indignation at certain statements which had appeared in a London paper about them, in a letter from its correspondent at Gemai, dated the day before their arrival there.
>
> His statement was that the Canadians, when coming up the river, were armed with either a bottle of rum or a revolver, or both. He also charged them with disorderly conduct. When taken to task for these statements by the late Colonel Kennedy and Dr. Neilson, his only excuse

was that "he had heard so," and yet upon mere hearsay evidence this gentleman wrote to an influential London journal that which was utterly untrue respecting a body of men who had come from their distant western home to serve the Queen and country on the Nile.[2]

Denison himself was equally indignant and disturbed by the unfounded reports that were appearing in certain London newspapers.

> I hear some lying accounts of my men have been telegraphed out from Assuan, saying they were mutinous etc. It is all manufactured. This is the worst country for lying reports I ever saw, and as it is full of correspondents, each anxious to get something new, they send it off without making any inquiries—and it serves its purpose of filling up their telegrams or letters—and when the denial comes it is forgotten.

Most of the charges made about the *voyageurs* were unfounded. Why the initial allegations continued to be made about the men even after they had begun to acquit themselves well remains at least partly inexplicable. One reason, as already noted, was the first impression made by the incompetence of some of the Winnipeg volunteers.[3] Another factor similarly distorted for the sake of a "story" was the easy-going attitude of the *voyageurs*. They were civilians throughout. Although theoretically under military discipline, they were almost never subjected to it. In short, they did not behave like British soldiers. Some of the London correspondents evidently believed that the Canadians should have emulated the British tommy in discipline and obedience. But the free and easy *voyageurs* themselves certainly did not see their role in that light. They looked upon the tactful Denison and their other officers in the same way as they regarded their "bosses" on the Canadian rivers: as men like themselves, sharing their hardships and dangers, and, by virtue of having proven their exceptional abilities, qualified to lead them. It was a subtle relationship which a British officer or war correspondent, accustomed to the clearly defined distinctions between officer and man in Victoria's army, would not readily appreciate.[4] The independence of the Canadians shocked the British officers as much as their resourcefulness impressed them. There was little love between most of the *voyageurs* and many of the British officers. The volunteers from Australia, Canada, or elsewhere in the Empire were generally more enthusiastic to serve in imperial campaigns than the War Office was to have them. Later, these attitudes would be reversed, but in 1884 many professional British officers resented the presence of colonial volunteers who did not seem to have the proper respect for military traditions and discipline among their forces.

Denison provided a rather more elaborate explanation of why adverse stories had appeared about the *voyageurs* in the British press. "That correspondent must be either a knave or a fool," he noted, speaking about the author of one such story,

> I rather fancy the man must be a fool—for his letter from Wady Halfa saying we carried bowie knives and were all drunk was written on the 25 October and we did not arrive there until the 26th October. So some one having a jealousy of us has been stuffing him—"pulling his leg" as they say here—and he was damn fool enough to believe it, and did not make the slightest effort to ascertain the correctness of the report. There was not the slightest atom of truth in it—not even enough to hinge a lie on. . . . I have not had the time or the inclination to answer all the lies that have been circulated against us. I would have had my hands full if I had attempted it. We had a good deal to contend with at first—two elements. First—a certain class who were jealous of us having been brought all the way from Canada to do what they thought was their work, and secondly, there is I see in England a good deal of politics as well as in Canada or the States, and as this Expedition has been started by Gladstone certain opposition papers consider it their duty to their party to abuse it, and find fault with every one connected with it. These papers seize any idle rumour that they think will please their party or readers and exaggerate it to make it readable—and interesting. But my men have done such good work and proved themselves such good men, they have been obliged—aye forced—to give them the credit, that they are now giving them.

Denison was never in any doubt about the value to the expedition of the work done by his *voyageurs*. He wrote to Lord Melgund, "I am glad to say that our men are doing excellent work here and are invaluable. Some of the 'hardest cases' make the best men on the river.[5] One officer . . . was so pleased with his men [i.e., the *voyageurs* assigned to his regiment] that he left a present of £1 apiece for them. Two other captains of the same Regiment spoke to me in highest terms of them and other officers the same." As the campaign lengthened, so the reputation of the *voyageurs* increased.

Lest Denison's account of their value be thought biased, four considered opinions might be noted. Brackenbury later wrote, "Without them, the descent of the river would have been impossible. Officers and men, they had worked with increasing energy and a complete disregard of danger."[6] Colonel Butler was in no doubt about the correctness of the decision to bring the boatmen to work on the Nile rapids. Wolseley agreed with him in a letter to Lord Lansdowne on 13 April from Cairo: "I desire to place on record, not only my own opinion, but that of every officer connected with the direction and management of the boat columns, that the services of these voyageurs had been of the greatest possible value, and further, that their conduct throughout has been excellent. They have earned for themselves a high reputation among the troops up the Nile."[7] One of the soldiers later recorded,

these imported voyageurs, greatly discredited by some of the commentators on this campaign, were absolutely indispensable. A few, it is true, were adventurers, humbugs, of no help whatever, but the main body of them were experts in the handling of boats in torrential waters, and had it not been for their guidance and help many boats would have been wrecked and countless lives lost.[8]

Finally, a British officer intimately "connected with the direction and management of the boat columns" stated, echoing Wolseley's praise,

the employment of the voyageurs was a most pronounced success. Without them it is to be doubted whether the boats would have got up at all, and it may be certain that if they had, they would have been far longer in doing so, and the loss of life would have been much greater than has been the case. There was, I imagine, no one connected in any way with the working of the whalers up the river, who did not feel that had double the number of voyageurs been available, work could have been found for them all, and the progress of the expedition would have been materially benefited thereby.[9]

But if the opinions of Wolseley, Denison, Butler, Grove, and Brackenbury are to be regarded with reserve because they were all connected with the original idea of recruiting the boatmen, one final comment might be noted. It came from a man who had at first maintained that the *voyageurs* were not needed since native Egyptian boatmen would do just as well or even better. However, John Cook, Thomas Cook's son, soon changed his mind after he had travelled to Korti on an inspection tour and had seen the Canadians at work. Later, during a lecture to the Royal Geographic Society in London, Cook paid high tribute to their skill. "At least half the Canadians sent out were the finest boatmen he had ever come in contact with, and he was satisfied that the work they did, and the impetus they gave to the other men, would fully repay the Government for the cost of conveying them from Canada to Egypt."[10]

The Canadians had proven their worth. Their work was almost always hazardous and demanding. And in meeting its challenge, several were injured, many became sick, and some lost their lives. Sixteen of the 386 *voyageurs* who sailed from Quebec died during the course of the campaign, six from drowning,[11] three from typhoid fever, three from smallpox, two from other diseases, and two from falling off a train (one of the men crushed to death between the rail carriages was found to have a half crown coin in his boot; it was used to pay the Egyptian gravediggers at the European cemetery at Assiout to bury his body). One *voyageur* became insane. The circumstances surrounding the fatalities were sometimes most disagreeable. Egerton Denison, writing one night from the stern of his boat by candlelight, described for his brother, Clarence, how a few days earlier,

> Just after lunch I noticed something drifting down stream. I said to my Voyageur that I thought it was a man's body, so he went up the hill to try and see what it was and I went down stream on the bank. After going about half a mile the current brought the object near shore and it turned out to be the body of one of our Canadian Indians who had drowned some days before. I got two natives to swim out for the body which they brought ashore. I got a spade, dug a grave with the assistance of my Voyageur and buried the body, which was not pleasant being very much decomposed.[12]

This incident occurred on 26 November 1884, near Ambako where an eighteen-year-old Iroquois, John Morris—whose father had begged him not to volunteer—had drowned on November 16. It was Morris's body that Egerton Denison buried on the bank after it had been in the river for eight days. Three weeks later, another *voyageur*, Leon Chatelain of Ottawa, drowned near the place from which Egerton had written to his brother. Chatelain's body was discovered by the Sudanese who took it to British officers to receive the reward promised for delivering the bodies of any drowned British personnel. They had, however, first stripped Chatelain's body of its pocket watch and most of its clothing.

Frederick Denison later explained in a letter the principal reason why six of his boatmen had drowned during the course of the expedition: "it is not surprising when you know that in all the bad places we put a Canadian in the bow and stern and turn out all the soldiers. In this way only Canadians are in the boat if it upsets and they run the risk of being drowned."[13] On in-numerable occasions when such risks had to be run, the *voyageurs* proved themselves worthy of the high praise that they won.

The *voyageurs* were, of course, the most numerous and important group of Canadians to participate in Wolseley's vain effort to rescue his old comrade-in-arms. But there were also several others: the wheelsmen from Ottawa and Winnipeg; Arthur Haliburton at the War Office; Commander Edmund Van Koughnet; Major "Cupid" Wilson; Surgeon Anthony de Lom, and war correspondents Alexander MacDonald and St. Leger Herbert.

Many other Canadians would have been there as well, if they had been able to have their way. From various parts of the Empire, men hastened to volunteer for service in the elaborate effort to rescue the eccentric British officer who had become something of an imperial institution. In addition to the Canadians and the British, the *kroomen* from West Africa and the Arabs from Aden have already been noted. On the Red Sea coast, where the port of Suakin was held against the desultory attacks of Osman Digna, soldiers from other British colonies served under Major-General Sir Gerald Graham. As part of the British government's short-lived intention to vanquish the Mahdi following Gordon's death, a brigade of three thousand Sikhs, Bengalis, and other Indians were sent to Suakin during late February 1885, where they reinforced twenty-seven hundred British troops already there under Graham and Sir John McNeill. This Anglo-Indian force was intended to join in an advance on Berber from the coast, to parallel an expedition with the same destination that Wolseley was planning to send up the Nile in the autumn. To join the Anglo-Indian combined force, there came from New South Wales in Australia a battery of artillery and five hundred infantry-men. The genesis of this New South Wales contingent was an indirect result of the recruitment of the *voyageurs*. An inaccurate report reached Sydney that six hundred Canadians would take over garrison duties in Britain to allow more regular troops to help in the rescue of Gordon. The news of the decision of the government of New South Wales to send to the Red Sea a contingent from its minute militia in turn encouraged Canadian militiamen to redouble their efforts to go to Egypt.

A mixture of imperial sentiment and practical politics had led New South Wales to offer its small force for service in the Sudan. For the same reasons, her sister-colonies of South Australia, Victoria, and Queensland made similar offers and even reached the point of contemplating the novel idea of a joint Australian force. In addition, the distant island of Fiji and the Malayan State of Perak announced their readiness to send a few soldiers. However, by the time these offers of service from outposts of the Empire were received in London in the spring of 1885, the British government had more than enough troops in the Sudan to hold the line until the proposed autumn campaign. Why the Australian colonies had been so forward in offering troops for the Sudan is explained implicitly in a shrewd and remarkably frank letter that Sir John A. Macdonald sent to his old friend and high commissioner in London, Sir Charles Tupper. The high commissioner had been impressed by the Australian offer and had urged the same gesture on Macdonald. After receiving the prime minister's letter of 12 March 1885, Tupper can have been in no further doubt about the reasons why the government of Canada did not share the Australians' partly self-interested enthusiasm. In sending him such a letter, Macdonald formulated an attitude of detachment which would be recalled by later Canadian statesmen such as Mackenzie King when in search of a precedent for their own desire to avoid any automatic involvement in Britain's wars.

the time has not yet arrived, nor the occasion, for our volunteering military aid to the Mother Country.

We do not stand at all in the same position as the Australasia. The Suez Canal is nothing to us, and we do not ask England to quarrel with France or Germany for our sake. The offer of those colonies is a good move on their part, and somewhat like Cavour's sending Sardinian troops to the Crimea. Why should we waste men and money in this wretched business? England is not at war, but merely helping the Khedive to put down an insurrection, and now that Gordon is gone, the motive in aiding in the rescue of our countrymen is gone with him. Our men and money would therefore be sacrificed to get Gladstone and Co. out of the hole they have plunged themselves into by their own imbecility.

Again the reciprocal aid to be given by the Colonies and England should be a matter of treaty, deliberately entered into and settled on a permanent basis. The spasmodic offers of our Militia Colonels, anxious for excitement or notoriety, have roused unreasonable expectations in England, and are so far unfortunate. I dare say that a battalion or two of venturous spirits might be enlisted, but 7d a day will cool most men's war-like ardour.

Our artillery batteries are not enlisted for foreign service, and could not be ordered to the Soudan. The Fenians are beginning to show signs of life again in the U.S.A. and there are so many unemployed there that they may become dangerous again. They threaten to invade Canada if she sends troops against the Mahdi. Most of this is nonsense, but we can never calculate on what these people may do.[14]

Macdonald was opposed to any suggestion that militia units or other forces raised at the expense of Canada should be sent to the Sudan. But many

Canadians felt differently. Even before the *Ocean King* had sailed from Quebec City, Lord Lansdowne had informed the Colonial Office that "The number of applications from officers desiring to accompany the party has been very large. I could with the greatest ease have obtained the services of upwards of 100 many of them in every way suitable for the purpose. In one or two cases whole corps have volunteered but I have explained that the voyageurs, being regarded as non-combatants I did not regard myself as at liberty to engage any body of men having a military organization of its own."[15] Gordon's fate and that of the expedition sent to rescue him was a matter of daily interest to newspaper readers in Canada. As the autumn of 1884 passed, news and rumours about the Sudan multiplied: Gordon had marched out of Khartoum; the Mahdi had marched in; Gordon was dead; the Mahdi was dead; Gordon had defeated the Mahdi; the Mahdi had defeated Gordon. It was all headline news. And it all whetted the appetite of young Canadians who still hoped to join the great adventure that was playing itself out within their Empire on the other side of the world.

Both Macdonald and Lansdowne, however, maintained their respective attitudes throughout the winter of 1884–85. Macdonald was not opposed to the recruitment of troops in Canada for the regular British army. But he was strongly opposed to the use of Canadian militia units in imperial adventures or attempts to involve Canada directly in the Sudan. For his part, Lansdowne, who had only been asked to recruit five hundred civilian *voyageurs* and eight wheelsmen, made no attempt to change the prime minister's attitude. Yet applications from Canadians to join the expedition continued to pour in, some to the Department of the Militia, but most direct to the governor general's office.[16] The news of Gordon's death only increased the flow of applications. There was no doubt in the minds of many Canadians that early retribution would be made.

Major-General J. Wimburn Laurie, a former British army officer who had served in Canada and had chosen to retire in Nova Scotia, was one of the first to offer "to raise troops or render any service." Arthur Williams of Port Hope, a member of parliament who was also a militia colonel, sent a telegram to the high commissioner in London, proposing recruitment from the 46th East Durham Regiment. All the attempts to see service in the Sudan were not, however, made by militia or retired officers: privates and non-commissioned officers also shared their imperial sentiments and sent their applications to the governor general. An offer to search for water in the desert was submitted by a Canadian company specializing in the drilling of artesian wells. A steamboat captain in British Columbia had heard that the British government was building fifty riverboats for service on the Nile. He not only offered to help navigate them but, after the Mahdi had been vanquished, he would volunteer "to join a company to run them on the Nile for commercial purposes."[17]

During the early spring of 1885, after the death of Gordon, a minor epidemic of volunteering swept over Canada. From Ontario, Manitoba, Quebec, the Maritimes, British Columbia, and even from the United States, offers arrived to aid in the rescue of Gordon or, later, in the punishment of those who had killed him. Lansdowne asked London what he should do. The Colonial Office advised him to discuss it with Sir John A. Macdonald. The prime minister remained consistent. He had not changed his mind. He replied to Lansdowne on 10 February 1885, "I think that if any volunteers are accepted from Canada, they must be enlisted as part of the Regular [British] Service and not as [Canadian] militia. Our militia cannot be called out as such except under the 61st clause of the Militia Act of 1883 and it would be straining the meaning of the clause to hold that the state of things in Egypt warranted such a call."[18] Macdonald suggested that if Britain really needed troops, they might be recruited in Canada as they had been at the time of the Indian Mutiny in 1858. Volunteers had then been enrolled for service in the regular British army, and Canada was not involved in their subsequent employment.

This cautious attitude on the part of the Canadian prime minister was, in fact, entirely satisfactory to London. Colonial troops were really neither welcomed by professional British officers nor required, but no one wanted to hurt the feelings of those offering them. At a meeting of the British cabinet on 9 February 1885, Joseph Chamberlain, the president of the Board of Trade, had raised the possibility of Canada being invited to send troops to reinforce Suakin, and five days later, Sir Charles Dilke, the president of the Local Government Board, supported such a request in a letter to Lord Rosebery, the Lord Privy Seal. On 20 February, however, the cabinet decided that any Canadian force would be too little and too late compared with the offer of a fully equipped contingent from New South Wales. Sir Charles Tupper nevertheless continued to urge that Canadian troops be offered for service in the Sudan at Canadian expense. For his efforts, he received from Macdonald the letter already quoted to the effect that Canadian men and money should not be "sacrificed to get Gladstone and Co. out of the hole they have plunged themselves into by their own imbecility."

Before long, Britain herself was withdrawing from the Sudan. The question of further Canadian participation disappeared as the British retreated down the Nile. By the autumn of 1885, while difficulties with Russia distracted the attention of the British public and a permanent defensive line was established near the present Egyptian-Sudanese border, the mass epidemic of imperial enthusiasm subsided in Canada. The Canadian *voyageurs* were already back at work in their woods. The militiamen had to be content with their drill halls.

Imperial enthusiasm had not saved Gordon. Too much procrastination on Gladstone's part, too little of Thomas Cook's coal between Assuan and Wadi Halfa, too many stores in the whalers, not enough camels in the desert, and too many responsibilities on Wolseley himself had combined to ensure the failure of the expedition. The staff organization of Victoria's army was so inadequate that Wolseley was required to be at several places at the same time to make a multitude of decisions necessary to maintain the momentum of the expedition, let alone its acceleration. Wolseley's "Ring" was no longer what it once had been. It was now top-heavy, riven with jealousy and dissension, and often a real hindrance to the swift progress of the relief force. Indeed, after a study of various accounts of the Nile expedition, it is surprising that it went forward as rapidly as it did rather than that it failed to save Gordon from the final onrush of the dervishes. Basically what was wrong was Wolseley's calculation that a large, fully equipped force could make its way up the Nile at a rate comparable to the rapid progress his Red River expedition had made fifteen years before. The seed of the trouble was in Butler's bland assumption that "water is water and rock is rock." In fact, as the elderly French Canadian Coteau had pointed out to Butler on Christmas Day, the rivers and lakes of Canada were frequently turbulent and dangerous, but it was also often possible, in smooth stretches, to move swiftly along them. The villainous Nile offered little such respite or opportunity to offset the delays of portages or rapids. In short, water was not water, and, ultimately, this erroneous belief was a major factor in the failure of the expedition.

But failure though the Gordon relief expedition was, it had been an occasion for gestures of imperial solidarity. It established a precedent. For another fourteen years, the possibility of large numbers of Canadians serving abroad in an imperial cause did not arise. During that time, however, the memory of military service—and even the offers of service—in an imperial venture did not die among Canadians. The great Sudan expedition in which the French-speaking and English-speaking Canadians had worked side by side became an event in the gradual evolution of Canadian nationhood. Memoirs and lectures by the participants and "Maxime Labelle; A Canadian Voyageur's Account of the Nile Expedition," the curious work of an admiring Canadian poet, W. H. Drummond,[19] did much to keep alive pride in the achievements of the *voyageurs* and to make it a factor in later stimulating other Canadians to volunteer for service in Britain's imperial enterprises. More immediately there remained the problem of what "Canadian" skills might be used in any future excursion into the Sudan.

11

Reculer pour Mieux Sauter

The country over which the breath of the West . . . has once passed . . . can never
be the same as it was before. The new foundations must be of the Western, not
the Eastern type.

EARL OF CROMER
ANCIENT AND MODERN IMPERIALISM

By the autumn of 1885, the *voyageurs* were back on those sparkling rivers
that they knew so much better than the muddy, treacherous Nile. Canadian militiamen had reluctantly given up their intoxicating ideas of imperial
adventures in distant Egypt. The Mahdists controlled the Sudan. And the
voyageurs once again had all the salt pork and beans that they could eat and
a medal to testify to their service to the Queen. The Mahdists continued,
however, to be an unpredictable threat to the future peace and security of
Egypt. Gordon had foreseen as early as February 1884 that the borders of
Egypt and, indeed, Egypt itself could not be secure until the Mahdi was
"smashed up." The British government, by its later actions, eventually
acknowledged that Gordon had been right.

The Mahdi himself eluded British revenge. Surrounded by his silks and
slaves, his wives and worshippers, he died suddenly in Khartoum on 22 June
1885 of the same disease which had caused the deaths of so many British
soldiers: typhoid fever.[1] There was something fitting in the death of the
Mahdi only five months after the death of his adversary, Gordon. The duel
between those two religious fanatics had been, to a degree, a personal one.
The Mahdi died at the pinnacle of his very considerable power. In less than
four years, he had risen from obscurity to reign over a land as large as India;
he had defeated soldiers from nations much more powerful than his; his
religious image, despite debaucheries, had remained unblemished in the eyes
of his followers. Yet if he had lived and had proceeded any further with his
ambitious plans to invade Egypt and then Europe (where he would, he said,
convert the pope), he would inevitably have been defeated before he had
advanced much farther northward. He stopped in time. Britain could not
have let him move down the Nile beyond Wadi Halfa or let him enter Egypt
proper, especially since the country was in such an unstable condition.

That "Bloody Halfway" marked the northernmost point to which the

British would tolerate an advance by the dervishes was made abundantly clear as early as 30 December 1885, less than four months after the departure of the last of Wolseley's troops. The Mahdi's successor, his most faithful lieutenant and disciple, the equally debauched and despotic Khalifa Abdu Allah, learned exactly the extent of British tolerance when he was decisively defeated at Ginnis, near Wadi Halfa, by a combined Anglo-Egyptian force commanded by General Stephenson with a brigade led by William Butler. The line had now been drawn and no dervish would ever cross it. As a biographer of Gladstone noted, the British government "decided to retire from the Sudan and to fix the southern frontier of Egypt where it was left for twelve years, until apprehension of designs of another European power on the upper waters of the Nile was held to demand a new policy."[2]

Despite this initial setback, the Khalifa was determined to continue his messiah's crusade against "the Turks." But before he could do so, he had to consolidate his own precarious position in the Sudan itself. He withdrew his troops back into the province of Dongola to assert his authority by the sword over a number of factions who were contesting his right to succeed the Mahdi. To quell all the rebels took four years. Then the Khalifa tried for a second time to invade Egypt. However, the destruction of his army at Toski on 3 August 1889, when twelve hundred of his warriors were slain, put to an end, for the time being at least, any plans for an invasion of Egypt.

That the Khalifa's attention was for four years fully engaged in countering internal dissension was entirely satisfactory to the British government and, in particular, to Sir Evelyn Baring in Cairo. During 1886, a strongly held defensive line had been established by an Anglo-Egyptian army in the arid, rock-strewn desert near the second cataract at Wadi Halfa. Once this border had been secured, a period of peace descended on Egypt. The *Pax Britannica* was able to begin to make its blessings felt where the *Pax Romana* long before had also brought order and prosperity. This was, after all, the advantage for Egypt that the occupation had all along been supposed to provide; a period of peace would provide the opportunity for the humanist ideals of liberal English gentlemen to be applied in tranquillity. There was no longer any talk of early British evacuation of Egypt. The Sudan apparently could be safely left in the hands of the Sudanese. But Egypt could not be left in the hands of Egyptians. No European power had yet evinced any close interest in the Sudan, but several, notably France, continued to envy Britain's position astride the Suez Canal. And Russia seemed to be constantly pressing in the direction of the eastern Mediterranean and India. Britain could no longer employ the declining Ottoman Empire as a first line of defence against Russian intrigue; increasingly the demands of imperial strategy as well as the omnipresent threat of internal anarchy in Egypt kept soldiers such as Kitchener and administrators such as Baring in Cairo. From their efforts flowed economic development and justice. Yet these material advances did not reconcile nationalist Egyptians to the presence of the British in their midst. The liberal dreams of Britain remained dreams. It gradually became evident that no sound, dependable, and independent ally would soon be fostered in Egypt. Britain was in Egypt for a long stay.

While the Khalifa gradually consolidated his rule on the Upper Nile, the British consolidated theirs on the Lower Nile. But by late 1890, after the Battle of Toski, the dervishes and the Anglo-Egyptian forces were once again eyeing each other warily. The reason the British in Egypt looked again southward was, simply, their conviction that their paramount position in India and the Far East would be threatened if any other European nation secured control of even part of the Nile Valley. From there it might threaten the Suez Canal. For years the Khalifa might go on imagining that the reason "the Turks" did not move against him was because they were afraid of him. But the day that another European power began to show an interest in the Sudan, the Khalifa received about as much respect from the British as a bankrupt tenant can expect from a powerful landlord bent on eviction. That the British regarded the Sudan as their own private preserve was never in doubt—at least not in London. The tenants might be the Mahdists, but the absentee landlord was Britain. "If the Dervishes have occupied the valley of the Nile, they do not pledge the future in any way," Salisbury wrote in his inimitable style to Baring on 21 November 1890,

> Whenever you have money enough to go to Khartoum, the resources of civilisation will be adequate to the subjugation of the country. If you leave them for the present where they are they can destroy nothing, for there is nothing to destroy: they cannot erect any domination which shall make the conquest of them a formidable task, for they have, practically speaking, neither cannon nor machine-guns, nor even the ammunition for ordinary rifles. Surely, if you are *not* ready to go to Khartoum, this people were created for the purpose of keeping the bed warm for you till you can occupy it.[3]

The prime minister's complacency about the dervishes was justifiable. It stemmed partly from the knowledge that the Sudanese were yet so primitive that they could not possibly tamper with the flow of the Nile or its annual cycle of rise and fall. The prosperity of Egypt depended almost entirely on the irrigation water provided by the Nile. Salisbury's fear, shared by many of his countrymen, that the flow of the river could be radically altered by the skill of modern European engineers was greatly exaggerated. But exaggerated or not, as soon as Italians from Ethiopia, French and Belgians from central Africa, and Germans from east Africa began to move in the general direction of the Sudanese vacuum, the reconquest of the country by Anglo-Egyptian forces began to be considered seriously. Some writers have maintained that retaking the Sudan was, to Englishmen, a necessary act of retaliation for Gordon's death and for the national humiliation of Wolseley's subsequent withdrawal. For Salisbury the reconquest was never so. He did not share such jingoist fancies. He did not move a finger to retake the Sudan until it seemed clear to him that another European power might attempt to establish its influence over the headwaters of the Nile. Then he moved suddenly. His mind once made up, Salisbury hastened to implement his essentially defensive policy.

Salisbury's decision to reconquer the Sudan was easier to make by 1895 than it would have been eight or nine years earlier when he had first come to power. By then it had become obvious to Major F. R. Wingate, the head of the Egyptian Army Intelligence Service, that despite the Khalifa's best efforts to maintain control of the whole of the Sudan from his capital at Khartoum, his empire was, in fact, gradually disintegrating. The Sudan was reverting to tribal factions. Wingate's analysis of its actual circumstances under the Khalifa was supported by the appearance of two highly dramatic books, Father Ohrwalder's *Ten Years' Captivity in the Mahdi's Camp* and Slatin Pasha's *Fire and Sword in the Sudan.* As well as being immediate best-sellers in Britain and, therefore, potent in reviving public interest in the Sudan, both books, written by Europeans who had escaped after having been held captive for many years by the Mahdists, contended that the dervishes had been seriously weakened by famine as well as internecine quarrels.[4] By 1895 anarchy was, apparently, not far off in the Sudan.

Salisbury had all long been alive to the danger of just such a situation. If tribal anarchy, instead of the Khalifa, ruled, other European powers would be all the more tempted to intrude. "The pivot of the whole question of a movement into the Sudan has always seemed to me to be the condition of the... Khalifa's power." The under-secretary at the Foreign Office, Sir Edward Grey, well summarized Salisbury's feelings when he wrote in January 1897,

> when the Khalifa's power breaks up anarchy must ensue. This anarchy produces such disorder and weakness on the Egyptian frontier that you are almost bound to interfere: but it does more than this, it creates a standing temptation and provocation for other powers, be they Belgians or French, or some devilry working through Abyssinian intrigue, to interfere, to occupy, and to establish claims for themselves. ... As long as the Khalifa was strong it did not so much matter.[5]

A subsidiary consideration which assisted Salisbury in his decision to begin the reconquest of the Sudan was the increasingly healthy state of Egyptian finances and, perhaps even more important, of the Egyptian army. That Salisbury was, if necessary, prepared to use British money and British soldiers to maintain his policy of excluding any other European influence from the Sudan was finally demonstrated by events. But he knew that the British public would be more willing to contemplate a campaign against the dervishes if it were paid for in Egyptian pounds and Egyptian lives. That Egypt was able to pay for a final showdown with the dervishes was a result of the efficiency of Baring[6] and his capable lieutenants, such as Alfred Milner. Milner wrote an account of his services under Baring, *England in Egypt*,[7] which, with the second volume of Baring's own *Modern Egypt*, gives a good picture of the strenuous—and largely successful—efforts that the British overlords made to move Egyptian finances from the debit to the credit side of the ledger and to bring the *fellaheen* a degree of justice and prosperity that had hitherto been unknown. Milner's book complemented the works of Ohrwalder and Slatin, which had made such a strong appeal to the British sense of pride and adventure. Milner appealed to British missionary zeal which found partial expression in the development of materially backward countries. *England in Egypt* enjoyed almost as great a popular success as the two earlier books. Winston Churchill has well described the impact of *England in Egypt*: "the book was more than a book. The words rang like the trumpet-call which rallies the soldiers after the parapets are stormed, and summons them to complete the victory."[8] The completion of the victory, the work of pacification and order, had been left undone, and few Englishmen can rest content with a job half-done. Credit for the fact that the job could now be finished, that the Egyptian army could now initiate the campaign, was not only Baring's and Milner's but also Herbert Kitchener's. It is well to pause here to look more closely at this veteran of Wolseley's expedition in whose hands the future of the Sudan was placed and under whom a Canadian officer was to win great fame by his engineering skill.

A thirty-five-year-old lieutenant-colonel in the Royal Engineeers when Gladstone had, as his critics said, "scuttled" the Sudan in 1885, Kitchener had doffed the Arab disguise he had worn during his service under Wolseley and cast about for new employment to help satisfy his vaulting ambition. First in Zanzibar, then as governor of Suakin, then as a cavalry officer at the Battle of Toski, and finally as adjutant general of the Egyptian army, Kitchener had added to his already formidable knowledge of the Middle East and to his reputation as a brave and extraordinarily competent officer. With the decisive support of Baring, he was appointed Sirdar or commander-in-chief of the Egyptian army at the early age of forty-two. "That appointment," one of his biographers has rightly noted, "which was dated 13 April, 1892, was received with surprise and disgust by the entire Egyptian Army."[9] Kitchener was a severe man, exacting and often harsh in his treatment of his subordinates. He would not tolerate weakness or even ill-fortune. If an officer achieved a reputation for bad luck, he was soon transferred to some insignificant post. Kitchener was, in short, self-centred, arrogant, and unpopular. However, none, not even the many enemies whom he had made during his scramble for promotion, could deny his energy, his efficiency, and his outstanding ability. The result was that Sirdar Kitchener successfully brought to completion the work of reorganizing and retraining the Egyptian army begun so ably by his predecessors, Generals Sir Evelyn Wood and Sir Francis Grenfell. Kitchener was determined to go to the top of the British army and win for himself a place in the innermost circles of the Empire. Egypt and the Sudan were two important stepping-stones on the way.

The ruthless Kitchener was seen by some as more like a machine than a man. A war correspondent later suggested that "he ought to be patented and shown with pride at the Paris International Exhibition. British Empire: Exhibit No. 1, *hors concours*, the Sudan Machine."[10] Kitchener ordered the strictest economies in the Egyptian army. He demanded unquestioning devotion and efficiency from all British officers serving under him. These he recruited personally when on leave in London, his back ramrod stiff and his great mustache carefully groomed, in a little room facing the top of the main staircase of the Junior United Service Club. Celibacy, efficiency, and loyalty Kitchener asked of all of his subordinates. In return, he gave them great responsibility and active support in forwarding their careers. Consequently, there grew around him a devoted group of young officers who became known as Kitchener's "band of boys." There were among them no fashionable young men such as had come out from London between "seasons" for the Battle of Tel-el-Kebir and no amateur soldiers such as had accompanied Wolseley up the Nile. Kitchener's career officers resembled more the heroes of the *Boys' Own Paper* or contemporary "penny dreadfuls." It was not the chance of a few months of adventure which had brought them to the Egyptian army. Ten years before, on his way to help rescue Gordon, Buller had written to his wife about some of the officers, "One thing amuses me and that is the way some of these gay young men who have come medal hunting have got sold. There are some real good soldiers among them, but there are others who would never have been here had they had the least idea they were going to be kept here this summer."[11] Kitchener's "band of boys" were, on the contrary, fully aware of the hardships which would face them during their years in Egypt, but they followed their machine-like general with all the devotion and efficiency of the ardent professional soldier.

In 1892 the new Sirdar was as convinced of the necessity and, indeed, the righteousness of the reconquest of the Sudan as he had been when he had reluctantly joined in the withdrawal of Wolseley's rearguard. Hence, during the four years between 1892 and 1896, Kitchener had trained his new army mercilessly. It soon differed greatly from the armed rabble that had once broken in the face of wild dervish charges. Under the bright Egyptian sun, both *fellaheen* from Egypt and "niggers" from the Sudan learned their drill to perfection. On the frontier at Wadi Halfa, they were occasionally engaged in small skirmishes which taught them what it was to be under enemy fire. By 1896 the Egyptian army was fully trained, thanks to the combined efforts of Wood, Grenfell, and especially Kitchener. The Egyptian treasury was full as a result of Baring's economies and development plans. Even various tribes in the northern Sudan, formerly loyal to the Khalifa, had been subverted by Wingate's secret agents. The time for reconquest of the Sudan was ripe. And imperial considerations now required it.

Action by Britain suddenly became imperative as a result of the crushing defeat an Italian army of thirty thousand suffered at Adowa, Ethiopia, on 1 March 1896. London was dismayed by the astonishing Ethiopian victory and horrified by such tales of Ethiopian cruelty as the castration of Italian prisoners. It seemed clear to many British that not only was the Italian colony of Eritrea threatened but also that Egypt itself might be endangered if the victorious Ethiopians and the dervishes once joined forces. Italy had been humiliated by her defeat. Her pro-British policies in Europe would now be in jeopardy if Britain did not come to her assistance. The time, it was clear, had arrived for Britain to act. "The decision [to which the Cabinet came yesterday]," Salisbury explained to Baring [now Lord Cromer], "was inspired specially by a desire to help the Italians ... and to prevent the Dervishes from winning a conspicuous success which might have far-reaching results. In addition, we desired to kill two birds with one stone, and to use the same military effort to plant the foot of Egypt rather farther up the Nile."[12]

The principal reason why Her Majesty's government sanctioned an advance up the Nile in 1896 by the Egyptian army was not, in fact, to help the Italians in Ethiopia but rather to use the Italian difficulties as an opportunity for moving back into the Sudan. "With the object of effecting a diversion in [the Italians'] favour," Lord Lansdowne, now the secretary of state for war, candidly noted in a cabinet memorandum, "we have announced to the European Powers that we intend to advance up the Valley of the Nile. . . . Our explanations to Lord Cromer have, however, been more specific for we have told him that while the movement was intended to help the Italians, the ulterior object was to restore a portion of her lost territory to Egypt."[13] It was believed by some in London that the victorious Ethiopians, united with the dervishes, might soon become the tools of the French. Already disturbing rumours of French intrigue on the Upper Nile were beginning to reach

London. Salisbury would not tolerate the French astride the Blue Nile, let alone the Nile itself. Both French influence and Ethiopian-Sudanese co-operation had to be forestalled.

The moment for such action was largely of British choosing. It was not, except in the immediate sense just noted, forced on the British. The decision to advance into the Sudan was based on dispassionate, objective calculations. It was, in a sense, like a business enterprise: for a long period the costs had been carefully weighed against the advantages to be gained. By 1896 the profits were calculated to be substantial. Only then were final plans made. That these plans were difficult to make was not the result of the actions of men; natural obstacles still posed the main problems for an advance up the Nile. Unlike Wolseley, Kitchener could make his plans without worrying very much about enemy attack for, except well into the Sudan, no threat existed. The frontier between Egypt and the Sudan was now a large no-man's land where tribal anarchy prevailed. On the other hand, Kitchener, unlike Wolseley, was not undertaking the campaign as a British general commanding British forces. He was Sirdar of the Egyptian army dependent upon Egyptian resources. Wolseley could draw upon the resources of the whole British Empire once his expedition was under way; Kitchener could not look with any assurance beyond the limited resources of Egypt itself. Wolseley's campaign of 1884–85 had been a War Office campaign, carried out at the express wish of Her Majesty's Government. Kitchener's campaigns were sanctioned by imperial interests, but they were carried out by Egyptian forces acting on Foreign Office instructions received through Lord Cromer.

Given the limited resources of Egypt and the unknown character of its new army—it had not yet been tested in a major battle—London decided that a small bite of the Sudan should be taken before any attempt was made to devour the whole. That first bite was naturally the northernmost of the Sudanese provinces. Since it bordered on the defensive line near Wadi Halfa, Dongola was the obvious target for the initial Egyptian advance. Such a limited movement had been anticipated by the Sirdar. He had long been convinced that, sooner or later, the Egyptian army would be called upon to reconquer the Sudan, province by province. The training of the Egyptian army, its supply organization, and its intelligence network had been organized in anticipation of those orders. By 1896, when the call came, the army was ready to put its plans and training to the test. Kitchener's intelligence staff, led by the capable Wingate, had collected enormous amounts of information of great value to an army marching through Dongola and beyond during the preceding years. Twelve years before, Wolseley's army had suffered from the prevailing ignorance about the Sudan. Kitchener could draw upon a mass of information which removed much of the guesswork that had hindered Wolseley's advance up the Nile.

Moreover, the two expeditions differed in spirit. Wolseley's had been an extemporaneous crusade hurriedly put together to rescue the man whom many Victorians had regarded as the "verray, parfit gentil knyght." It had been a race against time, an adventure in which every day counted if the Muslim besieging Khartoum was to be vanquished and Gordon rescued. There was none of this haste in the various stages of Kitchener's measured advance. Nor was there any of the romantic glamour of Wolseley's vain efforts. Time was on Kitchener's side. No undue haste complicated his operations, no ignorance of tribes or terrain impeded his progress, no besieged countryman awaited his rescue. He could set the pace of his army. Kitchener enjoyed yet another advantage over Wolseley. He could rely on the sympathy and understanding of the commander-in-chief of the British army since the commander-in-chief was no longer the crusty and conservative Duke of Cambridge but Wolseley himself. In August 1895 Wolseley had at last realized his lifelong ambition of being appointed head of the army.

Confidence spread through the whole of the Egyptian army in the spring of 1896 as orders for the reconquest of Dongola arrived in Cairo. Shortly before midnight on 12 March 1896, Kitchener received the anticipated orders from London. During the following days, as supplies were loaded on Messrs. Thomas Cook's pleasure steamers, as soldiers boarded trains, and as the last details of the advance were decided upon by Kitchener and his staff, the conviction spread throughout the Egyptian army that, although Dongola might be the immediate objective, there would really be no stopping until Khartoum itself had been retaken. Lord Cromer had no doubts about the outcome. "When once the British and Egyptian troops were brought face to face with the enemy," he later observed, "there could . . . be little doubt of the result. The speedy and successful issue of the campaign depended, in fact, almost entirely upon the methods adopted for overcoming the very exceptional difficulties connected with the supply and transport of troops. The main quality required to meet those difficulties was a good head for business. . . . Kitchener . . . was an excellent man of business; he looked carefully after every important detail."[14]

The Sudan campaign of 1896-99 was, in the sense that Cromer noted, a business undertaking. Its success would largely depend on its supply arrangements. Kitchener's steady advance up the Nile was in one sense the supreme proof of Napoleon's dictum that an army travels on its stomach. Neither the advance into the province of Dongola nor finally on Khartoum could be contemplated without the prior assurance of ample and uninterrupted supplies.

The essential differences between Wolseley's and Kitchener's campaigns manifested themselves in various ways but in no way more clearly than in their supply arrangements. Wolseley's measures, in comparison with Kitchener's, seem almost amateurish. Quickly conceived and implemented, Wolseley's plan to use whalers on the Nile to transport, feed, and supply his motley army was, perhaps, the most that could have been done in the urgent circumstances. Yet there remains something of a romantic sport, something even of a Sunday outing, in the scene of British soldiers and Canadian *voyageurs* struggling up the Nile in their whalers. The future commanding general of the Gallipoli expedition, Sir Ian Hamilton, later confessed that at first he and his fellow junior officers felt like "Boy Scouts dressed up like Red Indians let loose in a flotilla of canoes."[15]

There was nothing so colourful in Kitchener's careful plans. And something of the change in military life that had occurred between the two campaigns is evident. Only eleven years separated them, but while Wolseley's expedition looked back to the manpower and individual heroism of the Crimean War, Kitchener's looked ahead to the bigger wars, when machine power and all the scientific and technical advances of mankind were to be employed in the cause of destruction. Brawn and bravery carried Wolseley far up the Nile. But steam and careful staff work took Kitchener to Khartoum. The bullets and bandages, the pickles and champagne that Wolseley packed into his wonderful whalers, Kitchener simply loaded aboard a railroad that he had built across the desert.

Supplying an army is never glorious, but it is always essential. A secure supply line was, Kitchener knew, the one thing that would ensure his conquest of the Sudan. A railroad would be the ideal answer to all the logistic problems raised by a campaign across a desert. A railroad he was determined to have. In his *River War*, Winston Churchill described in his inimitable way this essential element in Kitchener's success.

It often happens that in prosperous public enterprises the applause of the nation and the rewards of the sovereign are bestowed on those whose offices are splendid and whose duties have been dramatic. Others whose labours were no less difficult, responsible, and vital to success are unnoticed. If this be true of men, it is also true of things. In a tale of war the reader's mind is filled with the fighting. The battle—with its vivid scenes, its moving incidents, its plain and tremendous results—excites imagination and commands attention. The eye is fixed on the fighting brigades as they move amid the smoke; on the swarming figures of the enemy; on the General, serene and determined, mounted in the middle of his Staff. The long trailing line of communications is unnoticed. The fierce glory that plays on red, triumphant bayonets dazzles the observer; nor does he care to look behind to where, along a thousand miles of rail, road, and river, the convoys are crawling to the front in uninterrupted succession. Victory is the beautiful, bright-coloured flower. Transport is the stem without which it could never have blossomed.[16]

Two fundamental problems faced both Wolseley and Kitchener: mobility and supply. To solve them, Wolseley had looked to Canada. And it was from that same source of transport expertise that Kitchener sought his solutions. There was no lack of Canadian volunteers. Colonel James Domville, the commanding officer of the 8th (New Brunswick) Hussars, offered to build and operate a steamboat, a railway, and a telegraph line for the British army advancing into the Sudan, a proposal for which he was warmly thanked by Joseph Chamberlain, the secretary of state for the colonies, and then heard no more. Colonel Sam Hughes, an ardent imperialist (who was minister of militia at the beginning of the First World War), urged in vain upon both Sir Wilfrid Laurier and Chamberlain that either a permanent force infantry battalion or a special unit of Canadian volunteers be sent. Neither London nor Cairo wanted any such units. Kitchener knew exactly what he wanted. The desert railroad was the stem of Churchill's bright-coloured flower. The gardener, to extend the metaphor, who caused that flower to flourish was a young Canadian, Percy Girouard.

12

On the Road to Dongolay

On the road to Dongolay
Where the dying camels lay,
And the sun comes down like hell-fire,
And grows hotter day by day.

BRITISH ARMY PARODY OF
KIPLING'S "ON THE ROAD TO MANDALAY"

Edouard Percy Cranwell Girouard was born in Montreal on 26 January 1867. His paternal ancestors had been settled in Canada for a century and a half, having arrived in Quebec from France in 1720. His mother, Essie Cranwell, the daughter of a physician from County Wexford, Ireland, had been raised in New Orleans. In 1863 she married a young Montreal lawyer, Désiré Girouard. Percy was the second of their four children. His Irish mother died when he was twelve, but by that time she had ensured that her four children were as fluent in English as they were in French. By the time of the death of his first wife, Percy's father had become a prominent barrister and the member of parliament for the Montreal constituency of Jacques Cartier.[1] He very much wanted his son to follow a similar career. However, in 1882, having recently remarried, Désiré Girouard decided that the best place for Percy and his brothers to receive the general education that was a necessary preliminary for a law career was in the public-school-*cum*-military-academy atmosphere of the new Royal Military College at Kingston. Hence Girouard, aged fifteen years and six months, was duly removed from the religious seminary in Trois Rivières where he had hitherto received his schooling and enrolled at Kingston. On 12 September 1882, the day that Gentlemen Cadet Girouard was taking his oath of allegiance, Garnet Wolseley was winning his decisive victory over Arabi at Tel-el-Kebir.

A good student, Percy Girouard received a sound education at R.M.C. The act establishing the small college in 1875 had outlined its proposed curriculum: "A complete education in all branches of military tactics, fortification, engineering and general scientific knowledge in subjects connected with and necessary to a thorough knowledge of the military profession." In practice, the new college provided all that and a liberal education as well, the Canadian government being aware that few of its graduates could hope to obtain one of the limited number of commissions available in either the permanent Canadian militia or the British army. Girouard's R.M.C. graduation diploma, in addition to describing him as five feet eight inches in height with fair hair and blue eyes, noted that he had distinguished himself in civil engineering, geology, and French. He had led his class of nine in his third and fourth years of the college and, in his final year, had been awarded prizes in military history, strategy, tactics, reconnaissance, military administration, law, and, not surprisingly, French. During summer vacations, Girouard had learned less formal but more practical lessons by working on Canadian railroads.

Girouard was offered one of the four commissions in the British infantry available annually to R.M.C. graduates when he completed his four years at Kingston in 1886. By then, however, it was clear that his father was more determined than ever that Percy should follow a career in law. Like many other Canadian fathers, Désiré Girouard had not sent his son to R.M.C. to become a soldier. He had sent him there because he believed that a military college would provide an environment more conducive to serious study than the large house in Montreal where his second wife was bearing him a second family. Percy, on the other hand, had decided long before his graduation that the British army was where he belonged. He was, nevertheless, prepared to compromise with his eminent father to the extent of declining the proffered commission and of accepting employment with the Canadian Pacific Railway until he and his father could finally agree upon his future.

Girouard worked for two years as a junior civil engineer with the C.P.R. Although only twenty years old, he was given heavy responsibilities in the survey and construction of a branch line through the State of Maine. It was there, near Greenville in the wild Aroostook country, that he learned of a limited number of commissions in the Royal Engineers being offered for the first time to R.M.C. graduates.[2] He immediately made up his mind, sent off his application, and, in early 1888, learned to his joy that he had been accepted as a subaltern in the Royal Engineers. Désiré Girouard was not at all pleased. He still so much opposed his son's decision that in June 1888 an aunt had to advance Percy £100 so that he could buy his passage to England and his uniforms.

Railway construction in the late nineteenth century engaged the interest and energies of young engineers in something of the same way that electronics now absorb the attention of their professional descendants. Some of the most aggressive and far-seeing men in Canada and the United States were then employed in opening up vast new territories both at home and abroad. Part of the great attraction that a career in the Royal Engineers held for Girouard was that the challenge of railroading could be joined with the adventure of military life. Because of his own inclination and his experience with the C.P.R., after he had completed at Chatham his introduction to the same corps from which such men as Gordon and Kitchener had come, Girouard was appointed traffic manager of the railways serving the Royal Arsenal at Woolwich. During the next five years, he increased his knowledge of military railroading not only by operating with great efficiency and economy the miniature line that carried the guns and stores of the great arsenal, but also by employing his leisure time in studying the railway achievements of army engineers in the American Civil War and the Franco-Prussian War. In the second half of the nineteenth century, the utilization of railways for military purposes was still a new and challenging possibility which occupied the minds of an increasing number of writers. Girouard showed imagination —if not great practicality—in a lecture to the Royal United Services Institution advocating construction of a railway encircling the British Isles on which armoured trains, complete with heavy guns, would defend Britain against invasion.[3] Girouard was already well on his way to establishing a name for himself as his tour in Woolwich drew to an end. Despite his junior rank, he had earned a reputation as a practical engineer by the competent way in which he had operated the arsenal railway; distinction as an imaginative railroader by his novel ideas; and popularity as an officer by never failing to lead vigorous renditions of "Alouette" at mess dinners.

In late 1895, Girouard was ordered to raise a company of engineers in that French-speaking colony in the Indian Ocean where Gordon had once served, Mauritius. Before taking up his new appointment, Girouard—now known widely as "Gerry"—travelled to Canada on leave. On his return to England in December 1895, while en route to Mauritius, he learned that the famous Kitchener wanted to see him in London. "Gerry's" growing reputation as a railroader had reached even Kitchener's ears. The Sirdar soon arranged with the War Office that the young Canadian's appointment to Mauritius should be cancelled and that he should instead be lent to the Egyptian army for railway work in Egypt. Kitchener had liked Girouard on sight. In addition to his reputation for professional ability and superabundant vitality, the Canadian engineer was also noted for an iconoclastic attitude. He stood in awe of no one. Colonels and generals were nothing to him. He addressed them in as direct a way as he had done his colleagues on the C.P.R. As an example of this attitude, upon being received briefly by the adjutant general before his departure for Egypt, Girouard offered him his left hand to shake while holding his right behind his back. The adjutant general enquired sympathetically whether he had injured his right hand. Girouard thereupon produced the still-glowing butt of a cigar from behind his back. "Nothing wrong; only a see-gar!" he explained, fixing the astonished general with the monocle he always wore to correct the deficient sight of his left eye.[4] Kitchener, for all his gruff exterior, liked such men.

"Gerry" arrived at the railway workshops at Wadi Halfa at the end of March 1896. The final orders for the advance on Dongola had only been issued ten days earlier when Girouard had been passing through Cairo, but Kitchener had known for a long time what he wanted in the way of a military railway in the Sudan. First of all, a line would have to be built from Wadi Halfa along the Nile as far south as Kerma from whence a force advancing on the initial target of Dongola could easily be supplied by boat over a flat stretch of the river. Kitchener intended to match the advance of his army to the speed of the construction of the railroad. The army would move forward by bounds and then pause while the railroad caught up to provide it with supplies for the next stage southward.

The problems that were presented to the twenty-nine-year-old Girouard when he accepted the appointment under Kitchener were formidable, certainly more than enough to cause anyone but such a bumptious young sapper to hesitate before accepting the work. Not only was Girouard charged with the construction of over one hundred miles of railway, but he was also faced with a much more challenging task which would continue until Khartoum itself had been taken: under most difficult circumstances, the trains had to run frequently and on schedule if, in Churchill's metaphor, the stem was going to support the blossom—if men in the desert fighting dervishes were not going to starve, die of thirst, or run out of ammunition.

When the advance on Dongola was first ordered in March 1896, there remained intact only thirty-three miles of railroad between Wadi Halfa and Sarras. Wolseley had used that track twelve years earlier to carry supplies before they were loaded aboard whalers. It was still in working order, although all its equipment was old. Ironically, Gordon's frugality was the reason why the Sudanese railway extended no further south than it did. Twenty years before Girouard arrived in Egypt, the Khedive Ismail had, characteristically, envisaged a great railway stretching from Wadi Halfa to Khartoum. At colossal expense—largely graft—the line had been completed only as far as Sarras by 1877 when Gordon recommended its abandonment. Along a newer section laid by Wolseley between Sarras and Akasha, a distance of fifty-three miles, the dervishes had torn up the track and, wood being very scarce, had burned the sleepers in their camp fires. But the embankment still remained. And it was already in Egyptian hands. Even before Kitchener and Girouard had reached the advance headquarters at Wadi Halfa, the vanguard of the Egyptian army had marched into Akasha. Kitchener had not planned on so rapid advance into Dongola province, but when the leading units of his army encountered no opposition, they continued into the town.

The stage was thus set for Girouard's first task. At the end of March he started the work of relaying the fifty-three miles of track south from Sarras to Akasha. It was an inauspicious beginning. Girouard had only a handful of fellow Royal Engineers, all even younger than he, to help him train his Railway Battalion, a rag-tag unit of eight hundred dervish prisoners, Egyptian soldiers, and local tribesmen. Some had never before even seen a locomotive.

Few, initially, had the slightest idea about the logic of machinery. Some were lazy and dishonest. Others were simply stupid. However, as the weeks passed and the narrow-gauge line was slowly extended along the Nile from Sarras, the Railway Battalion divided itself naturally into two groups: the intelligent, who quickly learned such trades as plate-laying, and the incorrigibly stupid who could not be trusted to do more than shovel the desert sands on the embankments. To operate the railway, selected officers and men from the Egyptian army were drafted as stationmasters, yard shunters, switchers, telegraphers, and telephonists. Even so, trained personnel were so scarce that Girouard had to establish two small vocational schools at Wadi Halfa. In them, many Egyptians had their first taste of a technical education. Girouard had not only to improvise with faulty human material; the equipment was also bad. "Kitchener had bought a mixed assortment of rails," one of his "boys" later noted,

> some from Syria, some from other light railways, which did not make the work of track-laying any easier. . . . Spiking and linking up the rails was done by some antiquated Soudanese. There were very few trained plate-layers. At first, the railway resembled parallel corkscrews. . . . For a time, owing to shortage of material, only two bolts were put into each fishplate, and when one of these worked loose it was no uncommon thing to have to clear a trainwreck. The Sapper subalterns became experts at this business. The engines suffered from every locomotive complaint, the only part that was never known to go wrong being the whistle. Comfort there was none. The subalterns had to supervise both shifts, and then be regaled during the night by dreadful telephones, staffed by Egyptians who tried to talk all at once.[5]

Despite the hardships resulting from bad equipment and a hostile climate, the effects began to be felt of the instruction provided by Girouard and his small staff and the example they set, new although they were to the desert. The line grew longer with increasing speed, the pace of construction heightened, and the young subalterns took heart, thinking that they also would soon reach Akasha and, not long after, be in Dongola itself.

Even before the railway reached Akasha, the Mahdists had suffered their first decisive defeat. The Egyptian army and the forces of the Khalifa had clashed for the first time. The Egyptian army had again demonstrated the superiority of discipline over fanaticism. On 7 June 1896, almost one thousand dervishes had been killed at the cost of a handful of Egyptians. In that first encounter with the Mahdists, Kitchener had reason to be satisfied with his army, its discipline, morale, and training. However, at that point, when the enemy had been temporarily thrust out of the way, natural calamities which set back by several weeks the progress of the new railroad suddenly struck. First, a cholera epidemic swept through the Egyptian army, killing more men than dervish bullets and spears were ever able to do and taking its toll among the engineers as much as among the infantry and artillery. Most of Girouard's subalterns were sick during July. At one point, when the number of Royal Engineers still on their feet had dwindled to almost nothing, Girouard himself had to leave his small headquarters at Wadi Halfa to assume command at the railhead. Sunstroke, however, overcame him too, and for a fortnight, he had to remain in his tent. No sooner had he recovered and the cholera epidemic subsided than a second calamity struck. A sudden desert storm washed away weeks of work. To save time and ignorant of the fact that cyclonic rainstorms very occasionally occur in the northern Sudan, Girouard had not left culverts under his track for the rivers of rainwater that might suddenly appear—and as quickly disappear. The result was that, when the torrents of rain fell on 27 August, the rails in many places were undermined or otherwise seriously weakened. In some places they hung like suspension bridges over small, newly cut gorges. Twelve miles of the line was swept away completely. It was not only the Egyptian members of the Railway Battalion who were learning from experience.

Kitchener and Girouard were nothing daunted, however, and both worked with five thousand soldiers night and day for a week to repair the line. Girouard, like Kitchener, had an unusual ability for inspiring confidence in his subordinates. On no occasion was it more useful than this. Soon all was well again, the systematic laying of track resumed. "We lay anything from a quarter of a mile to one and a half miles a day," one of Girouard's principal assistants noted in a letter home,

a trainload comes up and goes to the end of the line, as far as is safe. A gang of men unload sleepers, walk out in front, and throw them down roughly in the place of the bank. Another gang carry rails, and throw them down roughly in place on the sleepers. This is an amusing sight. The rail gangs are Sudanese pensioners, mostly old men, and they abuse each other all the time for not taking fair shares; and generally, after they have dropped the rail, they have to be separated by a spare gang from a sort of Donnybrook! Next come a gang of men with fish-plates, which join the rails together. Then a man with a piece of chalk, marking the position of the sleepers on the rail—a soft job. After him, a few men moving the sleepers correctly under the chalk marks. Then come 12 "work-shops," each consisting of five men—two with crowbars as levers, two with hammers, and one with a gauge to measure the correct width between the rails. The crowbar men lever the sleeper up, sitting on the end of the bar. After a man has sat on a crowbar for four months he wears out his breeches, so you can tell a crowbarman at a glance as generally he has no breeches left. The hammermen knock in the spikes, and the hardest worked man of the lot, who carries the gauge, measures to see if they have done right. You can always tell a gaugeman: his clothes are so good. The line is now laid, but it looks rather inebriated, and so a real *Osta*, or plate-layer, comes along with a party who move the whole thing sideways, one way or the other, until it is fairly straight. Then, as about 50 yards or so are finished, the material train moves over the line. Behind the train comes the remainder of the men, and a huge lever, with two men to sit on it, which is used to level the rails. Then about 20 men with shovels, who throw on the ballast; and another 20 with beaters, who pack it well into the sleepers. Finally there comes another *Osta*, who finishes up the straightening. It all goes like clockwork.[6]

In this methodical way the damage caused by the unexpected storm was, before long, only an unpleasant memory. Soon the way to Dongola lay open before the Egyptian army. On 19 September, the second and last battle on the route to Dongola was fought. In the middle of the desert, it was, paradoxically, largely a naval affair. The Battle of Hafir was simply an unequal duel between a small flotilla of Kitchener's gunboats, officered by the Royal Navy, and a large concentration of dervishes on the shore.[7] After the gunboats and Egyptian artillery had decimated the dervishes, there was no further opposition before Dongola was reached. On 24 September 1896, the provincial capital was entered unopposed. Thanks to Girouard's riverside railway, Kitchener had been able to carry out his orders with despatch and economy.[8] With the capture of Dongola, Salisbury's immediate goal had been achieved. Everyone in London was gratified about this initial step on the way toward the reconquest of the Sudan. Kitchener was promoted a major-general in the British army and Girouard was awarded the Distinguished Service Order.

In the late autumn of 1896 the British government, at the prompting of Kitchener acting through Cromer, decided to sanction an advance on Khartoum itself. Salisbury recognized that such an advance would exceed the limited resources of Egypt and eventually ordered both British soldiers and money to support the Egyptian army. The pressure on the Italians, it was true, had been in part relieved by the capture of Dongola, but that had always been only an ostensible reason for the initial campaign. The ulterior object, as Lord Lansdowne had noted, was to restore the control of the Sudan to Egypt (and, accordingly, indirectly to Britain) in an effort to ensure that no other European power seized the headwaters of the Nile. The ambitious Kitchener had, of course, long been anticipating the order to advance on

Khartoum. He envisaged a two-pronged attack, one up the Nile in gunboats and barges from Dongola to Merowe (an easily navigable stretch of the river) and then to Abu Hamed. His second force would travel across the desert by rail directly from Wadi Halfa to Abu Hamed. When his two small armies had joined forces at Abu Hamed, Kitchener would lead the advance first on Berber and then on Khartoum, supplied by the railway that he now confidently ordered "Gerry" to begin building across the desert, as if they were on the Canadian prairies and the line was the C.P.R.

13

The Desert Railway

Like the leaves of the forest when summer is green,
That host with their banners at sunset was seen:
Like the leaves of the forest when autumn has blown,
That host on the morrow lay wither'd and strown.

LORD BYRON
"THE DESTRUCTION OF SENNACHERIB"

Long before construction of the river railway south from Wadi Halfa had begun, indeed long before the Dongola expedition itself had been ordered, Kitchener had decided that the conquest of the Sudan, whenever it was sanctioned, would require a railroad across the desert from Wadi Halfa to Abu Hamed. Several of the Sirdar's confidants in Cairo had advised him against a scheme that would require a rail line being laid across an almost waterless desert in the face of a mobile and numerically superior enemy. But Kitchener was not a man to heed the advice of others once he was convinced of the correctness of his own ideas. He knew that the success of his expedition would depend entirely upon secure lines of communication. He had seen with his own eyes what had happened when Wolseley's extemporaneous arrangements had proven inadequate. However, when the advance on Khartoum was sanctioned, Kitchener could not immediately put into practice his daring plan to supply his army by rail across the desert. He first had to await permission from London for the expenditure and for the completion of the line along the river from Wadi Halfa toward Dongola. Priority had to be given to the river railway not only because Dongola was the immediate target but also because there were insufficient supplies and trained men to build two lines at the same time.

However, even before the river line of the Sudan Military Railway was completed, Girouard had turned his attention to arranging the details of the projected—and much longer—desert line. In his headquarters of crude brick in Wadi Halfa, he compiled exhaustive lists of the material he would require to carry out what seemed to many to be an impossible task. In the midst of his preparations, Kitchener departed for leave in England in November 1886, returning with the expected news that a further advance had been sanctioned and the unexpected news that he had already purchased six locomotives for desert work. As a result of Girouard's questions, it soon became obvious that Kitchener had bought engines too light for the heavy tasks that awaited them.[1] Girouard thereupon left for England himself in February 1887, taking with him his long shopping list of essential equipment for the desert railway and for expansion of its workshops at Wadi Halfa. With the Sirdar's admonitions about economy in mind, Girouard borrowed several heavy engines from Cecil Rhodes, the prime minister of the Cape Colony, who happened to be in London ordering equipment for the Cape railways. Kitchener had chosen a broader gauge than was standard in Egypt so that his railway might fit into Rhodes' imperial dream of a Cape-to-Cairo line. Rhodes, therefore, was ready to oblige when Girouard asked him to lend a few engines for several months. After ordering another fifteen engines, some of which had to come from the United States because of an engineering strike in England, Girouard returned to his new offices and workshops in Wadi Halfa in the early spring of 1887 when the construction of the desert railway was just beginning.

The story of the desert railway is not unlike that of the river line. Inefficiency and delays at first but increasing speed as the workmen became accustomed to their tasks in the scorching heat was as much the tale of the second railway as it had been of the first. The workshops at Wadi Halfa were rapidly expanded, and by working night and day, they provided essential support for the new line moving out into the desert. A great impetus to quicker construction was provided by the unexpected discovery of water at two points along the route, thus ameliorating the problem of supplying men and locomotives who were always thirsty. The track-laying thereafter became something of a routine; under the burning sun sometimes as much as a mile was laid every three hours as May passed into June and the 230-mile line was pushed farther and farther south across the desert. In his own small rail car, fitted as an office, "Gerry" became a familiar sight as he travelled up and down the line, praising, criticizing, exhorting, and encouraging. Delays still occurred as a result of faulty machinery and ignorance about its performance in the unknown conditions of the desert, but by 7 August, when Abu Hamed was captured by the river force working up the Nile from Merowe, 110 miles of line had already been completed. This was most satisfactory progress, but Girouard was fully aware that the final advance on Khartoum required the speedy completion of his desert railway. The remaining 120 miles clearly had to be built even faster. Kitchener, albeit cautious and deliberate, was a man in a hurry. Philip Magnus, who has described Girouard as possessing "rare good looks, bubbling high spirits, and that happy transatlantic ability to express himself crisply and tartly without causing offence," tells of an occasion when Kitchener became overly impatient about the rate of progress a heavily laden train was making over one particularly tortuous section of the railway.[2] He and Girouard both clambered from their carriage into the cab of the ancient engine. Kitchener ordered the astonished driver to detach the latter half of the train and to "Go like hell!" with the other half. "The train rocked like a ship in a storm, but it reached its destination in record time. Kitchener turned to Girouard and exclaimed with his habitual drawl: 'What a dreadful journey we have had, Girouard! A dreadful journey! Terrible! Terrible!' There was a pause, while Girouard adjusted his eyeglass before replying with an impudent and lazy smile: 'You'll break the record, and your own ruddy neck one day!' Kitchener's face flushed with rage, but he could never be angry for long with Girouard, who was the reigning favorite, privileged and indispensable." One of the war correspondents accompanying the expedition noted the same special standing that Kitchener accorded Girouard: "Conceive a blend of French audacity of imagination, American ingenuity, and British doggedness in execution and you will have.... The Director of Railways.... The Egyptian Army is a triumph of youth on every side, but in none is it more signal than in the Director of Railways. He never loses his head nor forgets his own mind: he is credited with being the one man in the Egyptian army who is unaffectedly unafraid of the Sirdar."[3] Adding to his labour force his original and experienced Railway Battalion from his now completed river railway, Girouard finished the remaining 120 miles across the sand by 31 October 1897. In five torrid summer months, a total of 232 miles of new railway had been constructed. An enthusiastic welcome greeted the first train as it steamed into Abu Hamed laden with men and supplies. Girouard's rapid construction of the desert railway was an engineering record. "The critics had been confounded by Kitchener's 'Band of Boys' who had accomplished what may justly be classed as one of the most remarkable engineering feats of modern times."[4]

Yet even in Abu Hamed there was to be no rest for Girouard and his staff. No sooner had they reached Abu Hamed than they learned that Berber, having been evacuated unexpectedly by the Mahdists, had already been occupied by Kitchener's advance force working up the river. They had encountered no opposition so, without specific orders to the contrary, they had occupied the town. Such rapid progress had been envisaged by none, not even by the aggressive Kitchener himself. The advance had been so quick that there were not enough rails and sleepers, signals and switches, fishplates and bolts, to extend the line beyond another seventeen miles from Abu Hamed toward the place where one of the Nile's few subsidiaries, the Atbara, flows into the great river. From October 1897 until January 1898, the railhead remained stationary while Kitchener obtained the final sanction of the British government for an advance on Khartoum and while Girouard ordered more construction material to be rushed from Britain. The delay was, of course, only temporary. By the time that the great Battle of Atbara was fought on 8 April 1898, the railhead was twenty-five miles from Berber and only forty-eight miles north of the battlefield itself. On 3 July 1898, after one final burst of engineering skill, Girouard completed his desert railway which now stretched 385 miles from Wadi Halfa to its temporary terminus at Atbara.

On the day that the first troop train steamed into the fortified camp at the confluence of the Nile and Atbara rivers the doom of the Dervishes was sealed. It had now become possible with convenience and speed to send into the heart of the Soudan great armies independent of the season of the year and of the resources of the country; to supply them not only with abundant food and ammunition, but with all the varied paraphernalia of scientific war. . . . Though the battle was not yet fought, the victory was won. The Khalifa, his capital, and his army were now within the Sirdar's reach. It remained only to pluck the fruit in the most convenient hour, with the least trouble and at the smallest cost.[5]

The steady stream of supplies now moving across the desert did indeed seal the fate of the Mahdists. The already high morale of the now-seasoned veterans of the Egyptian army was increased by the knowledge that their supplies were safe, but to provide stiffening, if any were needed for the crucial clash with the dervishes, and to demonstrate that Cairo was acting with the full support of London, a British infantry division, an artillery brigade, and a cavalry regiment were added for the final, terrible stage of Britain's conquest of the Sudan. For the advance on Khartoum, Kitchener's army was no longer immune from the presence in its midst of the type of fashionable soldier whom Wolseley had suffered in his army. H. H. Prince Christian Victor of Schleswig-Holstein and H. S. H. Prince Francis of Teck joined for the decisive stage of the long campaign. However, the British units whom Wolseley, in London, added to Kitchener's command also contained able professionals and, like Kitchener himself, veterans of the Gordon relief expedition. As a lieutenant-colonel Brigadier-General Wauchope had commanded the Black Watch in that expedition; Major Stuart-Wortley, now commanding local irregulars, had carried the news of the fall of Khartoum from Wilson to the Desert Column's camp at Metemmeh; Major Wingate, the former aide-de-camp of General Sir Evelyn Wood, now headed the intelligence service of the Egyptian army. Among the Cameron Highlanders, there were men who had fought at the Battle of Ginnis thirteen years before when the Khalifa had been turned back from the borders of Egypt.

No amount of fanatical courage, no amount of human flesh could stop the advance of a disciplined and mobile army, using to the full the impersonal forces of science. The Khalifa and his brave followers, armed with rifles, spears, and even pieces of medieval armour, may have guessed what lay in store for them after their crushing defeat at the Battle—or slaughter—of

Atbara on 8 April 1898. Like all battles the imperious Kitchener fought in the Sudan, the action at the confluence of the two rivers was really a carnage set to the tune of brass bands and bagpipes. The Battles of Atbara and, later, of Omdurman are reminiscent of the slaughter of game sometimes practised by European "sportsmen." The animals were herded together so closely that the hunters could hardly shoot fast enough to kill them all. It was the same at Atbara when the long, closely packed lines of dervishes rushed toward the Anglo-Egyptian squares, waving their long banners bearing quotations from the Koran. Soon the bodies of three thousand Mahdists were strewn across the desert. Total British and Egyptian losses were eighty-three. What force could stop this juggernaut? the Khalifa might well have asked himself after the Battle of Atbara. He had never seen a railway, but it was now obvious what it could do. Although his enemy was over one thousand miles from its principal base, the railroad brought seemingly inexhaustible supplies of ammunition and food, artillery and horses, men and machine guns. They were eroding his own badly armed forces at a fearful pace. There had been an opportunity, when the railhead was out in the desert between Wadi Halfa and Abu Hamed, for the Khalifa to have delivered a shattering blow to Kitchener's plans by cutting the line and tearing up the track. But the Khalifa did not know of the devastating effect commando raids can have on railways so he waited, for no particular reason, for his enemy to approach closer to Khartoum.

After the carnage at Atbara, the end was not long in coming. By late August 1898, with the eyes of all Britain on him, Kitchener was rapidly approaching Khartoum with his combined force of twenty-six thousand British and Egyptian soldiers. The Khalifa, now with his back to the wall, decided to give battle in the desert near Omdurman, across the Nile from Khartoum. The moment for which Kitchener had long been waiting finally arrived on 2 September. By 11:30 on the morning of what he later described as the proudest day of his life, eleven thousand dervishes lay dead amid the dust and smoke. Forty-eight British and Egyptians had been killed. When the massacre was over, the ambitious Sirdar put away his field glasses and was heard to remark complacently that the enemy had been given "a thorough dusting." Queen Victoria was equally satisfied. After thirteen years, she could finally write about "Chinese" Gordon in her journal, "Surely, he is avenged!"

Winston Churchill, a subaltern of the 4th Hussars who served with the 21st Lancers at Omdurman and who therefore participated in what has been described as the last cavalry charge of the British army, called the battle "the most signal triumph ever gained by the arms of science over barbarians. Within the space of five hours the strongest and best-armed savage army yet arrayed against a modern European Power had been destroyed and dispersed with hardly any difficulty, comparatively small risk, and insignificant loss to the victors."[6] And yet, the sheer courage of the Mahdists came close several times to breaking the British lines. As a British war correspondent reported,

the honour of the fight must still go with the men who died. Our men were perfect, but the Dervishes were superb—beyond perfection. It was their largest, best, and bravest army that ever fought against us for Mahdism, and it died worthily of the huge empire that Mahdism won and kept so long. Their riflemen, mangled by every kind of death and torment that men can devise clung round the black flag and the green, emptying their poor, rotten homemade cartridges dauntlessly. Their spearmen charged death at every minute hopelessly. Their horsemen led each attack, riding into the bullets till nothing was left.... Not one rush, or two, or ten—but rush on rush, company on company, never stopping, though all their view that was not unshaken enemy was the bodies of the men who had rushed up before them. A dusky line got up and stormed forward; it bent, broke up, fell apart, and disappeared. Before the smoke cleared, another line was bending and storming forward in the same track.[7]

The killing had been almost too easy. The getting to Khartoum had certainly been easy, thanks to the young Canadian engineer, Edouard Percy Cranwell Girouard. No one seemed to worry very much about whether it was all right or wrong. That was left for later generations. Girouard himself has left no record of his feelings, although he later wrote with some modest pride about how he had so successfully carried out his orders.[8] The most intransigent problem in the long campaign, that of transport and supply—the same that had bedevilled Wolseley—had been solved by Canadian application, skill, ingenuity and the inspiration of others to achieve the barely possible in the shortest possible time.

14

Canada on the Nile

What is the Soudan?

JOHN RUSKIN

Girouard was not, however, present at the dénouement of the long Sudanese drama which had begun with the defeat of Hicks in 1884 and had ended with Kitchener's victory at Omdurman fifteen years later. During the early spring of 1898, Kitchener began to receive reports that confirmed his own suspicions that the old Egyptian rail-line down the Nile between Luxor and Assuan was rapidly deteriorating and might soon prove to be an impossibly weak link in the chain that bound together his army with Cairo and the world beyond. He could take no chances with any part of that single track which was a vital link in the safety of his force. In March 1898, he sent "Gerry" to report on the line's true condition. Confident that Girouard's seasoned sub-ordinates could finish what little remained to be constructed of the desert railway, Kitchener ordered him to Egypt to inspect the line and to discuss with Cromer what could be afforded. The British agent and the Canadian engineer thus met for the first time. Cromer was as impressed with the Canadian's abilities as Girouard was with the agent's great intelligence and fore-sight. The result of their meeting was that Girouard never returned to the Sudan. After setting aright in a matter of weeks the Luxor-Assuan line, Girouard (who at 31 was still a lieutenant) was offered, through Cromer's personal intervention, the highly-paid post of president of the Egyptian state railways and of Alexandria harbour. Before accepting the £2,000-a-year appointment, "Gerry" prudently asked Kitchener for his advice. On receiving the Sirdar's approval, he immediately began an inspection tour of the whole twelve hundred miles of Egyptian railway that lay between the port of Alexandria and the Sudanese border. Hence Girouard missed the final carnage of Omdurman in September 1898, and he in turn was missed by those who were there. Girouard's new appointment was a great honour, but in the Sudan he was "inimitable and irreplaceable, and his departure was mourned by the remainder of Kitchener's 'Band of Boys' whom he had led with so much skill and energy across the Nubian Desert and up the Nile."[1]

Following the Battle of Omdurman, peace finally settled over the Sudan after fifteen years of warfare and anarchy. During the following year, Girouard worked steadily at increasing the efficiency of the Egyptian railway, visiting Britain, the United States, and Canada to purchase new equipment and to recruit engineers. Soon, however, the British army found that it again needed him and all the other military railway experts it could find. The Boer War had already begun when Girouard, by now a major, arrived in London in 1899 to advise the War Office on what construction equipment and rolling stock should be sent to South Africa to meet military needs. Soon Girouard himself was on his way to Capetown, appointed "Director of Railways for the South African Field Force" and charged with creating order out of the chaos that had suddenly overcome the South African railways as the result of the demands made on them by the British army. In South Africa, Girouard was able to apply lessons he had learned in the Sudan. And he again enjoyed the direct support of Kitchener, who was also serving in the war against the Boers. So successful was Girouard in his efforts to provide a dependable route for supplies and reinforcements that he was knighted in 1900, being made a K.C.M.G.[2] He was thirty-three. At the end of the Boer War, Lord Milner (who had in the meantime completed his apprenticeship under Cromer in Cairo and was now chief British administrator in South Africa) appointed Girouard commissioner of railways in the Transvaal and the Orange River Colony. Although again engaged in running a complex railway system recovering from the demands of a recent war, Girouard nevertheless found the time to court and marry the daughter of the attorney general of Transvaal. In 1904, he and his bride sailed for England where, during the next five years, Girouard filled various military engineering posts.[3]

In 1907, Girouard returned to Africa for a third time, this time as an imperial pro-consul. Winston Churchill had travelled on Girouard's wonderful Sudanese railroad upon his return to Egypt after the Battle of Omdurman. During the Boer War, while employed as a war correspondent, Churchill again saw the skills and talent for improvisation that Girouard brought to his tasks. By 1907, Churchill was under-secretary of state for the colonies and responsible for a decision to construct a railway to open up the interior of Nigeria. What better person than Girouard to build it? From his duties in southern England, he was called to London to discuss with Churchill the problems involved and to receive the appointment to succeed that famous imperialist, Lord Lugard, as governor of northern Nigeria. Once there, Girouard found that he had inherited a morass of trade and land tenure problems. But there was also an eight-hundred-mile railroad to be built between the navigable mouth of the Niger River and the northern capital of Kano. This was just the sort of challenge that Girouard relished, and it gave him deep satisfaction to master the problems involved. Yet he also made time to settle satisfactorily the disputes over land ownership. His success in northern Nigeria was such that Girouard was given a fourth senior appointment in Africa in the autumn of 1909, this time as governor of the Protectorate of Kenya. After a successful if controversial tour presiding over the protectorate's return to solvency, Girouard resigned his gubernatorial appointment in early 1912, partly over a difference with the secretary of state for the colonies concerning land grants (one such controversial grant was to Kitchener).[4]

Shortly after his return to London, Girouard resigned his army commission and accepted a directorship in the great engineering and arms company of Armstrong-Whitworth. In 1913 he established a Canadian branch at Longueuil in his home province of Quebec and became the new subsidiary's first president.

The First World War found Girouard back in England in uniform again, this time as a colonel in charge of munition supplies in the War Office. Kitchener had called upon his old friend to help him in the task of attempting to supply the insatiable British guns in France with adequate quantities of ammunition. In October 1914, when the war was not yet two months old, Kitchener sent Girouard (with the acting rank of brigadier-general) to report on the problems the fighting had placed on the Belgian railway system. From his recommendations came the International Railway Commission composed of British, Belgian, and French officers, which supervised all rail transport in that part of Belgium held by the allies. When Kitchener's plea to retain in the War Office the responsibility for ammunition supply was rejected in 1916 and a separate Ministry of Munitions was established, Girouard returned to Armstrong-Whitworth to help deal with a flood of war contracts. He remained a director almost until his death on 26 September 1932, at the age of 65.[5]

With Girouard's passing, one of the most prominent of the Canadians who had served on the Nile had died. Girouard was a remarkable example of that band of Canadians of outstanding ability who chose the imperial arena as the most challenging for their talents—and Girouard was a French Canadian, as had been so many of those serving with Wolseley on the earlier expedition. All the Canadians on the Nile had, however, played a singular role in the story of Canada's involvement in Victorian imperialism. Canadians had been on the Nile partly because they offered something unique. The forest, the rivers, and the plains of Canada had produced men who behaved differently from, and who knew different things than, Englishmen, Frenchmen, or Americans. No one else could do as well what the *voyageurs* did. No one else in the Royal Engineers had the same railroading skill, experience, and initiative that Girouard had. These were Canadians; their country was not many years old but they were gradually becoming an identifiable species.

In the Sudan in 1884, Canadians for the first time served abroad in circumstances which allowed them to realize better their own nature. It soon became clear to them—if they did not know it before—that they had unique skills, abilities, and attitudes. They were as much the product of the new world as their Yankee cousins. The *genus Canadenses* had begun to appear on the international scene. British officers and war correspondents on the Nile expedition were sometimes astonished at the easygoing attitudes of the boatmen. Others, serving under Kitchener, were perplexed by Girouard's indifference to rank and position. For their part, the *voyageurs* were pleased that fellow Canadians were to be their own officers, men who understood them, their needs, and attitudes. They did not want Englishmen who had different ideas and characteristics. Steamboat skipper Robinson thought that some of the British officers were surprisingly decent fellows, but he nevertheless looked forward to the day when he would be back again in "sweet Canada."

The growth of imperial sentiment was as strong, the infection of imperial enthusiasm was as contagious among some Canadians as it was among British. But no matter how often they proclaimed their loyalty to their imperial sovereign, their essential Canadian character kept emerging. They were different even from the Americans: their experiences at home were different; the challenges of their half of the continent were distinct. Their service abroad only confirmed what some had begun to suspect in their own country: they were becoming a nation. Rabid Canadian Tories might denigrate the idea of a Canadian nationality, but the *voyageurs* instinctively regarded themselves as an identifiable entity. French-speaking and English-speaking Canadians worked side by side without favour or prejudice. A lawyer from Toronto or an engineer from Montreal, a woodsman from Quebec or a boatman from Manitoba were all Canadians bringing their special skills to meet a challenge that faced them. Canadians of French and English descent talk of differences which distinguish them. In the Nile expedition—and in any such joint undertaking—they soon found that the talents they share and the common attitudes they embody are, in fact, what really matter.

The role of the military in developing a Canadian national consciousness, whether resulting from service in Canada or in imperial ventures abroad, had been neglected by historians. At home, the War of 1812, the Fenian Raids, and the two Riel expeditions were the most prominent occasions in stimulating a sense of disciplined service in a common interest. Abroad, service in Victoria's army and navy was seen as an adventure, but it was also a place where Canadians learned to know themselves. Their role in various campaigns is largely unrecorded—there was, in fact, a small legion of imperial "prefects" and officers from Canada—but yet more important is the sense of identity to which such imperial service gradually contributed. In different ways, the boatmen and Girouard set a precedent for Canadian participation in the Boer War when over seven thousand Canadian volunteers fought in their own battalions. When the war in South Africa began, Canadians could point to the earlier conflict in the Sudan when they had served as a separate, distinct entity within the imperial forces. Service on the Nile and in South Africa led on, in turn, to participation on a national scale in the First World War, when over six hundred thousand Canadians served in their own units and under their own generals. Only thirty years separated 1884 and 1914, but in that short time the evolution of Canada from a colony to a nation largely ran its course and the theory of a free-and-equal commonwealth began to emerge. The imperial service of Canadians on the Nile, stretching over a period of almost twenty years, contributed to this rapid evolution in a way which was at once significant and romantic, noteworthy and bizarre.

Notes

NOTES TO THE INTRODUCTION

1. G. M. Young, *Victorian England* (New York: Doubleday, 1954), pp. 265–66.
2. Garnet Wolseley, *The Story of a Soldier's Life*, 2 vols. (London: Constable, 1903), 1:229.
3. Carl Berger, *The Sense of Power* (Toronto: University of Toronto Press, 1970), pp. 257–58.

NOTES TO CHAPTER ONE

1. William Winwood Reade, "Preface," in George Schweinfurth, *The Heart of Africa: Three Years' Travels and Adventures in the Unexplored Regions of Central Africa from 1868 to 1871*, 3d ed., 2 vols. (London: Sampson, Low, Marston, Searle and Rivington, 1873), 1:iv.
2. For a discussion of the varying estimates of Gordon (1833–85) during his lifetime and since his death, see the Introduction to John Marlowe, *Mission to Khartum* (London: Gollancz, 1969), pp. 7–15.
3. Later Field Marshal Viscount Wolseley; he was born in Dublin in 1833 and died on the French Riviera in 1913. On the eve of the Boer War, he succeeded the Duke of Cambridge as commander-in-chief of the British army.
4. Wolseley, *A Soldier's Life*, 1:147.
5. Alan Moorehead, *The White Nile* (London: Hamish Hamilton, 1960), p. 190.
6. Marlowe, *Mission to Khartum*, p. 59.

NOTES TO CHAPTER TWO

1. Ronald Robinson and John Gallagher, *Africa and the Victorians* (London: Macmillan, 1965), p. 83.
2. Sir Charles Rivers Wilson (1831–1916) thus described the financial controls. Wilson, a commissioner of the British National Debt, was British financial controller from 1878 to 1880 and Egyptian minister of finance. Ismail had originally intended to appoint Gordon as controller. Wilson gives an amusing account of his Egyptian experiences in his autobiography, Everilda MacAlister, ed., *Chapters from My Official Life* (London: Arnold, 1916). In 1895, Wilson was appointed president of the Grand Trunk Railway of Canada.
3. Spencer Compton, the Marquess of Hartington (1833–1908), who became the eighth Duke of Devonshire in 1891, was the uncle of the ninth duke, who was governor general of Canada from 1916 to 1921. Lady Hartington was the daughter of another governor general, Lord Lansdowne.
4. The coastal defences of Alexandria had been greatly improved under the direction of several former Confederate Army officers who, after the end of the Civil War in the United States, were employed by the Khedive in train-

ing his army (see William P. Hasseltine and Hazel C. Wolfe, *The Blue and the Grey on the Nile* [Chicago: University of Chicago Press, 1961]).

5. Later Field Marshal Lord Kitchener of Khartoum (1850-1917).
6. Later Admiral Lord Charles William de la Poer Beresford (1846-1919).

NOTES TO CHAPTER THREE

1. George Arthur, ed., *The Letters of Lord and Lady Wolseley, 1870-1911* (London: Heinemann, 1922).
2. Wolseley dedicated his autobiography to George Stephen (Lord Mount-Stephen), the Montreal Scot who did so much to bring about the construction of the Canadian Pacific Railway and whom Wolseley had first met at the time of the Red River expedition of 1870.

   One of Wolseley's most trenchant literary critics was President Theodore Roosevelt of the United States, whom Ernest Morrison, an Australian journalist, recorded in his diary as stating, "Of Wolseley he spoke contemptuously, especially of his ignorance in his book on Lee.... It was wrong, unpardonably... he would attribute to the South what had happened to the North, and so on.... Wolseley wrote with astonishing ignorance.... I said all Wolseley's work was like that" (Cyril Pearl, *Morrison of Peking* [Harmondsworth: Penguin, 1970], pp. 156-57).
3. George Arthur and F. Maurice, *The Life of Lord Wolseley* (London: Heinemann, 1924), p. 337.
4. Wolseley, *A Soldier's Life*, 1:170.
5. Later Lieutenant-General Sir Gerald Graham (1831-99), and later General the Rt. Hon. Sir Redvers Buller (1839-1909). Buller served in China at the same time as Wolseley in 1860 and in Canada from 1863 to 1869. Buller, one of the most prominent of Wolseley's many protegés, eventually appeared as a challenger for the post of commander-in-chief at the same time as his mentor was seeking it himself. Wolseley's feelings may be judged from the fact that he then named a treacherous horse he owned "Sir Redvers." After a strenuous period in the War Office, Buller was appointed to command in South Africa at the beginning of the Boer War but badly handled what was already a difficult situation.
6. 10 September 1882 (*Letters*, p. 74). The duke's brigade major was Ivor Caradoc Herbert, later Major-General Lord Treowen, who commanded the Canadian militia from 1890 to 1895.
7. 26 August 1882 (ibid., p. 77).
8. The Earl of Minto (1845-1914) was governor general of Canada between 1898 and 1904. He partly owed his appointment to Wolseley, who urged his merits on the colonial secretary after the Queen had refused to allow her son, the Duke of Connaught, to accept the post and after several others had declined. His biography was written by another governor general of Canada, Lord Tweedsmuir (John Buchan), *Lord Minto: A Memoir* (London: Nelson, 1930). Buchan also wrote a brief account of Gordon's service in the Sudan: *Gordon at Khartoum* (London: Davies, 1934). Like several of his predecessors and successors in Ottawa, Minto was later viceroy of India (1905-1910). He was succeeded in Ottawa by his brother-in-law, Earl Grey.
9. Arthur and Maurice, *Wolseley*, p. 158.
10. For an account of Rawson's Arctic experiences, see Captain Sir George Strong Nares, *Narrative of a Voyage to the Polar Sea during 1875-76*, 2 vols. (London: Sampson, Low, Marston, Searle and Rivington, 1878), 1:135-40, 240-49, 280-308; and 2:90-113, 127-32.
11. Anon., "The Battle of Tel-el-Kebir," *Nineteenth Century Magazine*, March 1890.
12. 15 September 1882 (*Letters*, p. 79).
13. John Gordon, *My Six Years with the Black Watch, 1881-1887* (Boston: Fort Hill, 1929), p. 79.
14. Lieutenant-Colonel   C. F.   Winter

(1863-1947), "A Canadian's Recollections of Tel-el-Kebir," *Canadian Magazine* 39 (1912), p. 59. Although Winter purchased his discharge soon after his departure from Egypt, his military career was far from over. He joined the civil service upon his return to Canada but saw action again during the Northwest Rebellion and the Boer War. He was military secretary in Ottawa during the First World War and died a brigadier-general.

15. On 29 August 1882, the War Office informed Wolseley that "on the application of the Dominion of Canada, Her Majesty's Government has sanctioned an officer of the Canadian Artillery being attached to one of the Field Batteries of the Royal Artillery. ...you will attach [Hébert] for duty to such at the front as will enable him to see whatever service there may be going on....The Government of Canada...will defray all expenses in connection with his service in Egypt" (Public Archives of Canada [hereafter P.A.C.], RG 9, II A-1, vol. 206).

16. Ahmed Arabi was sentenced to death, but the sentence was subsequently commuted to exile in Ceylon. The judge advocate at the trial was Sir Charles Wilson, an officer who was later to play a leading role in the expedition to save Gordon. Arabi was permitted to return to Egypt in 1901, was eventually given a pension of £1,000 a year, and died in Cairo in 1911.

17. Queen Victoria to Sir William Harcourt, 22 September 1882 (Robinson and Gallagher, *Africa and the Victorians*, p. 123).

18. The official biography of Dufferin (1826-1902) is by Sir Alfred Lyall, *The Life of Lord Dufferin*, 2 vols. (London: Murray, 1905). A more informal and intimate portrait was sketched by his nephew, Harold Nicolson, in *Helen's Tower* (New York: Harcourt, Brace, 1938). After his service in Asia Minor, Dufferin, like several subsequent governors general of Canada, was named viceroy of India. Later he became British ambassador in Rome and Paris.

NOTES TO CHAPTER FOUR

1. Bernard M. Allen, *Gordon and the Sudan* (London: Macmillan, 1931), p. 181. William Hicks (1830-83) had entered the Bombay Army in 1849 and had served in India and Ethiopia.

2. The standard biography of Osman Digna is H. C. Jackson, *Osman Digna* (London: Methuen, 1926). The "Fuzzy-Wuzzies" about whom Kipling later wrote were Osman Digna's warriors.

3. Major Sir Evelyn Baring (1841-1917), later the first Earl of Cromer, was a scion of the famous banking family. He entered the Royal Artillery in 1858, but he eventually decided to leave the army, partly because of the knowledge that he had, by his reforming zeal, made many enemies among more conservative officers. Lord Northbrook, Baring's cousin, had been undersecretary when Cardwell was war minister; Baring became Northbrook's private secretary upon his appoint-

ment as viceroy of India (1872-76). Baring first served in Egypt in 1877-80 as a commissioner of the debt. He was again in India in 1880-83 as financial member of the viceroy's council. His two-volume account of his stewardship of Egypt between 1883 and 1907 (*Modern Egypt* [London: Macmillan, 1908]) gives, *inter alia*, a good account of the procrastination and doubt which beset Gladstone's cabinet whenever it attempted to deal with the complex problems of Egypt and the Sudan.

4. From a memorandum written by Gordon in October 1878 (Sir Henry W. Gordon, *Events in the Life of Charles George Gordon* [London: Kegan Paul, Trench, 1886], p. 114).

5. Allen, *Gordon*, p. 193.

6. Marlowe, *Mission to Khartum*, p. 102.

7. Philip Magnus, *Kitchener: Portrait of an Imperialist* (London: Murray,

1958), p. 41.

8. Lord Northbrook to the Marquess of Ripon, 13 February 1884 (Robinson and Gallagher, *Africa and the Victorians*, p. 135).

9. The four ministers present at the meeting with Gordon were the foreign secretary (Lord Granville); the secretary of state for war (Lord Hartington); the First Lord of the Admiralty (Lord Northbrook); and the president of the Local Government Board (Sir Charles Dilke). Wolseley also attended. There are good descriptions of the meeting and the general confusion surrounding Gordon's sudden departure for the Sudan in Allen, *Gordon*, pp. 219-34; Marlowe, *Mission to Khartoum*, chapter 3; and Julian Symons, *England's Pride* (London: Hamish Hamilton, 1965), pp. 19-31.

10. Allen, *Gordon*, p. 229.

11. Baring, *Modern Egypt*, 1:570-71.

12. A. Egmont Hake, ed., *The Journals of Major-General C. G. Gordon, C.B., at Khartoum* (London: Kegan Paul, Trench, 1885), p. 40. *Gordon's Journals* became one of the most popular books in later nineteenth-century Britain.

13. Lieutenant-Colonel John Donald Hamill Stewart (1846-84), 11th Hussars, had first met Gordon when he was a vice-consul in the Balkans. Stewart had also served in India and for several months in the Sudan in 1883 in an effort to determine what was happening in the Sudan. He wrote *Report on the Sudan* (London: H.M.S.O., 1883), which was tabled in parliament in 1883.

14. Marlowe, *Mission to Khartoum*, pp. 154-55.

15. Valentine Baker (1827-87) was a younger brother of Sir Samuel Baker, the great African explorer, who had preceded Gordon as governor of Equatoria and who had recommended his appointment to Khartoum in 1884.

16. Colonel Frederick Gustavus Burnaby (1842-85) is the subject of two biographies: Thomas Wright, *The Life of Colonel Fred Burnaby* (London: Everett, 1908); and Michael Alexander, *The True Blue* (London: Rupert Hart-Davis, 1957). Burnaby's description of the battle with the Mahdists is quoted on p. 157 of Alexander's biography.

17. The name "dervish," signifying a Moslem holy man who has taken vows of poverty and austerity, was generally applied by Tommy Atkins to the Mahdi's followers. It would be more correct, if pedantic, to call his followers what they called themselves, the "Ansar," or "Chosen Ones."

18. Allen, *Gordon*, p. 282.

19. A graphic, often amusing, sometimes pathetic and always interesting account of Khartoum besieged is contained in *Gordon's Journals*, which are as quixotic, perverse, and brilliant as the man himself. The entries in the diary begin on 10 September and end on 14 December 1884. Robin Maugham has based a novel on the imaginary contents of Gordon's later (and lost) diaries: *Search for Nirvana* (London: Allen, 1975).

20. Marlowe, *Mission to Khartoum*, p. 210.

21. Wolseley Papers, War Office Library (Joseph H. Lehmann, *All Sir Garnet* [London: Jonathan Cape, 1964], p. 345).

22. On 24 September 1884, after learning that an expedition was on its way to rescue him, Gordon recorded in his journal, "I altogether *decline* the imputation that the projected expedition has come to *relieve me*. It has *come to* SAVE OUR NATIONAL HONOUR in extricating *the garrisons etc., from a position our action in Egypt has placed these garrisons. I was relief expedition No. 1. They are relief expedition No. 2.* As for myself, I could make good any retreat at any moment if I wished.... We the *first* and *second* expeditions are equally engaged for the honour of England. ... I am not the *rescued lamb*, and I will not be."

23. Alexander, *True Blue*, p. 172.

24. Robinson and Gallagher, *Africa and the Victorians*, p. 141.

NOTES TO CHAPTER FIVE

1. Wolseley, *A Soldier's Life*, 2:148-50.
2. Captain G. L. Huyshe, *The Red River Expedition* (London: Macmillan, 1871), pp. 94-95. Huyshe was a British officer on the expedition and kept a journal that later formed the basis for his book. Huyshe died of fever in the Ashanti War of 1874 when he was again serving under Wolseley.
3. Wolseley, *A Soldier's Life*, 2:212.
4. Later Major-General Sir John Carstairs McNeill (1831-1904). In 1873-74, McNeill was Wolseley's chief of staff during the Ashanti Wars in West Africa where he was severely wounded. He was also with Wolseley in Egypt both in 1882 and 1884.
5. Later Lieutenant-General the Rt. Hon. Sir William Francis Butler (1838-1910). Butler's *The Great Lone Land* (London: Macmillan, 1872) and *An Autobiography* (London: Constable, 1911) together provide a revealing picture of the Northwest at Confederation. Butler again served under Wolseley in West Africa and in Egypt. During the Boer War, he was promoted lieutenant-general. He was a skilful and prolific writer and an early biographer of Gordon: *Charles George Gordon* (London: Macmillan, 1889). Lady Butler was a leading painter of military scenes.
6. Later General Sir James Alleyne (1843-99).
7. Arthur, *Letters*, p. 5. Wolseley gave an account of the expedition's experiences in "Narrative of the Red River Expedition," *Blackwood's Magazine*, December 1870, and January and February 1871.
8. Wolseley, *A Soldier's Life*, 2:212-14. When in London, one of Wolseley's favourite recreations was to shoot the larger weirs on the Thames in a birch-bark canoe that he had brought with him from Canada (Arthur and Maurice, *Wolseley*, p. 50).
9. General Sir Frederick Charles Arthur Stephenson (1821-1911) had known Wolseley in the Crimea and China. He commanded the British army of occupation in Egypt from 1883 to Wolseley's arrival in 1884, the troops in Lower Egypt during the Sudan expedition, and again the British army of occupation after the end of the expedition.
10. The full text of this earliest memorandum about the Nile expedition is given in Colonel (later Lieutenant-General Sir) Henry Edward Colvile, *History of the Sudan Campaign*, 2 parts (London: H.M.S.O., 1887), 1:26-30.
11. Wolseley Papers, Hove Public Library (Symons, *England's Pride*, p. 68).
12. Colvile, *Sudan Campaign*, 1:39.
13. Wolseley Papers, War Office Library (Lehmann, *All Sir Garnet*, p. 347).
14. Colvile, *Sudan Campaign*, 1:43.
15. From Wolseley's campaign journal (Adrian Preston, ed., *In Relief of Gordon* [London: Hutchinson, 1967], p. 5).

NOTES TO CHAPTER SIX

1. The fifth Marquess of Lansdowne (1845-1927) was governor general of Canada from 1883 to 1888 and viceroy of India from 1888 to 1894. A leading Whig and a member of one of Gladstone's early governments, he later split with his former leader over Irish home rule, became a Liberal Unionist and served in Lord Salisbury's and Balfour's governments as secretary of state for war (1895-1900) and foreign secretary (1900-1905).
2. P.A.C., Macdonald Papers, vol. 84.
3. Ibid.
4. The eighteen foremen in the contingent received seventy-five dollars a month.
5. Copy in P.A.C. of P.R.O., W.O.-32, bundle 124, no. 7700/495. There are records of at least two of Wolseley's Red River *voyageurs* serving in Egypt. The sons of another two participated.
6. P.A.C., RG 7, G-21, no. 162, vol. 1.

7. Lansdowne to Melgund, 24 August 1884, P.A.C., Minto Papers.
8. Sir Joseph Philippe René Adolphe Caron (1843-1908), minister of militia, 1880-92; postmaster general, 1892-96.
9. Lieutenant-Colonel George Taylor Denison (1839-1925) described his military family in *Soldiering in Canada* (Toronto: Morang, 1900). Denison was an indefatigable author and public speaker whose interests are reflected in the titles of several of his books: *The National Defences, or Observations on the Best Defensive Force for Canada* (Toronto: Leaderstean, 1861); *Modern Cavalry* (London: Bosworth, 1868); *The Struggle for Imperial Unity* (London: Macmillan, 1909); and *Recollections of a Police Magistrate* (Toronto: Musson, 1920). An active supporter of the Confederacy during the Civil War in the United States, Denison described his experiences in *A Visit to General Robert E. Lee* (Toronto, 1872). An ardent cavalry officer, Denison won a prize offered by the tsar of Russia in 1877 for the best history of cavalry written by any officer of any army. Denison's book, *A History of Cavalry from the Earliest Times with Lessons for the Future* (London: Macmillan, 1877), was subsequently translated into Russian, German, and Hungarian. Wolseley wrote of George Denison: "One of the ablest, and professionally one of the best read officers I ever knew.... The descendant of many generations of gallant soldiers, who have, during the eighteenth and nineteenth centuries, fought for the British Crown in Canada, he would have been a military leader of note in any army he joined. It is much to be regretted that he did not adopt the Army as a profession. Had he done so he must have risen to eminence" (Wolseley, *A Soldier's Life*, 2:148).
10. Melgund to Lansdowne, 5 September 1884, P.A.C., Minto Papers.
11. Neilson's diary, now in the Public Archives of Canada (MG-29, F 31), begins on 4 September 1884 at the Royal School of Artillery in Kingston, Ontario, where he was serving as medical officer. The diary abruptly ends exactly seven months later, on 4 April 1885, when Neilson was aboard the "Messageries Maritime" steamer *Sindh* outward bound from Marseilles for England. Neilson (1845-1925) became the first director general of the Canadian Militia Medical Service in 1898. He was also an amateur military historian, publishing privately *The Royal Canadian Voltigeurs (1794-1802)* (Montreal: Lovell, 1895) and translating and editing *Jacques Viger, Reminiscences of the War of 1812* (Kingston: News Printing Co., 1895).
12. A biography of Bouchard, *Le R. P. Bouchard*, was published by his friend, Monseigneur Henri Têtu (Quebec: Pruneau and Nirouac, 1897).
13. Gaston P. Labat, *Les Voyageurs canadiens à l'expédition du Sudan* (Québec: Demers, 1886). "Stature of a cuirassier, beard of a sapper, built like a Monitor, heart of a lamb."
14. After deciding to remain in the town of Winnipeg following the Red River expedition of 1870, Kennedy (1839-85) became one of its most prominent and respected citizens. He was the second mayor of Winnipeg and a member of the executive council of the Northwest Territories. He commanded at various times the Winnipeg Field Battery and the 90th Battalion of Rifles. While participating in the Nile expedition, Kennedy and several fellow Manitobans wrote about their adventures for the Winnipeg *Daily Times*.
15. Commanding officer of the Canadian Regiment of Artillery to the adjutant general, Canadian Militia, 9 March 1885 (P.A.C., RG-9, II A-1, vol. 207). Wilson's original application was dated 16 July 1884 (P.A.C., RG-7, G-21, vol. 162). Wilson (1852-1911) was born in Kingston, Ontario, and had joined the embryonic Canadian army as an ensign in 1871. Melgund had raised with Lansdowne the possibility that Wilson should command the *voyageurs*, but Wolseley preferred Denison, whom he had known on the Red River expedition. Wilson's distinguished later career made him one of Canada's leading soldiers. As a lieutenant-colonel, he commanded the Royal School of Artillery in Kingston from 1897 to 1905, when he was ap-

pointed colonel commandant of the Royal Canadian Artillery. Shortly before his retirement in 1908, Wilson, by then one of the best known and most popular figures in Canadian military circles, was promoted major-general.

16. Ottawa *Daily Citizen*, 15 October 1884.

17. 16 September 1884.

18. Lord George Hamilton, *Parliamentary Reminiscences and Reflections*, 2 vols. (London: Murray, 1917), 1:223.

19. Labat, *Les Voyageurs canadiens*, p. 63. "On Saturday evening when almost all the voyageurs were aboard, a squaw appeared wanting to see her man. Having perceived her he leaped over the side and then was in the arms of his better half. I assure you this better half was a complete whole, the size of a Chinese and weighing at least 200 pounds. There they are then embracing each other like Daphnis and Chloe, these two children of our forests, when to put an end to this tenderness, someone obliged our man to go back on board. Since he resisted, she did likewise.... Finally, in a last, too close embrace where the lips were on lips, the husband's hands disappeared into the corset of the squaw and seek to find.... what?... shocking!... a false manoeuvre having taken place, one heard a noise of broken glass and a bottle of whisky struck the pavement. The squaw began to cry, him too, to melt into tears and I believe one could find there the origin of the expression 'crocodile tears.'"

20. Têtu, *Bouchard*, p. 127. "Father Bouchard had no confidence in this expedition which was too late to be of any use. How many times he spoke to me in this way. And he opened his mind clearly in the presence of the governor and some officers.... he was convinced that it was too late and that Gordon would be betrayed by them and killed or delivered alive to the Mahdi. His repugnance was so great that, in my opinion, the sacrifice that he made in accepting the title of chaplain was the greatest in his life, and I can speak of it with full knowledge of the case."

21. Ibid., pp. 123-24. "I must say in truth that I was not very enthusiastic nor

very proud at the sight of the three hundred voyageurs who were on the deck and who were going to represent the country in Egypt. What a strange assembly. No uniforms—clothes of every colour—tanned faces, some with hard and fierce features—here and there the sinister faces of Iroquois from Caughnawaga — a half-silence — the weary attitude of men who wait; all that had a terrible and funereal aspect which I will never forget."

22. Toronto *Globe*, 15 October 1884.

23. Louis Jackson, *Our Caughnawagas in Egypt: A Narrative of What Was Seen and Accomplished by the Contingent of North American Indian Voyageurs Who Led the British Boat Expedition for the Relief of Khartoum up the Cataracts of the Nile* (Montreal: Drysdale, 1885), pp. 22-27.

24. John Pudney, *The Thomas Cook Story* (London: Michael Joseph, 1953), p. 86.

25. Unless otherwise indicated, unattributed quotations in this and following chapters are from Denison's diary in the Denison Papers, Toronto Public Library.

26. Labat, *Les Voyageurs canadiens*, p. 72. "He was seized by nostalgia, homesickness, two days after departure. Very superstitious, he wanted to return home to see his wife and children."

27. Ibid., p. 81. "You know, these big spoiled children like dirty jokes, to fight, to laugh, to sing, and this is what two of our hardy fellows did at the time of our stay in Gibraltar, routing the police, and crying 'we have conquered Gibraltar!'"

28. Ibid., p. 83. "Almost all the real dangers that we will have to meet are summed up in a single word: Intemperance. Don't think that I am going to make you a sermon on temperance; that would be to trespass on the terrain of our eloquent and devoted chaplain. Besides, I cannot pose as an apostle of temperance, but I am convinced of one thing; that is that the greatest moderation in the use of spirits is necessary at all times, and if this moderation is necessary in a salubrious country like ours, the greater reason is there for the greatest urgency of being temperate in hot regions of doubtful wholesomeness like the Nile."

NOTES TO CHAPTER SEVEN

1. Toronto *Globe*, 5 December 1884.
2. Three years later Van Koughnet achieved the goal of all ambitious naval officers, his own sea-going command. His ship, the sloop *Wild Swan*, was stationed at Esquimalt, British Columbia, from where he sailed it back to England for service with the Home fleet. Van Koughnet's naval career ended in 1894, when he retired with the rank of captain. He volunteered to act as transport officer in Durban during the early part of the Boer War and was awarded the C.M.G. for his services. He died in Gibraltar in 1905 during a return voyage from Australia.
3. Preston, *In Relief*, p. 48.
4. Butler, *Campaign of the Cataracts*, p. 214.
5. Ibid., pp. 142–43.
6. Charles Beresford, *Memoirs*, 2 vols. (London: Methuen, 1914), 1:232. There were no regulations in Victoria's reign which prevented a serving officer from sitting in parliament; see, for example, W. S. Jameson, *The Fleet That Jack Built* (London: Longmans, 1962), pp. 61–89.
7. Gordon, *My Six Years*, p. 142.
8. Letter from Louis Hylas Duguay of Trois Rivières, 16 November 1884 (Têtu, *Bouchard*, pp. 133-34). "We had still a day's march to reach Wadi Halfa, when the mail steamer came alongside, on which is the abbé Bouchard, our chaplain. The good father, who had left us at Cairo to give an account of his two years of absence to his bishop, brought us news of home. He had in his hands several letters which he distributed to whom they concerned. In the evening he disembarked to shake hands with all the Canadiens by whom he is adored. Our bishops could never put us in better hands. Apart from his ministry, he has a marvellous knack of making come to him not only the meek but also the most rebellious. You can imagine that among a composite of voyageurs, men from timber yards, rafters, leapers of rapids like this one, there will be present those who don't follow the cross of St. Louis. I have met several of them who, after an interview with this good missionary, exclaim with joyful heart, 'That is a good father!'

Apart from this role, he also fills that of interpreter, because the abbé Bouchard speaks very well the language of the country that he has travelled over, as apostle of Negritia [the Sudan], for several years. How many times has he not been of the greatest use to our officers in a thousand unforeseen circumstances which are encountered and which will be encountered often in this expedition. It is true that he has become indispensable and that he is considered among us like an envoy of Providence."

9. Ibid., p. 135. "If you had seen us Canadiens, you would have been really proud of it; the officers in charge were amazed by it.... At the time when I am writing to you, all the boats which were brought to Aswan have come up, and I am certain that there are several of them which have already been transported to Dongola. Captain Butler, who is commandant of our encampment, said yesterday that it was extraordinary to see the rapidity with which the expedition travels since the Canadiens have arrived, and we are so much the more surprised by this compliment since we find that the work has not strained us. It has only provided us with a diversion."
10. Butler, *Campaign of the Cataracts*, p. 178.
11. Denison first delivered his lecture, "Reminiscences of Egypt and the Sudan," in Toronto on 22 December 1885. The text is among the Denison Papers, Toronto Public Library.
12. Ottawa *Free Press*, 3 December 1884.
13. Several *voyageurs* wrote accounts of their experiences for Canadian newspapers or for their friends at home. John Andrew Sherlock of Peterborough, Ontario, sent home a diary account of the expedition's progress. Some of his letters were later published

in T. Arnold Haultain, *The War in the Soudan* (Toronto: Grip, 1885); the quotation is from pp. 96-97. Sherlock remained with the expedition to the end, dying of smallpox in Egypt on 26 March 1885. He won Major-General Sir Evelyn Wood's posthumous praise as "a most active and skilful boatman."

14. Alexander, *True Blue*, p. 189.
15. Gordon, *My Six Years*, p. 154.
16. Colvile, *Sudan Campaign*, 1: appendix 4, pp. 186-87.
17. Butler, *Campaign of the Cataracts*, pp. 231-32.
18. For an account of Kitchener's daring work, see Willoughby Verner, "With Kitchener in the Gordon Relief Expedition," *Nineteenth Century Magazine*, August 1916.
19. Allen, *Gordon*, p. 414.
20. Gordon had sent four of his eight small steamers to help bring Wolseley's troops to Khartoum. The armament of the steamers were able to keep the dervishes at a respectful distance. One steamer had aboard Gordon's journals, which he had placed there for safe-keeping; they were carried to England upon the return of the expedition.
21. Colvile, *Sudan Campaign*, 1:139.
22. Egerton Denison to his brother, Lieutenant John Denison, R.N., 27/28 January 1885, Denison Papers, Toronto Public Library, vol. 3.
23. Like Lord Dundonald after him, Lieutenant-General Sir Edward Thomas Henry "Curly" Hutton (1849–1923), a veteran of Tel-el-Kebir, acted as if he had assumed an independent military command when he became commanding general of the Canadian militia in 1898. He soon ran afoul of political considerations, and in 1900 Laurier had to ask Hutton's friend Melgund, by then the Earl of Minto and governor general, to arrange his recall (Norman Penlington, "General Hutton and the Problem of Military Imperialism in Canada, 1898–1900," *Canadian Historical Review* 24 [1943]; and H. Pearson Gundy, "Sir Wilfrid Laurier and Lord Minto," Canadian Historical Association, *Report* [1952]).
24. Labat, *Les Voyageurs canadiens*, p. 181. "The moment of departure arriving, I see some of our voyageurs who are proceeding to the station. They are proceeding in the company of some affectionate Egyptians whose hearts they have known how to touch. French gallantry!

These women accompanied them smoking cigarettes. I see one of them who is smoking a cigar. Horror! How long before they chew it? The machine warms up, it waits for us; the curious too. An old woman, the wife of a Protestant minister probably, to judge from her costume, gesticulates, is enraptured, salutes the passage of the voyageurs with her handkerchief.

'Hurrah boys!' cries the good woman. Everyone looked at her and despite the exhortations of her husband who said to her 'Don't excite [yourself] Kate!' She was flared up, became very enthusiastic, and we left to the cries of the old woman who shouted: 'Hurray for the Canadian boys!'"
25. Ibid., p. 123.
26. Ibid., p. 125. "Since I speak of deaths, let me tell you in conclusion that I have just seen the chaplain and the surgeon who attended the lamented Major Hébert, of Battery B. They gave me a cordial eulogy of him and keep so moving a memory that it is an honour for Canada. It is for that reason that I am happy to tell you meanwhile that I may be able to make the pilgrimage to his grave that my heart has promised itself....

I add here a paragraph to let the reader know that not being able myself to accomplish this desire of my heart on my return to Cairo, it was the bishop of Cairo, accompanied by Father Bouchard, who accomplished this holy mission, laying on the grave of Hebert a wreath of everlasting flowers in the name of the Canadian brothers in arms of this excellent fellow."
27. From notes which Melgund prepared about a conversation with Aumond in Ottawa on 14 March 1885, P.A.C., RG 7, G-19, vol. 37.
28. Winnipeg *Daily Times*, 9 March 1885.

NOTES TO CHAPTER EIGHT

1. Later Major-General Sir Herbert Stewart (1843-85). A protegé of Wolseley, Stewart was one of the youngest and most able field officers of the British army. Having served in India and West and South Africa, he was already a seasoned veteran of colonial wars by 1884. (He was no relation of Gordon's aide, Colonel Donald Stewart.)

2. Later Major-General Sir Charles Wilson (1836-1905). When a subaltern in the Royal Engineers, Wilson had served as secretary to Captain (later General Sir) John Hawkins in his delimitation of the Canadian-United States boundary from Lake of the Woods to the Pacific Ocean during the years 1858-62. Wilson had later become a close friend of Gordon.

3. Lord Edward Gleichen (later Admiral Prince Victor of Hohenlohe-Langenburg), *With the Camel Corps up the Nile* (London: Chapman and Hall, 1888), p. 71.

4. C. H. Melville, *Life of General the Right Hon. Sir Redvers Buller*, 2 vols. (London: Arnold, 1923), 1:185.

5. Winston S. Churchill, *The River War* (London: Eyre and Spottiswoode, 1899), p. 63.

6. Alexander, *True Blue*, p. 203.

7. Preston, *In Relief*, p. 128.

8. Ibid., p. 202.

9. Colvile, *Sudan Campaign*, 2:81-89.

10. Major-General William Earle (1833-85) served in Canada between 1862 and 1863 and again between 1866 and 1870 (the same time as Wolseley). He commanded the British garrison in Alexandria from 1882 to 1884. Wolseley and Earle were old friends, but Wolseley was not enthusiastic about giving Earle a major command: "my own opinion... is, that good an officer as Earle undoubtedly is, he will never rise to the position of commander. He has not it in him to influence troops or to inspire them with any enthusiasm" (Preston, *In Relief*, p. 7).

11. Colvile, *Sudan Campaign*, p. 84.

12. De Lom (1855-1929) first served abroad in Egypt, but later in 1885, he gained further experience of tropical diseases by serving in British Honduras and, after two years there, in Barbados. After sixteen years in the army, he resigned his commission in 1899 and entered private practice in England.

13. Ottawa *Free Press*, 2 January 1885. McLaurin was called MacLaren by the *Free Press*.

14. Hake, *Gordon's Journals*, p. 134.

15. Allen, *Gordon*, pp. 450-55.

16. Wilson wrote to Kitchener on 10 April 1885 stating that, while he might appear responsible in the public eye for Gordon's death, and implying that he knew he would be made a scapegoat, he could not properly defend himself. "I cannot say to the public, 'If Stewart had been allowed to carry out the original plan and march straight to Metemma [*sic*]... there would have been no desert fight and Khartoum would have been saved'; nor can I talk about contradictory orders relating to the purchase of camels which upset the transport; nor again, that everyone, knowing in November that Gordon could only hold out to Xmas day, no special efforts were made to perfect the desert column and transport; nor that the force which reached the Nile was too weak and composed of too many regiments to attempt an important enterprise" (Magnus, *Kitchener*, p. 62).

17. Hake, *Gordon's Journals*, p. 275.

18. Later Major-General the Hon. Edward James Montagu-Stuart-Wortley (1857-1934).

19. Preston, *In Relief*, p. 136.

20. Later Field Marshal Sir Evelyn Wood (1838-1913). After a distinguished career in India where he had won the Victoria Cross, Wood had been given command of the new Egyptian army in 1882 following Arabi's defeat. Wingate (later General Sir Reginald Wingate, [1861-1953]) had also begun his military career in India. Serving with the Egyptian army, he, like Kitchener, had learned to speak fluent Arabic. He had been present at the Cairo railway station in 1884 when Gordon set off for Khartoum. His subsequent adventures in Egypt and the Sudan are described

in his biography written by his son, Sir Ronald Wingate, *Wingate of the Sudan* (London: Murray, 1955). Wingate was author of *Mahdiism and the Egyptian Sudan* (London: Macmillan, 1891) and a great-uncle of Major-General Orde Wingate, the leader of the "Chindits" in Burma during the Second World War.

21. Preston, *In Relief*, p. 5.
22. One of Buller's first acts upon taking command of the desert column was to send to Korti all the wounded and most of the cavalry in order to be rid of as many useless mouths as possible. He retained a small cavalry detachment under the command of Major J. D. P. French, later Field Marshal the Rt. Hon. the Earl of Ypres, of Boer and First World War fame. In the Camel Corps was Captain (later Lieutenant-

General) the Earl of Dundonald (1852–1935), who commanded the Canadian militia during 1903–4, and Lieutenant (later General Sir) E. H. Alderson, a veteran of the Battle of Tel-el-Kebir, who was later to become the general commanding the First Canadian Division at the outbreak of the First World War. Dundonald describes his experiences on the expedition in chapters 3, 4 and 5 of his autobiography, *My Army Life* (London: Arnold, 1936).

23. Colvile, *Sudan Campaign*, 2:57.
24. Entry for 18 February 1885, A. B. Cooke and J. R. Vincent, eds., *Lord Carlingford's Journal* (Oxford: Clarendon Press, 1971), p. 67.
25. G. M. Trevelyan, *Grey of Fallodon* (London: Longmans, Green, 1937), pp. 29–30.
26. Preston, *In Relief*, p. 190.

NOTES TO CHAPTER NINE

1. Colvile, *Sudan Campaign*, 2:98.
2. Ottawa *Free Press*, 25 April 1885.
3. Later General the Rt. Hon. Sir Henry Brackenbury (1837-1914). He had served as an infantry subaltern during the Indian Mutiny. A military historian of note, in less than twenty-one weeks he wrote the definitive history of Wolseley's campaign in West Africa, *The Ashanti War*, 2 vols. (London: Blackwood, 1874). Brackenbury was promoted major-general for his services in the Sudan and general for his later services in India and at the War Office. He described his Sudan experiences in *The River Column* (London: Blackwood, 1885).
4. Gordon, *My Six Years*, pp. 221-22.
5. "Introduction," in C. P. Stacey, ed., *Records of the Nile Voyageurs* (Toronto: Champlain Society, 1959), p. 39.
6. Both orders are included in Colvile, *Sudan Campaign*, 2:124-25.
7. Brackenbury, *River Column*, pp. 277-79.
8. *Too Late for Gordon and Khartoum* was published in London by Murray in 1887 and *Why Gordon Perished* by W. H. Allen in 1898. Two of MacDonald's other books are *The Land of*

Ararat; or, Up the Roof of the World (London: Eden, Remington, 1893) and *In the Land of Pearl and Gold: A Pioneer's Wanderings in the Backlands and Pearling Grounds of Australia and New Guinea* (London: Unwin, 1907). It is not surprising that MacDonald was elected a Fellow of the Royal Geographical Society in 1887.

9. MacDonald, *Land of Ararat*, pp. 57-58.
10. Interview with Denison in the Ottawa *Free Press*, 24 April 1885.
11. John Denison's subsequent career was more spectacular than that of his naval colleague and Canadian contemporary, Van Koughnet; he commanded his own gunboat on the China station in 1887 and, as the years passed, assumed other commands and was promoted at frequent intervals until he retired with the rank of admiral on 7 December 1913. But a sixty-year-old admiral was not one to miss the First World War even though it meant serving as a commodore in the Royal Navy Reserve. For his wartime services, he was awarded the D.S.O. He lived almost long enough to see the beginning of the Second World War,

dying in England on 8 March 1939, at the age of eighty-six. In 1900-1902 he had commanded H.M.S. *Niobe*, which later became the first cruiser in the new Royal Canadian Navy.

12. Major-General Septimus Julius Augustus Denison (1859-1937) was, as his name suggests, the seventh son of Colonel G. T. Denison. He served with distinction in the Canadian Contingent in the Boer War.

13. One of his grandsons, the Earl of Athlone, became Canada's sixteenth governor general (1940-46).

14. Haliburton (1832-1907) was knighted for his services and, in 1895, made under-secretary of state for war, the most senior permanent post in the War Office. He was raised to the peerage in 1900.

15. Father Bouchard never returned to Africa. Between May 1885 and October 1888 and October 1889 and October 1891 and again between April 1894 and November 1895, Bouchard was the vicar of various parishes in Quebec. From November 1891 until January 1893, he was a member of the Fathers of the Holy Sacrament in Brussels. From November 1888 until July 1889 and again from December 1895 until

his death in September 1896, at the age of fifty-one, Bouchard was a parish priest in Trinidad.

16. Both the War Office's telegram and Melgund's reply are in P.A.C., RG 7, G-19, vol. 39.

17. 25 October 1884, written at sea aboard S.S. *Apollo*, outward bound from Trieste for Alexandria, in the possession of Mrs. B. Cummings of Grenville, Quebec, a daughter of Captain Cummings (1850-1933).

18. Robinson (1856-1936) was an imaginative and determined entrepreneur on the rivers and lakes of Western Canada, both as the owner of a major transport company and, later, as a director and partner in a Winnipeg bank, an insurance company, and a trust company.

19. P.A.C., RG 7, G-19, vol. 34.

20. Ibid.

21. The War Office was as pleased with their services as was Robinson himself. Melgund was asked to recruit for the projected autumn campaign another twelve wheelsmen, who "should be made clearly to understand that they may be required to go under fire" (P.A.C., RG 7, G-21, vol. 72).

NOTES TO CHAPTER TEN

1. P.A.C., RG 7, G-21, no. 162, vol. 1.

2. MacDonald, *Too Late*, p. 87.

3. In a telegram dated 23 February 1885, the Colonial Office informed Lansdowne that approximately 7 per cent of the boatmen had proved to be worthless, 25 per cent excellent, and the remaining 68 per cent "good" (P.A.C., RG 7, G-19, vol. 39). In a longer report by Lieutenant-Colonel (later Lieutenant-General Sir) Coleridge Grove, assistant adjutant general for boat service on the Nile expedition and later secretary to Wolseley, the number of "unsuitable" men among the 372 *voyageurs* (excluding officers and foremen) was placed at 45 (Colvile, *Sudan Campaign*, 1: appendix 6).

4. Typical adverse newspaper comment

about the alleged indiscipline of the *voyageurs* was placed in a more permanent form in Charles Royal, *The Egyptian Campaign 1882-1899 (New Revised Edition, Continued to December, 1899)* (London: Hurst and Blackett, 1900). "It subsequently transpired that many of the 'voyageurs' had absolutely no experience in the management of boats, and were worse than useless. There were some excellent men amongst them, and more particularly among the Indians, but the general opinion was that the blue-jackets from the fleet could have performed the work far more effectively, besides being sober and amenable to discipline. When, in addition, it is stated that the Canadians received very high salaries, the wisdom of engaging these men for the Nile expedition appears open to much doubt" (p. 316n.).

5. For example, the two Indian brothers, Alfred and Joseph Ayotte, who had caused such a disturbance in Gibraltar, evoked Denison's admiration on the Nile.

6. Brackenbury, *River Column*, p. 228.

7. Great Britain, *Parliamentary Papers* (Commons), Cmd. 207 (1885) (Stacey, *Nile Voyageurs*, p. 210).

8. Gordon, *My Six Years*, p. 180.

9. Report by Lieutenant-Colonel Grove of 19 June 1885 on the *voyageurs* (Colvile, *Sudan Campaign*, 1:appendix 4, p. 188).

10. Quoted in Pudney, *Thomas Cook*, pp. 206-7. Cook published his lecture to the Royal Geographical Society as *The Nile Expedition, 1884-85*; *Mr. John M. Cook's Visit to the Soudan* (London, 1885).

11. It was rumoured that the first *voyageur* to drown, Louis Capitaine, one of the Caughnawaga Iroquois, had in fact committed suicide. On 3 November 1884, Dr. Neilson noted in his diary, "Sir R. Buller . . . says it is now certain that Louis Capitaine contemplated suicide as the day previous he had thrown his cup in the river, remarking that he would follow it soon. Whether he jumped or fell off is not clearly known; he was an excellent swimmer." At the time of his death, Capitaine was twenty-eight years old and the father of three children.

12. 3 December 1884, Denison Papers, Toronto Public Library, vol. 3.

13. Letter to George Denison, 11 December 1884, ibid. The risk to the *voyageurs* had been, to some degree, foreseen. As early as October 1884, Lord Lansdowne had written to the Colonial Office querying "the manner in which relatives of any men who may lose their lives during their service with

the expedition are to be dealt with. It would in my opinion be advisable to deal liberally with such cases should they unfortunately arise. I would suggest that in all such cases the family of the deceased man should be allowed the whole of his pay due to him in respect of the unexpired portion of his engagement" (copy in P.A.C. of the original letter in P.R.O., W.O.-32, bundle 124, No. 7700/495). The British government concurred in Lansdowne's suggestion and, moreover, generally made an additional grant of £100 to widows.

14. 12 March 1885 (Sir Joseph Pope, ed., *The Correspondence of Sir John Macdonald* [Toronto: Oxford University Press, 1921], p. 337).

15. Letter to secretary of state for the colonies, 12 September 1884, P.A.C., RG 7, G-21, no. 162, vol. 1.

16. Applications to the Canadian Militia authorities can be found in P.A.C., G-9II, B 175, G 19, vols. 35-50, no. 162, vols. 1 and 2.

17. Letter to secretary of state for the colonies, 12 September 1884, P.A.C., G-21, no. 162, vol. 1.

18. P.A.C., Minto Papers, film A-130. For a discussion of the issues involved in raising British troops in Canada in 1884-85, see C. P. Stacey, "Canada and the Nile Expedition of 1884-85," *Canadian Historical Review* 23 (1952), pp. 319-341; and "John A. Macdonald on Raising Troops for Imperial Service, 1885," *Canadian Historical Review* 38 (1957), pp. 37-40; and C. P. Stacey and E. Pye, "Canadian Voyageurs in the Sudan, 1884-85," *Canadian Army Journal* 7 (1951), pp. 61-73; 8 (1951), pp. 56-68; and 9 (1951), pp. 16-26.

19. William Henry Drummond (1854-1907); "Maxime Labelle: A Canadian Voyageur's Account of the Nile Expedition."

NOTES TO CHAPTER ELEVEN

1. The cause of the Mahdi's death is open to question. Edward Dicey, *The Story of the Khediviate* (London: Rivington, 1902), p. 391, states that he died of smallpox. Reginald Wingate had a more sensational story to advance: "A

woman, daughter of a townsman who had lost children, wives, property and all, in the long siege, submitted to outrages and obtained a terrible revenge. On the night of the 14th of June she gave the effeminate and debauched prophet a deadly poison, and, after lingering in great agony, he died on the 22nd of the month" (*Mahdiism*, p. 228). While this account has a circumstantial ring about it, so do Father Joseph Ohrwalder's and Sir Rudolph Slatin's much different stories. The former insists that the Mahdi died of "fatty degeneration of the heart" (Major F. R. Wingate, trans. and ed., *Ten Years' Captivity in the Mahdi Camp, 1882-1892* [London: Sampson, Low, Marston, Searle and Wington, 1892], p. 160), while the latter asserts that typhoid was the cause (*Fire and Sword in the Sudan* [London: Arnold, 1896], p. 369). This latter theory was subsequently supported by Winston Churchill (*River War*, p. 71); Jackson (*Osman Digna*, p. 109); and Thomas Archer (*The War in Egypt and the Sudan*, 2 vols. [London: Blackie and Son, 1902], 1:261). It is impossible to reconcile these several theories, but, given the prevalence of typhoid fever and the belief that the Mahdi had already had smallpox, it seems that Slatin's statement is probably correct. There is no corroborative evidence for Wingate's dramatic story.

2. John Morley, *The Life of William Ewart Gladstone*, 3 vols. (London: Macmillan, 1903), 2:420.

3. The last sentence is typical of the somewhat detached approach that Robert Arthur Gascoyne Cecil, the third Marquess of Salisbury (1830-1903), took towards politics and international affairs. He was prime minister from July 1885 until February 1886; from July 1886 to August 1892; and again from June 1895 to July 1902. On three different occasions during these periods, Salisbury was his own foreign secretary. A *grand seigneur* who believed that the aristocracy had been made to rule, Salisbury had, consequently, distinct limitations, but he also had a clarity and cynicism which give his letters, speeches, and actions sardonic touches which are often amusing, if sometimes disconcerting. The example is quoted from Robinson and Gallagher, *Africa and the Victorians*, pp. 304-5.

4. The authors are identified accurately on the title pages of their books: Ohrwalder as "Late Priest of the Austrian Mission Station at Delen, Kordofan," and Slatin as "Formerly Governor and Commandant of the Troops in Darfur."

5. Trevelyan, *Grey*, pp. 62-63.

6. Baring had been created a baron in June 1892. He became a viscount in 1899 and an earl in 1901.

7. Alfred Milner, *England in Egypt* (London: Arnold, 1893).

8. Churchill, *River War*, p. 90.

9. Magnus, *Kitchener*, p. 80.

10. George W. Steevens, *With Kitchener to Khartoum*, 23d ed. (London: Blackwood, 1901), p. 46.

11. C. H. Melville, *Sir Redvers Buller*, 1:238.

12. 13 March 1896 (Robinson and Gallagher, *Africa and the Victorians*, p. 348).

13. 24 March 1896 (ibid., p. 349).

14. Cromer, *Modern Egypt*, 2:107.

15. Sir Ian Hamilton, *Listening for the Drums* (London: Faber and Faber, 1944), p. 175.

16. Churchill, *River War*, p. 162.

NOTES TO CHAPTER TWELVE

1. The Hon. Désiré Girouard (1836-1911) was a member of parliament from 1878 until 1895, when he became a judge of the Supreme Court. He resigned in 1910 to become deputy governor general. Désiré Girouard was also the author of several regional histories of French Canada.

2. Hitherto only commissions in the infantry and artillery had been offered to R.M.C. graduates.

3. Percy Girouard, "The Use of Railways

for Coast and Harbour Defence," *Journal of the Royal United Service Institute* 35 (1891).

4. Brigadier-General R. B. D. Blakeney, "K. and Gerry," *National Review* January 1936. Blakeney, who was one of Girouard's Royal Engineer sub-alterns, tells several such anecdotes in his article.

5. Lieutenant-Colonel E. W. C. Sandes, *The Royal Engineers in Egypt and the Sudan* (Chatham: Institute of Royal Engineers, 1934), p. 179.

6. Lieutenant (later Major-General Sir) M. G. E. Bowman-Manifold, 31 July 1896 (ibid., p. 181).

7. One young Royal Navy officer commanding a gunboat was Lieutenant David Beatty, later Admiral of the Fleet Earl Beatty of the North Sea (1871–1936). Another gunboat captain was a veteran of Wolseley's expedition, Commander Colin Keppel, later Admiral Sir Colin Keppel (1862–1947).

8. The line to Kerma (from whence the Dongola garrison could be supplied by riverboat) was not, in fact, completed until 4 May 1897, by which time Girouard had long since concentrated his attention on building the desert railway.

NOTES TO CHAPTER THIRTEEN

1. In addition to pulling great quantities of men and stores, the locomotives had to draw heavy tanks of water behind them for their own use.

2. Magnus, *Kitchener*, p. 104.

3. Steevens, *With Kitchener to Khartoum*, pp. 26–27.

4. Sandes, *Royal Engineers*, p. 236.

5. Churchill, *River War*, p. 182.

6. Ibid., p. 300. The good-natured prime minister, Lord Salisbury, had asked Kitchener to appoint Lord Randolph Churchill's younger son, Winston, to temporary duty with the 21st Lancers. Kitchener refused but Winston

Churchill managed nevertheless to induce the War Office to appoint him. Another young cavalry officer who later won fame was Lieutenant Douglas Haig, later Field Marshal Sir Douglas Haig, who had already attracted attention by taking a camel-load of claret with him on the campaign.

7. Steevens, *With Kitchener to Khartoum*, pp. 282–83.

8. Percy Girouard, "The Railways of Africa," *Scribner's Magazine* (1906), pp. 553–68.

NOTES TO CHAPTER FOURTEEN

1. Sandes, *Royal Engineers*, p. 242.

2. Girouard wrote an account of his work during the Boer War under the title *History of the Railway during the War in South Africa* (London: H.M.S.O., 1903).

3. Girouard was invited to lecture the members of the Royal Engineers Institute on his South African experiences in March 1905. His lecture was subsequently published as "Railways in War," *Royal Engineers Journal*, July

1905.

4. For more details of Girouard's term as governor of Kenya, see volume 1 of Elspeth Huxley, *White Man's Country; Lord Delamere and the Making of Kenya*, 2 vols. (London: Macmillan, 1935); and Lord Cranworth, *Kenya Chronicles* (London: Macmillan, 1939).

5. An obituary by Major-General H. L. Pritchard giving some details of Girouard's later life is in *Royal Engineer's Journal*, June 1933.

Bibliography

1. *Manuscript Material*

Public Archives of Canada
  RG-7 G-19, vols. 34–50
  RG-7 G-21, vols. 28, 72, 162
  RG-9 II A-1, vols. 206, 207
  RG-9 II B-1, vol. 75
  RG-26 A, vol. 84 (Macdonald Papers)
  RG-27 II B-1 (Minto Papers)
  RG-29 F-12, F-13, F-31
Toronto Public Library. Denison Papers

2. *Books*

Alexander, Michael. *The True Blue*. London: Rupert Hart-Davis, 1957.
Alford, Henry S. L., and Sword, W. Dennistoun. *The Egyptian Sudan: Its Loss and Recovery*. London: Macmillan, 1898.
Allen, Bernard M. *Gordon and China*. London: Macmillan, 1929.
———. *Gordon and the Sudan*. London: Macmillan, 1931.
    Arthur, George. *Life of Lord Kitchener*. 3 vols. London: Macmillan, 1920.
Arthur, George, ed. *The Letters of Lord and Lady Wolseley, 1870–1911*. London: Heinemann, 1922.
Arthur, George, and Maurice, F. *The Life of Lord Wolseley*. London: Heinemann, 1924.
Atlay, J. B. *Lord Haliburton: A Memoir*. London: Briggs, 1909.
Atteridge, A. Hilliard. *Towards Khartoum: The Story of the Sudan War of 1896*. London: Innes, 1897.
Barris, Theodore. *Fire Canoe*. Toronto: McClelland and Stewart, 1977.
Bennett, Geoffrey. *The Life of Admiral Lord Charles Beresford*. London: Dawnay, 1968.
Berger, Carl. *The Sense of Power*. Toronto: University of Toronto Press, 1970.
Bermann, Richard A. *The Mahdi of Allah*. London: Putnam, 1931.
Beresford, Charles. *Memoirs*. 2 vols. London: Methuen, 1914.
Brackenbury, Henry. *The River Column*. London: Blackwood, 1885.
Butler, Lewis. *Sir Redvers Buller*. London: Smith, Elder, 1909.
Butler, William. *The Great Lone Land*. London: Macmillan, 1872.
———. *Campaign of the Cataracts*. London: Sampson, Low and Marston, 1887.
———. *Autobiography*. London: Constable, 1911.
Buckle, George Earle. *The Letters of Queen Victoria. Second Series*. 3 vols. London: Murray, 1926–28.
Churchill, Winston S. *The River War*. London: Eyre and Spottiswoode, 1899.
Collins, Robert O. *The Southern Sudan 1883–1898*. New Haven: Yale University Press, 1962.
Colvile, Henry Edward. *History of the Sudan Campaign*. 2 Parts. London: H.M.S.O., 1887.
Cooke, A. B., and Vincent, John. *The Governing Passion*. Brighton: Harvest, 1974.

Cooke, A. B., and Vincent, J. R., eds. *Lord Carlingford's Journal: Reflections of a Cabinet Minister, 1885*. Oxford: Clarendon Press, 1971.
Crabites, Pierre. *Gordon, the Sudan and Slavery*. London: Routledge, 1933.
Cromer, Earl of. *Modern Egypt*. 2 vols. London: Macmillan, 1908.
Dundonald, Earl of. *My Army Life*. London: Arnold, 1928.
Elton, Lord. *General Gordon*. London: Collins, 1954.
Farwell, Byron. *Prisoners of the Mahdi*. London: Longmans, 1967.
Gleichen, Lord Edward. *With the Camel Corps up the Nile*. London: Chapman and Hall, 1888.
Gordon, Donald C. *The Dominion Partnership in Imperial Defence*. Baltimore: Johns Hopkins University Press, 1965.
Gordon, John. *My Six Years with the Black Watch, 1881-1887*. Boston: Fort Hill, 1929.
Hake, A. Egmont. *The Story of Chinese Gordon*. 2 vols. London: Remington, 1884.
Hake, A. Egmont, ed. *The Journals of Major-General G. C. Gordon, C.B.* London: Kegan Paul, Trench, 1885.
Harries-Jenkins, Gwyn. *The Army in Victorian Society*. London: Routledge and Kegan Paul, 1977.
Haultain, T. Arnold. *The War in the Soudan*. Toronto: Grip, 1885.
Hill, R. *Egypt and the Sudan, 1820-1881*. London: Longmans Green, 1952.
Hodgson, Pat. *The War Illustrators*. London: Osprey, 1977.
Holland, B. *The Life of Spencer Compton, Eighth Duke of Devonshire*. 2 vols. London: Longmans, Green, 1911.
Holt, P. M. *The Mahdist State in the Sudan, 1881-1898*. London: Weidenfeld and Nicolson, 1958.
Jackson, H. C. *Osman Digna*. London: Methuen, 1926.
Jackson, Louis. *Our Caughnawagas in Egypt: A Narrative of What Was Seen and Accomplished by the Contingent of North American Indian Voyageurs who led the British Boat Expedition for the Relief of Khartoum up the Cataracts of the Nile*. Montreal: Drysdale, 1885.
Labat, Gaston P. *Les Voyageurs canadiens à l'expédition du Sudan*. Québec: Demers, 1886.
Lehmann, Joseph H. *All Sir Garnet*. London: Jonathan Cape, 1964.
MacDonald, Alexander. *Too Late for Gordon and Khartoum*. London: Murray, 1887.
Magnus, Philip. *Kitchener: Portrait of an Imperialist*. London: Murray, 1958.
Marlowe, John. *Mission to Khartum*. London: Gollancz, 1969.
McCourt, Edward. *Remember Butler*. Toronto: McClelland and Stewart, 1967.
Melville, C. H. *Life of General Sir Redvers Buller*. London: Arnold, 1928.
Moorehead, Alan. *The White Nile*. London: Hamish Hamilton, 1960.
Morley, John. *The Life of William Ewart Gladstone*. 3 vols. London: Macmillan, 1903.
Ohrwalder, Father. *Ten Years' Captivity in the Mahdi Camp, 1882-1892*. London: Sampson, Low, Marston, Searle and Wington, 1892.
Penlington, Norman. *Canada and Imperialism*. Toronto: Univeristy of Toronto Press, 1965.
Pratt, Edwin A. *The Rise of Rail-Power in War and Conquest, 1833-1914*. London: King, 1915.
Preston, Adrian, ed. *In Relief of Gordon*. London: Hutchinson, 1967.
Preston, Richard A. *Canada and Imperial Defence*. Durham, N. C.: Duke University Press, 1967.
Pudney, John. *The Thomas Cook Story*. London: Michael Joseph, 1953.
Robinson, Ronald, and Gallagher, John. *Africa and the Victorians*. London: Macmillan, 1965.
Sandes, E. W.C. *The Royal Engineers in Egypt and the Sudan*. Chatham: Institute of Royal Engineers, 1934.
Shibeika, M. *British Policy in the Sudan 1882-1902*. London: Oxford University Press, 1952.
Slatin, Sir Rudolph. *Fire and Sword in the Sudan*. London: Arnold, 1896.
Stacey, C. P., ed. *The Nile Voyageurs, 1884-1885*. Toronto: Champlain Society, 1959.
Stanley, George F. G. *The Birth of Western Canada*. Toronto: University of Toronto Press, 1936.
―――. *Louis Riel*. Toronto: Ryerson, 1963.
Steevens, George W. *With Kitchener to Khartoum*. 23rd ed. London: Blackwood, 1901.
Stephenson, Sir Frederick. *At Home and on the Battlefield*. London: Murray, 1918.
Symons, Julian. *England's Pride*. London: Hamish Hamilton, 1965.
―――. *Buller's Last Command*. London: Hamish Hamilton, 1962.
Têtu, Henri. *Le R. P. Bouchard*. Québec: Pruneau et Nirouac, 1897.

Vetch, R. H., ed. *The Life, Letters, and Diary of Sir Gerald Graham.* London: Blackwood, 1901.
Watson, Sir Charles M. *History of the Corps of Royal Engineers.* Vol. 3. Chatham: Royal Engineers Institute, 1915.
Wilson, Sir Charles. *From Korti to Khartoum.* London: Blackwood, 1885.
Wingate, F. Reginald. *Mahdiism and the Egyptian Sudan.* London: Macmillan, 1891.
Wolseley, Garnet. *The Story of a Soldier's Life.* 2 vols. London: Constable, 1903.

3. *Articles in Periodicals*

Anon. "Diary of an Officer with the Khartoum Expedition." *Royal Engineers Journal* 22 (1892).
Anon. "The Advance on the Nile." *Royal Engineers Journal* 27 (1897).
Anon. "The Battle of Tel-el-Kebir." *Nineteenth Century Magazine*, March 1890.
Blackburn, J. E. "From Gemai to Debbeh in a Whaler"; "From Debbeh to Hanbad with the Nile Column"; "With the Nile Column from January 17 to March 7, 1885." *Royal Engineers Journal* 15 (1885).
Blakeney, R. B. D. "K and Gerry." *National Review*, January 1936.
Carr-Harris, C. G. M. "Un Bâtisseur d'Empire: Sir Percy Girouard." *Le Magazine MacLean*, November 1961.
———. "Africa—The Girouard Story." *Professional Public Service*, October 1960.
———. "The Girouard Story." *Royal Military College of Canada Review* 42 (1961).
———. "Dans le génie militaire." *Le Soleil*, 28 January 1953.
Girouard, Percy. "The Railways of Africa." *Scribner's Magazine* (1906).
MacLaren, Roy. "Canada's First Foreign War Heroes." *MacLean's Magazine*, 25 January 1964.
Pritchard, H. L. "Memoir of Sir Percy Girouard." *Royal Engineers Journal* 63 (1933).
Stacey, C. P. "Canada and the Nile Expedition." *Canadian Historical Review* 33 (1952).
———. "John A. Macdonald on Raising Troops for Imperial Service." *Canadian Historical Review* 38 (1957).
Stacey, C. P., and Pye, E. "Canadian Voyageurs in the Sudan, 1884-1885." *Canadian Army Journal* (1951).
Winter, C. F. "A Canadian's Recollections of Tel-el-Kebir." *Canadian Magazine* 39 (1912).

Index